TRIUMPH
350/500 Unit Construction Twins Bible
1957-1974

Peter Henshaw

Justin Harvey-James

Also from Veloce Publishing

Enthusiast's Restoration Manual Series
Beginner's Guide to Classic Motorcycle Restoration, The (Burns)
Classic Large Frame Vespa Scooters, How to Restore (Paxton)
Classic Small Frame Vespa Scooters, How to Restore (Paxton)
Classic Off-road Motorcycles, How to Restore (Burns)
Ducati Bevel Twins 1971 to 1986 (Falloon)
Honda CX500 & CX650, How to restore – YOUR step-by-step colour illustrated guide to complete restoration (Burns)
Honda Fours, How to restore – YOUR step-by-step colour illustrated guide to complete restoration (Burns)
Kawasaki Z1, Z/KZ900 & Z/KZ1000, How to restore (Rooke)
Triumph Trident T150/T160 & BSA Rocket III, How to Restore (Rooke)
Yamaha FS1-E, How to Restore (Watts)

Essential Buyer's Guide Series
BMW Boxer Twins (Henshaw)
BMW GS (Henshaw)
BSA 350, 441 & 500 Singles (Henshaw)
BSA 500 & 650 Twins (Henshaw)
BSA Bantam (Henshaw)
Choosing, Using & Maintaining Your Electric Bicycle (Henshaw)
Ducati Bevel Twins (Falloon)
Ducati Desmodue Twins (Falloon)
Ducati Desmoquattro Twins – 851, 888, 916, 996, 998, ST4 1988 to 2004 (Falloon)
Harley-Davidson Big Twins (Henshaw)
Hinckley Triumph triples & fours 750, 900, 955, 1000, 1050, 1200 – 1991-2009 (Henshaw)
Honda CBR FireBlade (Henshaw)
Honda CBR600 Hurricane (Henshaw)
Honda SOHC Fours 1969-1984 (Henshaw)
Kawasaki Z1 & Z900 (Orritt)
Moto Guzzi 2-valve big twins (Falloon)
Norton Commando (Henshaw)
Piaggio Scooters – all modern two-stroke & four-stroke automatic models 1991 to 2016 (Willis)
Royal Enfield Bullet (Henshaw)
Triumph 350 & 500 Twins (Henshaw)
Triumph Bonneville (Henshaw)
Triumph Trident & BSA Rocket III (Rooke)
Velocette 350 & 500 Singles 1946 to 1970 (Henshaw)
Vespa Scooters – Classic 2-stroke models 1960-2008 (Paxton)

Those Were The Days ... Series
Café Racer Phenomenon, The (Walker)
Drag Bike Racing in Britain – From the mid '60s to the mid '80s (Lee)

Biographies
Chris Carter at Large – Stories from a lifetime in motorcycle racing (Carter & Skelton)
Edward Turner – The Man Behind the Motorcycles (Clew)
Jim Redman – 6 Times World Motorcycle Champion: The Autobiography (Redman)
'Sox' – Gary Hocking – the forgotten World Motorcycle Champion (Hughes)

General
BMW Boxer Twins 1970-1995 Bible, The (Falloon)
BMW Cafe Racers (Cloesen)
BMW Custom Motorcycles – Choppers, Cruisers, Bobbers, Trikes & Quads (Cloesen)
British Café Racers (Cloesen)
British Custom Motorcycles – The Brit Chop – choppers, cruisers, bobbers & trikes (Cloesen)
Bonjour – Is this Italy? (Turner)
British 250cc Racing Motorcycles (Pereira)
BSA Bantam Bible, The (Henshaw)
BSA Motorcycles – the final evolution (Jones)
Ducati 750 Bible, The (Falloon)
Ducati 750 SS 'round-case' 1974, The Book of the (Falloon)
Ducati 860, 900 and Mille Bible, The (Falloon)
Ducati Monster Bible (New Updated & Revised Edition), The (Falloon)
Ducati Story, The – 6th Edition (Falloon)
Ducati 916 (updated edition) (Falloon)
Fine Art of the Motorcycle Engine, The (Peirce)
Franklin's Indians (Sucher/Pickering/Diamond/Havelin)
From Crystal Palace to Red Square – A Hapless Biker's Road to Russia (Turner)
Funky Mopeds (Skelton)
India - The Shimmering Dream (Reisch/Falls (translator))
Italian Cafe Racers (Cloesen)
Italian Custom Motorcycles (Cloesen)
Japanese Custom Motorcycles – The Nippon Chop – Chopper, Cruiser, Bobber, Trikes and Quads (Cloesen)
Kawasaki Triples Bible, The (Walker)
Kawasaki W, H1 & Z – The Big Air-cooled Machines (Long)
Kawasaki Z1 Story, The (Sheehan)
Lambretta Bible, The (Davies)
Laverda Twins & Triples Bible 1968-1986 (Falloon)
Little book of trikes, the (Quellin)
Moto Guzzi Sport & Le Mans Bible, The (Falloon)
Moto Guzzi Story, The – 3rd Edition (Falloon)
Motorcycle Apprentice (Cakebread)
Motorcycle GP Racing in the 1960s (Pereira)
Motorcycle Racing with the Continental Circus 1920-1970 (Pereira)
Motorcycle Road & Racing Chassis Designs (Noakes)
Motorcycles and Motorcycling in the USSR from 1939 (Turbett)
Motorcycling in the '50s (Clew)
MV Agusta Fours, The book of the classic (Falloon)
MV Agusta since 1945 (Falloon)
Norton Commando Bible – All models 1968 to 1978 (Henshaw)
Off-Road Giants! (Volume 1) – Heroes of 1960s Motorcycle Sport (Westlake)
Off-Road Giants! (Volume 2) – Heroes of 1960s Motorcycle Sport (Westlake)
Off-Road Giants! (Volume 3) – Heroes of 1960s Motorcycle Sport (Westlake)
Peking to Paris 2007 (Young)
Racing Classic Motorcycles (Reynolds)
Racing Line – British motorcycle racing in the golden age of the big single (Guntrip)
The Red Baron's Ultimate Ducati Desmo Manual (Cabrera Choclán)
Scooters & Microcars, The A-Z of Popular (Dan)
Scooter Lifestyle (Grainger)
Scooter Mania! – Recollections of the Isle of Man International Scooter Rally (Jackson)
Slow Burn - The growth of Superbikes & Superbike racing 1970 to 1988 (Guntrip)
Suzuki Motorcycles - The Classic Two-stroke Era (Long)
Triumph Bonneville Bible (59-83) (Henshaw)
Triumph Bonneville!, Save the – The inside story of the Meriden Workers' Co-op (Rosamond)
Triumph Motorcycles & the Meriden Factory (Hancox)
Triumph Speed Twin & Thunderbird Bible (Woolridge)
Triumph Tiger Cub Bible (Estall)
Triumph Trophy Bible (Woolridge)
TT Talking – The TT's most exciting era – As seen by Manx Radio TT's lead commentator 2004-2012 (Lambert)
Velocette Motorcycles – MSS to Thruxton – Third Edition (Burris)
Vespa – The Story of a Cult Classic in Pictures (Uhlig)
Vincent Motorcycles: The Untold Story since 1946 (Guyony & Parker)

www.veloce.co.uk

First published in September 2019, reprinted September 2022 by Veloce Publishing Limited, Veloce House, Parkway Farm Business Park, Middle Farm Way, Poundbury, Dorchester DT1 3AR, England. Tel +44 (0)1305 260068 / Fax 01305 250479 / e-mail info@veloce.co.uk / web www.veloce.co.uk or www.velocebooks.com. ISBN: 978-1-845849-03-0; UPC: 6-36847-04903-4.
© 2019 & 2022 Peter Henshaw, Justin Harvey-James and Veloce Publishing. All rights reserved. With the exception of quoting brief passages for the purpose of review, no part of this publication may be recorded, reproduced or transmitted by any means, including photocopying, without the written permission of Veloce Publishing Ltd. Throughout this book logos, model names and designations, etc, have been used for the purposes of identification, illustration and decoration. Such names are the property of the trademark holder as this is not an official publication. Readers with ideas for automotive books, or books on other transport or related hobby subjects, are invited to write to the editorial director of Veloce Publishing at the above address. British Library Cataloguing in Publication Data – A catalogue record for this book is available from the British Library. Typesetting, design and page make-up all by Veloce Publishing Ltd on Apple Mac.
Printed and bound by CPI Group (UK) Ltd, Croydon, CR0 4YY.

TRIUMPH

350/500 Unit Construction Twins Bible
1957-1974

VELOCE PUBLISHING
THE PUBLISHER OF FINE AUTOMOTIVE BOOKS

Peter Henshaw
Justin Harvey-James

Contents

Acknowledgements 5
About the authors 5

1. Year by Year: 1957-1974 7
2. What Might Have Been: the C Range Replacements 111
3. Living with a 350/500 Triumph 114
4. Modifications and Improvements 127
5. How Meriden Worked 133

Appendices
 I Specifications 137
 II Contacts, Clubs and Sources 141
 III Production and Sales Figures 143
 IV The Triumph Factory Records 146
 V Magazine Road Tests/Features 151
 VI Bibliography 154

Index 159

Acknowledgements

This book, and the website from which it has grown, would not have been possible without the help of a great many people, all of whom we thank sincerely. So, in no particular order, thanks go to staff at the Vintage Motorcycle Club library in Burton upon Trent, a superb resource for countless makes of old motorcycle, not just the Triumph C range.

Russ Gurney of the Triumph-Daytowners group (plus Matt Watkins and Roy Keegan) provided information on the T100D. Richard Wheadon (Triumph Owners' club) gave details of engine/frame numbers of machines involved in the Meriden sit-in, while Andy Burbidge is the source of the TR5T production figures. Stuart MacAulay provided information on the 1969 oil pressure switch threads.

Pictures come from a variety of sources, but thanks go to Jane Skayman at Mortons for searching out suitable period pictures from the archives. Bill Greene kindly provided pictures taken by his dad at Kelso Dunes, California in the 1960s, while, more recently, Gary Catterick took the picture of a TR5T in action at the 2018 Beamish Trial. In Holland, Erik Breedijk runs an excellent website (http://www.triumph3ta.nl) all about the Dutch military 3TAs, and obtained pictures and permissions. Thanks also go to H&H Auctions for the use of catalogue pictures, to Dave at 303 Motorcycles for the early Daytona, and, of course, to all those C range owners, some of whose bikes we snapped while they were away!

Peter Henshaw & Justin Harvey-James

About the authors

Justin Harvey-James

My love for C range Triumphs was started by my late father in the 1970s. He owned and rode a 1968 Tiger 90 and it was on this bike that I had my first solo ride. This placed a T90 high on my list of desirable bikes and when I started this journey in 1990 the model was overlooked and good surviving examples difficult to find. Lacking also was any good information on the range and this led me to searching out road tests, parts books, bulletins, catalogues, photographs and especially other bikes and owners.

This book and my website could not have been created without the help of my Triumph friends, owners, individuals and organisations spread across the world. All I have done is to collate their information and knowledge into a single source which I hope you find useful.

There is an amazing amount of material to research when you go looking for it, long lost photographs, publications and letters are still out there waiting to be discovered and I know of several collections that survive but have not yet been catalogued. Meanwhile, look at my website at www.triumph-Tiger-90.com, for additional information and useful links to help you with restoring, maintaining and enjoying your Triumph. I regularly update the information as new details come to light and my research continues.

Triumph 350/500 Unit Construction Twins Bible 1957-1974

Justin Harvey-James, co-author of this book and the man behind tiger-90.com.

My own Tiger 90 is an early 1966 model (H42001), not a perfect example I admit but it's fun to ride, easy to keep and has been a faithful companion and friend for over 25 years and thousands of miles.

I hope that the information in this book and on the website useful and informative and look forward to meeting with you and your Triumph some time.

Justin Harvey-James
*Tiger 90 Man at www.triumph-tiger-90.com
& www.triumph-tiger-100.com*

Peter Henshaw

Like Justin, one of my formative experiences was a Tiger 90. In 1981, the British motorcycle industry was all but dead and Triumph's Meriden factory on its last legs. Aged 19, I should have lusted after an RD250LC, or maybe a Superdream. But I wanted to ride British, and bought a 1968 T90 in a leafy side street of Solihull – it was one of the last Tiger 90s made.

I rode everywhere on it – two-up to Le Mans with my brother, around the coast of Britain for charity, and some freezing mid-winter commutes across the south of England. It taught me a lot, but eventually I sold it to move on to (I thought) bigger and better things. Should have kept it, of course.

What I didn't know was that writing about transport in general and motorcycles in particular would turn into a career. A stint at *Diesel Car* magazine (you've got to start somewhere) was followed by the editorship of *Motorcycle Sport & Leisure* magazine before going freelance, writing for a whole range of transport magazines and websites including *The Vintagent*, *A to B*, and *Tractor & Machinery*. In between times, I edit *Vintage & Classic Motorcycle*, the house magazine of the VMCC. The Tiger 90 is long gone, but I've ridden two-wheelers of all sorts (powered and unpowered) ever since, and still don't own a car, so that 1968 Triumph has a lot to answer for. Hope you enjoy the book.

Peter Henshaw

*Visit Veloce on the web – www.velocebooks.com
Details of all books • Special offers • New book news • Gift vouchers*

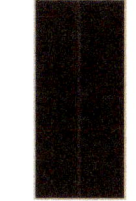

Year by Year: 1957-1974

1957

Models covered: Triumph T21
Production: 760
Engine/Frame Numbers: H1-H760
Price (new): £217

The Triumph T21 was designed from the outset to attract new buyers looking for neat, inexpensive transport. The design brief was for a clean, high-performance 350cc roadster, and the components and specifications used reflected this. Named in honour of the company's 21st anniversary, it was the first Triumph model to be fitted with the bathtub enclosure.

Many of the parts for the T21 were taken from the T20 Cub and the 500cc and 650cc twins – the abridged parts list published in April 1957 detailed all the parts shared with the other ranges.

Engine

Although the T21's engine followed the familiar Triumph pattern – vertical twin with twin camshafts and pushrods – it was actually all new. It was the first Triumph twin to feature unit construction, with the gearbox housing as part of the right-hand crankcase casting. The design allowed the gearbox to be dismantled without disturbing the remainder of the engine. Although described as unit construction, this was only partly true – the gearbox was cast in with the right-hand crankcase, but it had a separate oil supply, as did the primary drive. True unit construction engines share their oil between engine, gearbox, and primary drive.

The perfect lightweight tourer? This was Triumph's original vision for the Twenty One.

The 348cc capacity was achieved with a bore/stroke of 58.25 x 65.5mm, and the crankshaft was a single forging (another first for Triumph), the central flywheel being attached by radial bolts (very early machines featured straight-sided crankshaft webs). The crankshaft had a removable sludge trap designed to assist in the filtration of the engine oil by separating out particles via the centrifugal action of the crankshaft – an important component to clean during rebuilds!

Oil was fed to the big-end bearings through drillings associated with the sludge trap. Main bearings were a single-row

Triumph 350/500 Unit Construction Twins Bible 1957-1974

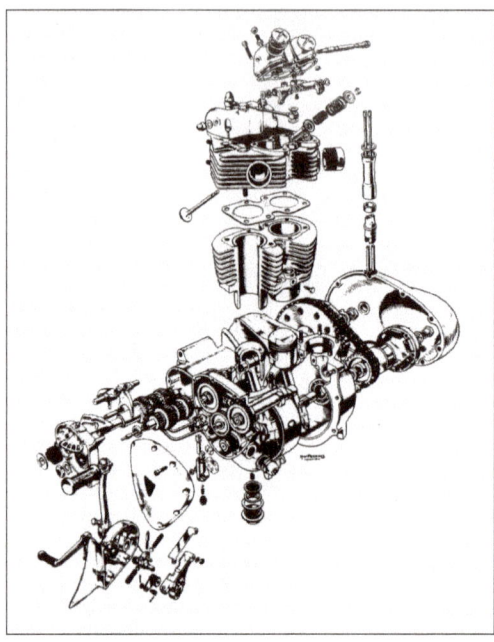

C range twin engine and gearbox, in all its exploded view glory.

Recessed cylinder head bolts on early engines.

ball-bearing (a Hoffman Metric 330) on the drive side and a plain bearing (VP3 copper lead) on the timing side – the plain bearing was perforated so as to provide pressurised oil to the crankshaft. From engine number H500 the timing side crank journal was heat treated and ground.

The connecting rods were steel stampings instead of the more usual forged alloy, split to hold the white metal thin-wall big-end bearings, and fixed with special high tensile blind bolts and locknuts. The small-ends were pressed-in phosphor bronze bushes.

The finned iron barrels were painted in silver heat resistant finish (see notes below) and attached at their base by eight short studs and nuts. Between the barrels fore and aft were the chromed pushrod tubes, which contained short pushrods operating on paired tappets, these housed within removable blocks in the cylinder base.

The pushrod tubes were sealed at each end by specialised silicone rubber washers. The sealing arrangement was altered many times over the years, and there are numerous variations in parts. Sealing the tubes and the barrels always presented problems, and was never really overcome successfully. Careful assembly using sealing compounds and new correct parts will minimise leaks, but may never completely eliminate them.

The well-designed alloy cylinder head was fixed by eight bolts, four of which pass through the rocker boxes (these accommodate paired rockers moving on hollow, hardened shafts). The rockers featured drillings to allow oil to be fed to the adjustable tappets, the adjusters reached via removable caps on the rocker boxes. A branched oil feed pipe supplied oil to the rocker shafts via drillings within each box. Each pipe was attached by a shouldered bolt running through the box and sealed with soft copper washers and domed, cadmium-plated nuts. A pair of head steadies attached the forward head bolts to an attachment point on the frame, readily visible in period photographs.

Early cylinder heads appear to have smaller exhaust ports and stubs than later heads (the casting number 3699 identifies an early example). On the cylinder head near the right inlet valve there is a stamped alphanumeric code, which refers to the batch of cylinder head castings. Triumph contracted out the casting to High Duty Alloys of Slough and Aircraft & Motor of Redditch.

The paired, case-hardened nickel steel camshafts ran in plain bronze collapsible bushes on the left, and were unbushed in the right-hand crankcase – oil scrolls assist lubrication. The inlet camshaft also operated the paired plunger oil pump, the distributor drive, and the timed breather system. The camshafts, keyed to the timing pinions, were located with steel plates and screws, punched on assembly to prevent them coming loose.

Oil pressure relief valve – if the plunger was exposed, you had pressure.

The paired oil pump fed pressurised oil via drillings to the oil pressure relief valve located in the front of the crankcase, and which featured a tell-tale plunger to indicate the presence of oil pressure: if the plunger was sticking out while the engine was running, then all was well. From the relief valve, drillings took oil to the timing side crankshaft bush.

Having made its way from the crankshaft to the sump, oil was collected by the return pump via a filter gauze and curved pipe fixed within the right-hand crankcase casting, to be returned to the oil tank. The filter here was accessed via a removable cap underneath the engine.

Transmission

The primary drive was by a ⅜in, non-tensioned, non-adjustable duplex chain to the Triumph four-spring clutch of the period. The hub was fixed to the gearbox main shaft by a taper, and located with a woodruff key, while the clutch featured four bonded and four plain plates, plus a rubber shock absorber in the hub. The Lucas three-wire alternator also lived inside the primary chaincase, the rotor keyed to the crankshaft and secured with a shouldered nut and locking washer. Access to the final drive sprocket was via a removable plate (with oil seal) behind the clutch basket. The small attachment screws were punched to prevent them coming loose.

The Parts Book indicates that there was an oiler jet for the final drive chain, but this isn't illustrated, and Tri-Cor, Triumph's USA Eastern distributor, described the chain oiler tube in a service bulletin dated 21st July 1961, but also recommended that it be blocked off to prevent oil leaks. This blocked-off tube remained on the C range for several years, and is the small hollow stud found behind the clutch, corresponding with the lower part of the final drive sprocket. Later bikes had an oil feed to the final drive chain from the return feed to the oil tank.

The clutch cable entered the gearbox via a simple grommet on top of the outer cover, and connected to the clutch release lever via a threaded spoke. Replacing the cable required removal of the entire outer cover, and extracting the cable through the rubber cover of the distributor as well.

The four-speed gearbox featured plain bushes for the layshaft and ball bearings for the main; the gears were built up onto an intermediate cover while the outer cover contained the positive-stop mechanism and clutch release screw. A useful gear indicator was attached to the selector quadrant.

Fuelling & ignition

The carburettor was an 375 Amal Monobloc $^{13}/_{16}$ with no choke, though the carb featured the usual tickler arrangement, and received its air via a rubber hose from an oblong air filter attached forward on the left of the vertical main frame rail.

The twin exhaust down pipes were 1in diameter, terminating in Triumph-style tubular silencers, and without the offset entry of later items. The silencers were originally supplied by Burgess, one of the many Birmingham-based parts suppliers for the British motor industry. One factory photograph does show a T21 with extended cylindrical silencers, as well as a radio and handlebar fairing, part of a 1958 display to encourage sales to the police.

The silencers were attached to the frame by short lengths of tubing with trapped ends – the same support was used to attach the pillion footrests if these optional extras were fitted.

The short, chrome-plated kickstart folded at the top, its 'Triumph' monogrammed rubber closed at the end, while the chromed gearlever rubber also showed 'Triumph.'

The distributor, located behind the right-hand cylinder, was the Lucas 18D2 (reference 40573) driven by a skew gear from the inlet camshaft, neatly covered and protected from the elements by a large rubber sleeve. The

Triumph 350/500 Unit Construction Twins Bible 1957-1974

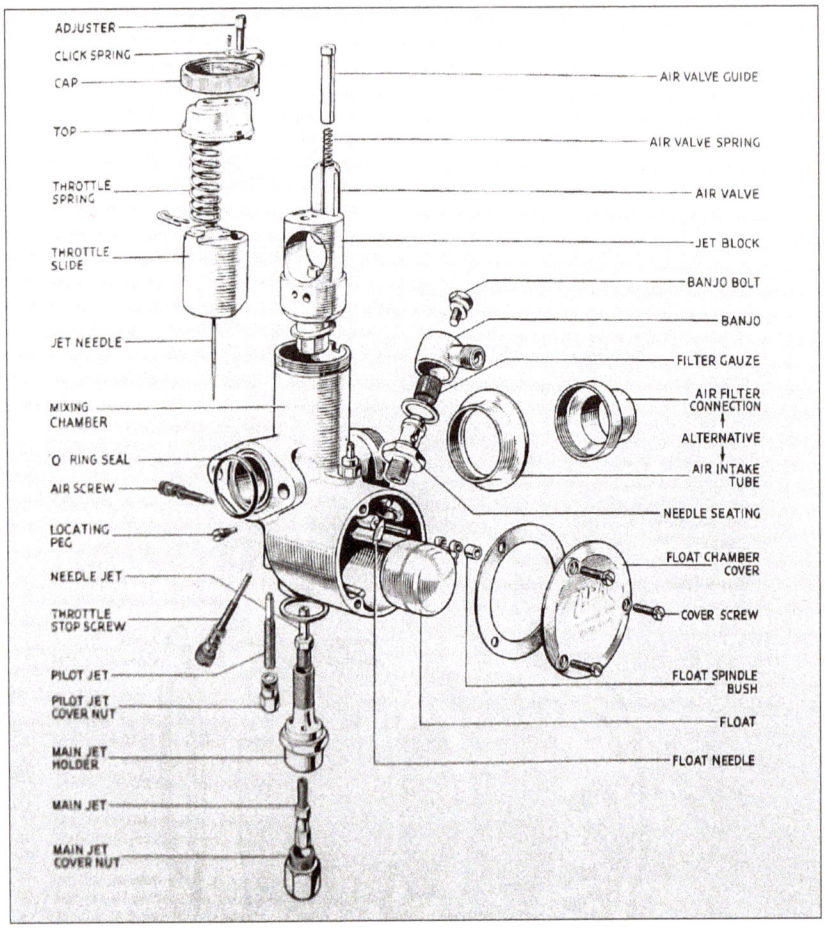

Amal Monobloc carburettor was a British industry stalwart.

Distributor date marking (1958 shown).

ignition timing was adjusted by loosening the mounting clamp and rotating the distributor body. A Lucas MA6 coil was attached by loop bracket to the inner rear mudguard, angled to allow the HT cable to exit to the left.

Electrics

Six-volt electrics were based around a three-cell Lucas PUZ7E/11 battery and Lucas alternator, which was a composite of an RM13 stator and RM15 rotor, lighter than the RM15 but efficient at lower engine speeds. Alternator wiring was arranged in combination with the ignition/lighting switch to provide adequate charging depending on load, with an 'emergency start' circuit in case of a flat battery. Photographs showing the seat base of the early factory machines (Gloss Black) show a foam rubber extension to retain the battery in position when the seat was closed.

Lighting comprised a Lucas 700 headlamp with pilot light – look carefully for 'Motorcycle' written on the glass. There were variations for export bikes and the period Lucas catalogue details these. At the rear, mounted on the number plate was (you guessed it) a Lucas 564 combined tail/brake/reflector light – look for the Lucas part numbers.

The Lucas brake light switch was the then new 6SA unit, operated by movement of a small 'ear' on the brake lever, the switch itself attached to the brake torque stay nearby. The cables to the switch passed through a moulded rubber cover.

Wheels, brakes & tyres

The wheels consisted of 17in Dunlop WM2 chrome rims front and rear, with a front 3.25-17 Dunlop tyre, ribbed in the pattern of the Avon Speedmaster. The rear tyre was a 3.25-17 Dunlop Universal, with the tread pattern of the (still available at the time of writing) Avon SM.

The front hub was painted silver, with a 7in single-leading-shoe drum brake with non-fully floating shoes. The alloy brake plate on the right was complemented by a shaped chromed hub on the left, with pressed concentric circles. The brake cable stop was located on the lower fork, and the cable had extra support from a small 'P' bracket on the mudguard. The rod-operated rear brake was also 7in SLS, in a hub that was common to other Triumph models, the adjuster a simple 'T' shape, cadmium- or chrome-

Rear hub was shared with other Triumphs.

Frame & controls

The frame (pinned and brazed) comprised a single tube loop main frame, with castings for the headset and rear engine support/swing arm. A bolted-on subframe supported the seat and rear suspension, while welded brackets were provided for other components.

The main frame was of 1⅜in OD 12-gauge tubing, and the duplex frame tubes for supporting the engine ⅞in 14-gauge, while the subframe was a combination of 1in 15-gauge tubing for the uprights and ⅞in 14-gauge for the seat support base. The headset and engine bridge support were malleable iron castings. The steering head angle was 64.5 degrees, matching Triumph practice for the period.

The engine/gearbox unit was held in the frame at the front by shaped plates, with studs with distinctive dome headed nuts. Underneath, behind and above the gearbox, were spacers and plates fixed by studs with conventional nuts.

A centre stand was fitted, but not the 'Easylift' type shown in the 1958 catalogue. From H434, the side stand was recorded fitted as standard, though this and the pillion footrests were advertised as 'extras'!

plated. The tubular brake torque stay and lower chain guard were combined.

Both sides of the rear axle had shaped spacers, and the effective Triumph-type chain adjuster, all parts cadmium-plated, and nuts were an early type of Nyloc – it is important to use this type. It is quite normal for the left adjuster to foul the brake plate when set to the minimum chain length. The Smiths speedo drive unit was mounted on the rear hub in the early angular form, and appears to be upside down!

Schematic of the twin's lubrication system. Note the plain timing side main bearing and two coarse filters.

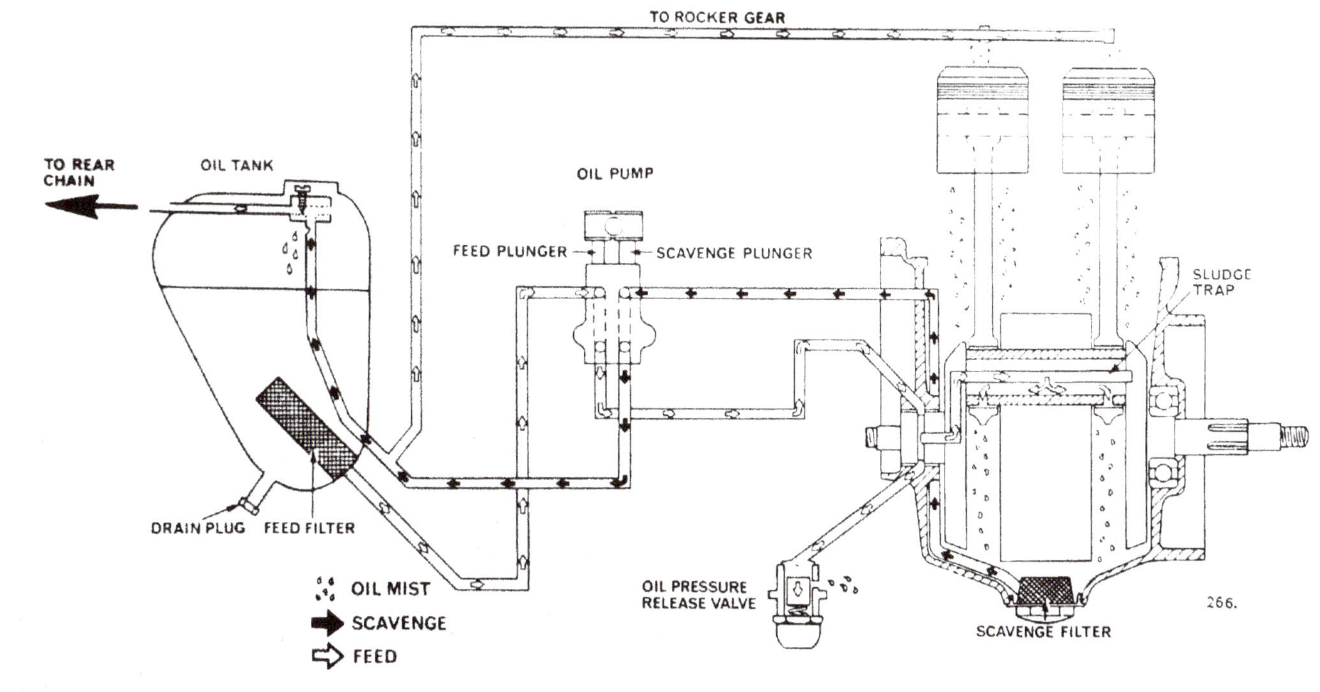

Fig. A2. Engine lubrication diagram

The forks were oil damped of conventional BSA/Triumph design, featuring chromed stanchions held in by cast iron steering yokes, with the sliders supported by sintered bronze bushes. The lower sliders featured cast clamps, with a mudguard support which could be hinged down to support the front wheel off the ground to assist in wheel removal. Recommended quantity of SAE 30 oil for each fork leg was 150cc, while Girling rear shocks (SB3 4234) used 100lb springs and painted/chromed covers. The shocks' corrected length was 11.9in extended, 9.4in compressed.

The headset was enclosed by the trademark Triumph nacelle, made in two parts with chrome trims disguising the joins. The nacelle housed the headlamp with pilot light, combined ignition and lighting switch on the right, ammeter on the left, the speedometer and the horn, as well as the steering damper knob. Rubber grommets were used where the handlebars pass into the nacelle, also supporting the control cables and wiring. The steering stops were associated with the lower fork bridge, and there was a facility to lock the steering with a padlock.

The slightly upswept 1in handlebar was attached by U-bolts to the upper fork yoke, while the brake and clutch levers were plain with vertical clamps, and feature distinctive 'one finger adjustment' of the clutch and brake cables. This type of adjuster slides easily within the lever clamp, and had a knurled adjuster turning half a turn at a time to adjust the cable tension.

On the left was a Lucas 25SA combined dip/horn switch attached to the clutch lever by a specialised clamp (alloy casting) – the wiring was grey. The twist grip featured a curved sleeve so that the cable entered the nacelle smoothly, the throttle friction clutch operated by a small adjusting knob. The grips were similar to the Amal pattern – black, quite thin, with a fine raised finish and embossed with the Triumph logo.

The ignition/lighting switch was the Lucas PRS8 type, the three-position switch controlling the pilot lighting and headlamp. The speedometer was a 120mph Smiths chronometric with the trip meter operated by an extension accessible within the nacelle. The ammeter was the black Lucas BM4 8-0-8 type, while the hidden horn was the Lucas HF1441. Look carefully on the reverse for the date code applied to all Lucas components.

Tinwork

The 3.5-gallon fuel tank had fore and aft mountings, but no tank top grid or central styling strip, though it did have chrome styling strips on each side of the mouth organ-type tank badge. Black rubber knee grips featuring the Triumph motif were attached by two screws. The fuel tap was the Ewarts type, with separate plungers for main and reserve leading to a single clear plastic fuel pipe.

The ribbed and flanged front mudguard was the fully valanced 'Roman helmet' style, attached to the lower fork sliders by a shaped brace. The lower mudguard stay looped within the mudguard and, when released by a single nut, was (and still is) able to act as a stand to help with wheel removal. The front number plate was fitted within a stylish chrome surround.

The rear mudguard was hidden by the bathtub enclosure; a new Triumph feature for the T21. The bathtub was formed from two 22-gauge steel pressings bolted together, with a rubber strip between them (the bolts carefully hidden to present a neat finish). These panels were supported and fastened by four self-tapping screws around the seat loop, with additional brackets associated with the fuel tank mount. Hidden underneath the pressings was a support stay running from the suspension mounts to a point at the rear of the panels, nicely illustrated in *The Motorcycle* 28th February 1957. The stay rarely survives, however, and many restored machines don't have it. It's an understandable mistake as the stay is not illustrated or mentioned in the Parts Book!

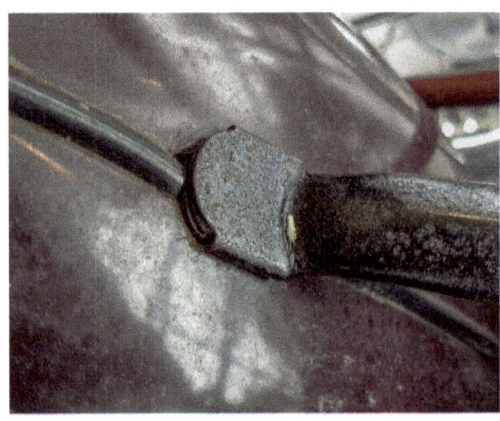

Detail of number plate bracket on the bathtub ('59 5TA shown).

Year by Year: 1957-1974

Bathtub, generous front mudguard and nacelle – the first Triumph C range was designed to be clean and fuss-free.

The Twenty One, 3TA and 5TA's beautifully presented toolkit – it didn't last long.

The rear number plate was attached by two nuts and bolts at the lower edge, the single upper mounting fitting neatly between the bathtub panels, with no fixing visible from the top. Each side of the bathtub had chromed 'Twenty One' script, while a chromed knob on the right released the seat.

In keeping with Edward Turner's yen for enclosure, the oil tank was hidden behind the bathtub, suspended at the top by two flat steel strips bridging the frame, with a lower mount to the rear engine plate. The cap included a dipstick, while the bottom of the tank had an extension to allow access to the drain plug, removable filter, and connection for the oil pipes.

A single-piece upper chainguard attached to the left side of the swinging arm, and could swing up to assist wheel and/or chain removal.

The seat (supplied by Motoplas) had a shaped metal base topped with latex foam, and covered by black Vynide for both the top and sides, separated by white piping. The lower fringe of the seat cover nearest the base was grey, and there was a centrally fixed passenger strap. The early seat base is nicely illustrated in the Parts Catalogue, also showing the rubber pad for the battery and safety strap. The seat hinged on the left to give access to the air filter, oil tank, battery, rectifier, coil and the tools, which were housed in a moulded tray covering the rear mudguard.

The inner mudguard extended forward, and attached to the frame at several points, using a tapped hole in the main frame forging as one of the locations – this hole survived for many years, and can be seen on all models up to 1967.

Finally, pannier brackets. Photographs of H120, a very early production bike, show external pannier brackets fitted, but these do

The nacelle's square rubber grommets supposedly kept out the weather.

not appear in the 1957 brochure, the Parts Book, or on period shots of other machines. From H301, pannier brackets were recorded as fitted to the frame, but holes were not provided in the bodywork – owners were expected to pierce the panels themselves to fit panniers. The holes that corresponded in the upper suspension gussets were part of the pannier fitting arrangement, and these would continue for years to come.

Colours

The finish for the T21 was confusing, to say the least. The first hundred bikes came in Metallic Silver Grey, including the frame and engine mounts. From H101 the finish was Shell Blue Sheen, again, including the frame parts and engine mounts, with only the number plates in black. Some time later the frame parts became black, possibly from H288, as there is a note in the front of Triumph Record Book 147.

The cylinder barrels were shown finished silver in the brochures, but one road test machine had black ones. The majority of the engine cases were unpolished, apart from the three covers and the rocker boxes, which had a satin sheen, not a high polish. Outer engine/gearbox covers were fastened by Phillips screws, though many owners have since swapped these for Allen bolts, which give a tighter seal. Triumph's distinctive triangular patent plate on the timing cover read 'Triumph 350 Twin,' and included the patent numbers.

Notes for 1957

The reasons for the introduction of the bathtub are complex. Scooters had become popular in late 1950s Britain, and were seen as clean and inexpensive transport. Many British motorcycle manufacturers attempted to enter the scooter market with new products, and this included Triumph with the Tina, and later the Tigress.

Parallel to this, there was a theme of British factories attempting to make motorcycling a clean, civilised and fuss-free affair. The dream, a recurring one in the industry, was to open it up to the proverbial 'man on the Clapham omnibus.' Of course, motorcycling was already being

"Smooth, Silent, Clean" – the brochure blurb said it all.

used as cheap transport by thousands right through the 1950s, but these users accepted that bikes needed more intensive maintenance than cars, and that the British climate ensured that sooner or later one got cold and wet, and often oily into the bargain.

The dream of extending the motorcycle market beyond this core resurfaced several times. The 1921 Ner-a-Car enclosed all components except the engine, and the Francis-Barnett Cruiser of 1933 was similar, though less radical. Postwar, Velocette unveiled its LE in 1949, a quiet, water-cooled flat-twin with more rider protection – the company also partly enclosed the engine and gearbox on some of its famous four-stroke singles with fibreglass panelling. In 1959, Ariel launched the Leader, designed from the ground up as a fully enclosed motorcycle, and using glassfibre and steel bodywork to hide the box section frame and 250cc two-stroke twin power unit.

By then, Triumph had already launched the T21. It wasn't as radical as the Leader, being based around a conventional tubular frame and running gear, but the bathtub certainly cleaned up its appearance, and the optional screen and leg shields could drastically improve weather protection. But Triumph did have form here.

Early nacelle (here on a 5TA) was neat and clean.

Edward Turner had conceived a forerunner to the T21 ten years earlier. The prototype 3TU was designed to be clean running, cheap to make and to own, with pressed steel wheels, huge mudguards, and an enclosed chain. Like the T21, it was a 350cc twin, but performance was limited, and, at the time, Triumph was far too busy meeting the demand for conventional motorcycles to attempt anything out of the ordinary. So the 3TU was shelved, though its concept arguably reappeared with the T21 a decade later.

Before the T21 was launched Edward Turner had already begun to clean up the appearance of Triumph singles and twins. Whatever his shortcomings as an engineer, there's no denying that Turner had a real artistic flair for design. It was his good looking bikes – the restyled Tiger 70, 80 and 90, followed by the milestone Speed Twin – which turned around Triumph's fortunes in the mid-1930s. The company became known as a seller of flash, fast, sporting motorcycles.

By the late 1940s, Edward Turner wanted to add smoother styling, and the result was the famous nacelle, which enclosed the headlamp, steering head, speedometer, ammeter and light switch in a smooth, rounded enclosure, with neat chrome strips to hide the joins. In its own way, the nacelle was a masterpiece of design, and became a Triumph trademark, fitted to every bike except the Trophy through the 1950s. The T21's bathtub was really an extension of the same look, seeking to clean up and enclose the 'bitty' look of the average motorcycle.

None of these sanitised motorcycles, it has to be said, succeeded in their aim of making motorcycling more mainstream. The Velocette LE certainly remained in production for 22 years, and became a favourite with UK police forces as the 'noddy bike,' but, like the Leader and others, it was built in relatively small numbers, never breaking into the mass market which the British factories dreamt of.

In fact, throughout the 1950s, they could only stand by and watch as Italian and German manufacturers made the dream a reality. Vespa had launched its iconic scooter in 1946, swiftly followed by Lambretta. Just the thing for an impoverished, transport-starved Italy of the late 1940s. Their popularity soared, encouraging German manufacturers to follow suit. In both countries, thousands of people needed transport but could not afford a car, and this new generation of lightweights offered cheap, stylish and independent transport. British buyers took to scooters and mopeds, too, imports booming from the mid-1950s. Some British manufacturers attempted to compete with home-designed tiddlers, but they never met with much success, lacking the style of the Continentals. The enclosed motorcycles meanwhile, such as the Ariel Leader and Velocette LE, were more expensive than the true scooters.

Overwhelmingly, the British industry concentrated on larger, conventional motorcycles, and the market for these was changing. Traditional markets for British bikes, such as Australia, which at one time took 20 per cent of UK motorcycle exports, were collapsing as buyers moved on to cars. These markets were being replaced by North America, which turned out to be a vast, affluent and profitable market for big bikes as a leisure item. Over there, motorcycling was about weekend sport, not day-to-day practicality, and buyers demanded performance and rugged style over weather protection. So, while the Americans loved the power and agility of a lusty Triumph twin, they didn't like nacelles and bathtubs. The same trend followed on in the UK, and, if that's what the customers wanted, who could blame Triumph for dropping both of these? The bathtub did linger into the mid-1960s (see below) but Edward Turner's enclosures ultimately turned out to be a fairly short lived experiment.

Early production

Engine production officially began with H1 to H4 sometime after 15th February 1957, though there would have been several months of activity previously to design and arrange a supply of parts. These first engines were built in the experimental department rather than the production engine workshop.

Like all new Triumphs, the prototype T21s were tested on the roads of the Midlands and beyond, and the Meriden factory had its own team of road testers whose job was to put miles on prototype, pre-production and production bikes. As was well known in the factory, they were envied by everyone in summer and no one in the winter! Percy Tait was one of the best known testers, with a racing background and skills to match. The T21 could manage 80mph, and Percy apparently used all this performance to the full on one occasion to escape the pursuing press, who were interested in this new and as yet unidentified bike!

The next batch of engines – H5 to H36 – were built on 19th March 1957. H36 was sent to the experimental department, and production then did not start again until 13th April when new flywheel balance weights were applied, presumably as a result of tests on H36. The engine record book during this early period is fascinating as it details a number of small changes and details. Machines destined for Australia, for example, were fitted with +10 thou pistons and barrels.

Complete machines H1 and H2 are recorded as having been assembled on 22nd February 1957, with H3 on the 28th and H4 on

Urban myth!

When the T21 was launched in the USA, no one failed to notice that 'Twenty One' matched the 350 twin's engine capacity in cubic inches – so that's what it was named after, right? Actually, no. No Triumph's sales literature of the time mentions this, as the T21 was named after the 21st anniversary of the Triumph Engineering Co Ltd. In the early 1930s, Triumph had nearly disappeared for good. It was part of Ariel, whose parent company, Components Ltd, went bankrupt in 1932. Jack Sangster – son of the Chairman – saved the motorcycle side of the business and, in 1936, set up Triumph Engineering Co, with Edward Turner at the helm. Nineteen fifty-seven marked its 21st.

Meanwhile, in America, the focus was on the bigger twins.

8th March – the first two machines were shown at the RAI Motorcycle Exhibition in Amsterdam from 28th Feb-10th March 1957. Destinations of the early production bikes were as follows:

H1 H2, H5 and H6 – Stokvis & Zonen, Holland (H5 and H6 known to survive – H5 was sold at a Bonham's auction in April 2017).

H3 – Germany.

H4 – Sweden.

H7 and H8 – Norway, while other early machines went to dealers in Denmark, Malta, Japan, Singapore, Chile and Algiers.

H39, H41, H45, H50-H52 and H88 were possibly test machines as, though made in early 1957, they are not recorded as dispatched until November. All of these were sent to UK dealers with the factory records amended to suit.

H39 – Elite Motors Tooting Ltd, despatched 15th November 1957.

H41 – Harveys, Lambeth SW8, 15th November 1957.

H45 – Pride & Clark, London, 15th November 1957.

H50 – Kings of Oxford, 22nd November 1957.

H51 – W Shearings, 23 North Street, Bishops Stortford, 16th November 1957.

H52 – Pride & Clarke, London, 14th November 1957.

H71 – Marble Arch Motor Supplies, 27th May 1957. Appears to be the first official UK machine.

H85 – Johnson Motors, USA. Appears to be the first T21 sent to the USA. Very few T21s were exported to North America, and most of the early production bikes were sent to varied export markets, such as Costa Rica, Algeria, Borneo, Mexico, Japan, South Africa, Australia, etc, as well as Europe. Triumph clearly thought the T21 had export potential, and wanted to get early bikes into the hands of importers before going into full-scale supply of UK dealers. Of the 760 T21s built for 1957, some 485 were exported, but only 11 of these went to North America. Five went to Johnson Motors, and six to Tri-Cor.

H96 – Tri-Cor (Triumph Corporation, USA). Publicity pictures of a T21 taken in Baltimore could have been of H96.

H120 (WAC 574) – Cliffe & Sons, London SE1, 15th May 1957. Pictures of this factory/press machine survive in the VMCC archive.

> ## What the press said
> T21 – *The Motorcycle*, 7th March 1957
> Alan Baker's first road test of the T21 started in a blizzard. At least, it was snowing as he rode up to Meriden to collect it. The weather had cleared by the time he headed south on the first T21 to be road tested by the press, but the wet roads gave him reason enough not to probe the limits of braking and handling. Triumph also asked him not to thrash the bike as it had covered little over 100 miles from new. Oh, and the carburation and ignition auto-advance were not quite to production standards so could he make allowances?
>
> Actually, all of that was probably true, as the bike would have been assembled only a matter of days before Baker arrived to collect, though you might think the first press bike of a brand new model would have been made a priority for 500 miles' running in, a check over and a service.
>
> But none of that mattered, because Mr Baker loved the little 350. It was light, with a low seat and low centre of gravity, all confidence building stuff on the damp and slimy tarmac of a wet English spring. It also came over as very civilised, even gentlemanly – quiet and with 'no vibration of note' between 15mph and 65mph in top gear. Sixty-five was as fast as Alan Baker wanted to go with such a tight engine.
>
> And the verdict? 'A big step forward by one of Britain's foremost manufacturers. With its modern styling, excellent handling and sprightly performance for its capacity, it should fulfil the needs of many discriminating motorcyclists.'

Naturally the motorcycle magazines wanted to get their hands on a T21 for road test, and arch-rivals *The Motorcycle* and *Motorcycling* both carried detailed and beautifully illustrated write-ups on 28th February 1957. The machine featured would have been one of the very early machines (H1 to H4) as no others had been assembled at the time. *The Motorcycle* appears to have scooped the first proper road test, though, this appearing in the 7th March issue (see box), which again would have been one of the early bikes. Early American road tests included one by *Cycle* in its December 1957 issue, which had a nice picture of Gill Stratton (actor and sports reporter, according to the caption) on his new T21.

1958

Models covered: Triumph T21, 3TA, 5TA
Production:
T21	4720
3TA	2
5TA	2

Engine/frame numbers: H761-H5480
Price (T21): £228/5s/11d (USA – $818)

Up hill, down dale with your chums in '58 (with a bit of artistic licence).

"... turbine-like smoothness, extreme ease of starting, silent performance ..."

Many of the details for the 1957 T21 apply for the 1958 model, and only the differences are listed here. The most significant changes were a new frame with revised steering angle, and a new 'stressed' fuel tank, now showing the raised central seam covered by a chrome trim, with the addition of a parcel grid on the tank top. The new tank was semi-stressed by the inclusion of a squared beam running longitudinally between the fixing points, the top of the beam visible through the filler cap aperture. Unfortunately, in practice the tank added little stiffness to the frame, and as more powerful 500cc C range bikes appeared, their handling came under fire. Triumph's solution was first seen in 1960, with an extra top tube added to US competition bikes to stiffen things up, though it was several years before this was fitted across the range.

The front brake hub was now painted black, and has a fluted chrome cover on the left – this was only applied this year.

New silencers were now asymmetric, and mounted slightly higher than before. The brackets to attach the silencers to the machine and to support the pillion footrests changed to an improved shape, which remained in place until 1963.

Main stand was now the 'Easylift' stand indicated in the 1958 brochure and displayed in the 1959 brochure – an extension pedal made it easier to use. The Amal's carburettor choke was slightly smaller at $^{25}/_{32}$in after H3330, and now had a plunger choke fitted, though this was likely to have been added earlier in production.

The dualseat illustrated in the 1958 catalogue shows the seat strap, but this is inaccurate on UK machines (it may remain on some export machines). Finally, the finish was Blue Sheen with Black frame and ancillary parts (including hubs). Cylinder fins were generally Silver Sheen.

Parts Book No: 1.

Notes for 1958

This is a summary of other modifications made during 1958 and the engine numbers they apply from. Details are taken from the Factory Engine Build Records.

H1584 – Modified valve springs.
H2297 – Primary chaincase metering jet reduced.

H2458 – Modified big-end bolt (shorter).
H2769 – Battery securing method changes to rod across battery.
H2828 – Endless primary drivetrain.
H3663 – Longer distributor clamp bolt fitted.
H4184 – New pattern tappets.
H5169 – New clutch inserts on all machines (Neolangite).
H5015 – Modified lower oil seal on the pushrod tubes.

A Tri-Cor bulletin of 10th January 1958 described a plastic battery cover that should be fitted before the machine was sold, and warned to not overfill the battery. This probably covered machines before H2769, when the battery tray was changed to eliminate the earlier issues of acid vapour causing corrosion.

Production

Production for 1958 began on 10th September 1957, with H761 despatched to Hacks Cycle Store, British Guiana, ten days later. The first UK machine was H774, sent to FH Blackpool and Co Ltd, Stanstead Road, Forest Hill, London, on the 18th. Only 637 machines (about 13 per cent of that year's production) were sent to the USA, with approximately equal numbers to Johnson Motors and Tri-Cor.

Thirty-three T21s were supplied to UNICEF in Kenya, news of which was illustrated in the BSA Group News Centenary booklet. This rare and fascinating book can be viewed at the VMCC library in Burton on Trent.

Police-specification 3TA for 1958. Police forces the world over took to the 5TA, in particular.

Other notes

There were no UK road tests of the T21 in 1958, but in *The Motorcycle* 24th October 1957 issue there was an article on 'Improvements to the Triumph Range for 1958.'

At the time of writing, a well restored 1958 T21 (H2158) was on display in the Barber Museum in Birmingham, Alabama, USA, along with several other Triumphs. The museum is a motorsport Mecca, housing a diverse collection of rare motorcycles and cars; well worth a trip, especially for the Barber festival held each October.

"Now in its second season" went the brochure, but looking much the same as in the first year.

Triumph 350/500 Unit Construction Twins Bible 1957-1974

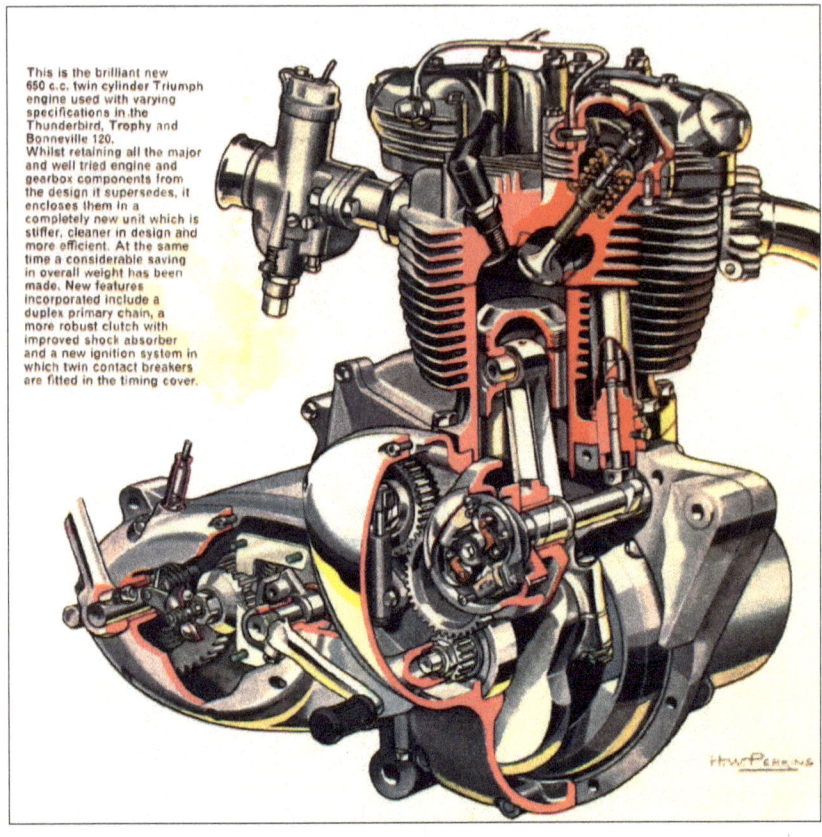

Big brother. The 650cc twin took another six years to follow the 3TA into unit construction.

New 500cc 5TA roars in to '59, with a Tiger Cub in a supporting role.

1959

Models covered: Triumph T21, 3TA, 5TA
Production:

T21	34
3TA	2802
3TA Police	59
5TA	3112
5TA Police	18
1960 T100A (converted)	2
1960 TR5AR (converted)	1
Engine/frame numbers:	H5481-H11511
Prices:	
3TA	£228/5s/11d
5TA	£245/15s/2d

The big news for 1959 was the launch of the 5TA Speed Twin, alongside the renamed 3TA, which replaced the T21. The 5TA was more or less a 500cc version of the 350, the engine bored out to 69.0mm to give a capacity of 490cc. Unusually, for a British twin of the time, that made it oversquare, as the stroke remained at the 350's 65.5mm. Other changes were few, though the stamped steel con-rods of the 3TA were replaced with forged alloy H-section items, and the carburettor was the slightly larger 375/3 (⅞in) Amal Monobloc. With 7:1 pistons, the 5TA produced 27bhp at 6500rpm, substantially more power than the 350. Gearing was raised to make the most of this extra urge, with a 20-tooth gearbox sprocket replacing the 18 teeth of the 3TA. The internal gearbox ratios were unchanged, but overall ratios went up to 11.56:1, 8.35:1, 5.62:1 and 4.8:1. The rear tyre was slightly wider as well, at 3.5in.

Triumph was keen to emphasise the new 5TA's links with the original Speed Twin of the 1930s, so it came in the same Aramanth Red (nickname 'Ammer and Thread') colour, though with the 3TA's nacelle and bathtub tinwork. Just to underline the point, this deep red was used

5TA combined the 3TA concept with a bigger, oversquare version of the small twin.

as an overall colour, applied to the frame, hubs and rear brake drum, as well as the tinwork.

The end result was a bike that weighed only a little more than its little brother (350lb dry), but could top nearly 90mph, cruise at 70mph, and return 70mpg. But it wasn't a sports bike – that role was left to the Tiger 100, which, for 1959, stuck with the older pre-unit engine. Instead, the 5TA was more of an ultimate all-rounder, with more torque and performance than the 3TA, especially useful two-up, but with the same emphasis on ease of use.

For both models the air filter mounting was new, illustrated in the *The Motorcycle*, 23rd October 1958. This allowed the filter to be extracted through the seat opening rather than removing the left-hand bathtub panel. The same article indicated that the front brake cam lever was altered to improve the action, and that plain chrome covers on the hub replaced the fluted covers fitted for 1958 (the picture showed a fluted cover). Optional extras remained advertised as prop stand and pillion footrests – no QD (quickly detachable) rear hub as yet.

As for colours, the 3TA stuck with its Shell Blue Sheen, black frame, with Silver Sheen for the front hub and cylinder fins. North American customers got different names, if not colours, with USA brochures describing them as Continental Red and Azure Blue. A few machines were supplied in other colours, and 3TA H8946 went to the Ministry of Supply in London in Charcoal. The Ministry also received H8945, though apparently in the standard colour. Like other manufacturers, Triumph was happy to supply bikes in different specs and colours if a fleet order was on the cards.

Parts Book No: 2 (actually starts from H5485).

Notes for 1959
Engine modifications made during 1959 model year.
H5785 onwards – Modified kick starter shaft bush.
H7039 onwards – Shorter valve guides.
H7116 onwards – Tapered piston rings (5TA).
H8141 onwards – Modified tappet guide blocks and thicker oil seals to improve sealing of the pushrod tubes.
H9001 onwards – New alternator grommet.
H10049 onwards – Modified distributor oil seal.

Production
Production for 1959 began 17th September 1958, with show models for the Paris Show (3rd October) and the Earls Court Show (15th-22nd November).
H5481 (3TA) – Eventually sent to Nigeria (10th December).
H5482 (3TA) – Sent to Decat of Belgium, 6th December.
H5483 (5TA) – To Campbell & Cameron.
H5484 (5TA) – To F Llewellyn & Co Ltd, Liverpool on 18th December. Believed to be the 5TA shown at Earls Court with a radio in the tank top.
H5485 (3TA) – First UK market 3TA of the year, sent to Kingston Motors, Kingston on Thames.

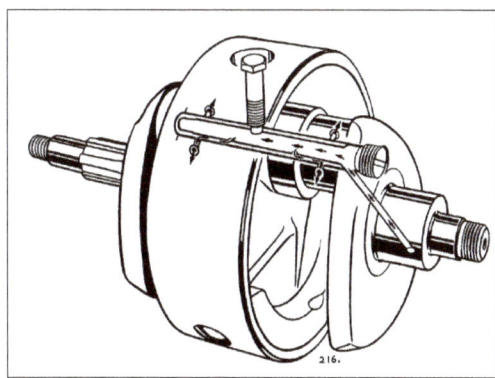

350/500 crankshaft. If the sludge trap was neglected, it would eventually block the oilways.

Americans called the 5TA Speed Twin the 'Streamliner.'

H5486 (5TA) – Sent to Julius Martinez, Nicaragua as part of a batch of 23 machines.

H5881 (5TA) – Built by the experimental department, eventually dispatched to J Surtees on 23rd October 1959.

H5939 (5TA) – Possibly a press or factory machine, eventually dispatched to Slocombes of Neasden (3rd October 1960).

H6187 (5TA) – Sent to The Daimler Company, Coventry for a Mr Hopper on 18th February 1959.

H6549 (3TA Police) – Thought to be the first Police Specification 3TA, supplied to the Buckinghamshire Constabulary 21st November 1958.

H6550 (Police) – Retained by Triumph until March 1959 when it was sent to Surtees, West Wickham.

H8656 (5TA Police) – Thought to be the first Police-specification 5TA, supplied to Hadlers of Chelmsford and followed later by H8900.

H6159 (5TA) – Converted to a TR5AC by the Competition Department, and registered to the Factory as 565 AAC.

H6282 (3TA) – Originally a 3TA but taken from its production batch 12th November 1958 and transferred to the experimental department for conversion to a T100A. This machine was eventually sent to Slocombes of Neasden on 16th November 1959.

Export order to Aziz, South Vietnam consisted of 3TAs H6237 and H6557-H6585 and 5TAs H6938 & H6955-H7088. One of these survives in the UK!

H11511 (3TA) – Final production bike for 1959, built 4th September 1959 and despatched to Austria; one of a group of six.

T100A prototype

With the launch of the 5TA, Triumph was naturally planning to replace its other 500cc twins with the newer unit construction engine. The T100A prototype was H9480, taken from a batch of 5TAs on 22nd May 1959, transferred to the experimental department and rebuilt with high compression pistons. Two sets of photographs of this machine survive in the VMCC archive: in one it's finished in Blue over Silver Sheen (unregistered); and in the other it's set in Black over Ivory (registered 148 AUE). The road test in *Motor Cycling* 10th March 1960 featured this machine. Both sets of photographs clearly show the engine stamped as 5TA H9480. It was later sent to Jack Surtees, West Wickham on 8th July 1960. At the time of writing, the whereabouts of this one-off prototype are unknown, even if it still exists. So that's one to look out for.

Racing the 5TA

Tri-Cor sent out a regular series of bulletins to keep dealers and customers up to date with what was happening at Triumph. One of these described a race kit to convert the 5TA into a racer eligible for the American Motorcycle Association's (AMA) Class C, both road racing and dirt track racing. The Americans could see the tuning potential of the oversquare 500cc twin, and a modified 5TA ridden by Ralph Tysor set up the second fastest qualifying time at Daytona in 1959, at 120mph. Two 5TAs were also reported as entered for the National Championships at Laconia in June. If you own a 5TA, especially in the USA, it would be worth looking into its history via the engine number, as it may have been converted with a race kit earlier in life.

Of course, the British raced the 5TA, too, and one was entered in the 1959 Thruxton 500, coming seventh in the unlimited multi-cylinder event. The same bike was used in other production racing events at Silverstone and Snetterton before being converted to a track machine by Cyril Jones in 1962, covered by an article in *Motorcycle Mechanics* September

This is the prototype T100A – more power but retaining the bathtub and nacelle.

1965. Interestingly, one modification was to the swinging arm to frame support, the same as used on the later Daytona T100Rs and 1967 production machines.

More exports

Triumph might have been losing its traditional export markets, such as Australia, while European demand for big bikes continued to decline, but it was always looking for new outlets. In 1959 Triumph began operations in South Vietnam and Peru. The Vietnamese Customs service took 30 3TAs, while other departments bought 137 Speed Twins. Another batch of C range twins went to Peru that year, 30 Speed Twins destined for the police in the capital, Lima. The Pakistan Army took delivery of 100 TRWs (the side-valve pre-unit twin, not part of the C range), which means that the army now had nearly 1000 Triumphs in service. The Jamaican police was also an established Triumph customer, and ordered 21 Speed Twins to replace earlier bikes. Ghana, too, was a user of Triumphs, and President Kwame Nkrumah's motorcade of 1959 included a number of 3TAs.

> ## What the press said
> 5TA Speed Twin – *The Motorcycle*, 15th January 1959
> "Compact and Stylish Roadster, Light for its Engine Size, Lively yet very Tractable" went the standfirst for *The Motorcycle*'s first brief test of the unit construction 500. Road tests in those days, as is well known now, were usually couched in glowing terms, with any criticisms heavily veiled and made in the most polite fashion possible.
>
> Still, David Dixon did seem genuinely impressed by the Speed Twin, pointing out that the bathtub enclosure meant it could be thoroughly cleaned in just 10-15 minutes. He liked the low seat height of 28½in, combined with a riding position roomy enough for long legs. The bike was "whistling along at 60 to 65mph," was happy in top at 25mph, would 'comfortably' clock eighty-five, and could 'beat that speed if you squeeze it.' He loved the light gear change but thought the steering was a little too light on greasy surfaces, but otherwise handling and braking got a thumbs up. Weather protection from the bathtub and valanced front mudguard got 99 marks out of 100.
>
> Read more closely, and the Speed Twin seems to have suffered a flat battery at one point – Dixon mentioned that it needed push starting in the Emergency Start mode. It also used a pint of oil over 600 miles, but it did average 75mpg through rain, fog, sleet and high winds. Ah, to be a storm-suited road tester in 1959.

Still relatively few 350/500s were exported to North America, where most interest was focused on the bigger 650s, and, of course, all attention was on the Bonneville, launched in '59.

1960

Models covered: Triumph 3TA, 5TA, T100A
Production:

3TA	2758
3TA Police	6
5TA	2172
5TA Police	42
T100A	2120

Engine/frame numbers: H11512-H18611
Prices:

3TA	£227/19s/8d
5TA	£237/12s/8d
T100A	£247/17s/9d

The C range expanded again for 1960, this time with the T100A, which replaced the successful pre-unit T100. High compression pistons (9:1) and sports camshafts (E4022/E4023) boosted power to 32bhp at 7000rpm, making this the fastest, most powerful C range Triumph yet. As a precaution against extra stress on the timing side main bearing bush, this was located by a plate and screw, rather than just a peg

In 1956, Johnny Allen's 650cc Streamliner had clocked 214mph on the Bonneville Salt Flats – Triumph made the most of it.

Back in 1960, Triumphs were fun.

Tiger 100 T100A was the first performance variant of the C range, though short lived.

and cut-out, to prevent it turning (though this could still happen when racing). Otherwise, the T100A was mechanically identical to the 5TA, with the same cylinder head, valves, tappets, carburettor, and gear ratios.

The T100A also had energy transfer ignition, which allowed the battery, lights and rectifier to be dispensed with for racing. The Lucas RM13/15 alternator, instead of being keyed to the crankshaft, was driven by a dowel which would fit in one of two sockets – 'S' for road use and 'R' for racing, which also advanced the ignition timing. That was the theory, but in practice the system depended on very accurate timing, which the distributor could not deliver, and so either cold or hot starting could be very difficult. The ET system was soon dropped. The ignition coil was also different – Lucas 2ET instead of MA6 – as was the distributor, with the 3TA using Lucas part number 40573, the 5TA 40646, and the T100A 40710 (40710B after engine H17466).

The T100A also had less restrictive absorption-type silencers (E4157.8) with removable mutes for racing, while the 3TA/5TA stuck with the more restrictive but also more civilised silencers with permanent baffles. New clutch components allowed two extra plates to be fitted, which necessitated a deeper clutch sprocket and housing, clutch centre, springs, spring cups and clutch operating rod, as well as modified mountings and primary chaincase to give the required extra clearance. Complete clutches are, therefore, interchangeable between the T100A and its softer brothers, but individual components are not.

The T100A was certainly faster than the Speed Twin – it could hardly be otherwise – and it was lighter than its pre-unit predecessor. Oddly, though, for a sporty 500 taking over from a long line of Tiger 100s, it kept the

sober-sides tinwork of bathtub and nacelle, along with the voluminous 'Roman helmet' front mudguard. (Actually, there was a slight change – the T100A's nacelle top was altered to accommodate the smaller Lucas SA41 light switch). Clean and practical they might be, but they made Triumph's hottest 500 look like a 3TA in different colours. These, incidentally, were all black apart from an ivory lower fuel tank.

Theories as to why the company kept the enclosure are varied. Edward Turner ruled Triumph with an iron hand, and the bathtub was his baby; or it may be that with the enclosure being phased out the following year for export markets, the factory needed to use up existing stocks of tinwork. Either way, the T100A didn't look like the sporting bike that it was – many lost their bathtubs, others had their engines transferred to competition bikes.

Other changes

All C range bikes saw changes for 1960. The primary chain could now be adjusted via a tensioner, consisting of a spring steel blade faced with synthetic rubber. Turning the adjuster (a screwed sleeve inside the primary drive drain plug), caused the blade to bow upwards into the chain until tension was correct. It wasn't a perfect system, though, as access through the drain plug meant the oil had to be drained every time. Furthermore, if amateur mechanics weren't careful with the screwdriver, they could damage the threads on the drain plug hole, which would then leak. All in all, though, it was probably better than not being able to tension the chain at all. The differences meant a different part number for the chaincase (E4122 instead of E3107), and at first the adjuster was fitted to the 5TA and T100A only – the 350 followed later in the year, from H18392.

All bikes now had the QD rear wheel as an option: the wheel was mounted on splines so that it could be removed without disturbing the chain or disconnecting the brake. Interestingly, most bikes of this age seem to have had this option. Rear shock absorber springs were

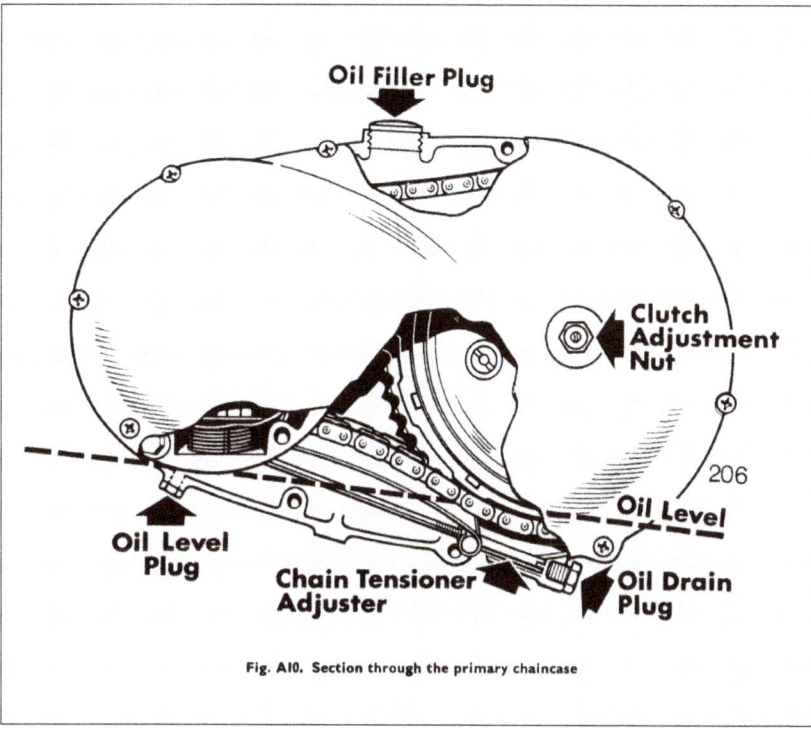

Fig. A10. Section through the primary chaincase

Primary drive sectioned, showing chain tensioner fitted from 1960 – awkward access through the drain plug hole.

Meanwhile, the original 3TA still outsold the newer 500s for 1960.

uprated to 130lb, though 110lb and 145lb were optional.

There were changes for the bathtub as well, and, from H13116, the panels had external fixing flanges which were easier to take apart and assemble, for which a new number plate design was needed. The front hub cover changed to the non-fluted type. US models featured higher bars, with cables to suit.

Police machines were supplied with a high output alternator, with additional wiring and a switch to enable the higher charge rate to be brought in at any time. Alternative Lucas parts are provided on these machines – contact Justin Harvey-James via his website www.triumph-tiger-90.com. Police-spec bikes and those supplied to overseas governments often had differing specifications from standard. If you have one it's worth contacting the VMCC or Triumph Owners' club to confirm the original destination of your bike and how it might have differed from standard.

Colours

3TA : Shell Blue Sheen, Black frame and ancillary components, Black hubs; Silver cylinder barrel fins.
5TA : Ruby Red overall, Black cylinder fins.
T100A: Black over Ivory separated by Gold lining on the petrol tank, all other cycle parts Black, Black hubs, Silver cylinder fins.

Parts Book No: 3 (covers machines from H11512). While the earlier Parts Books are not fully illustrated, Parts Book 3 is, and shows the components for each of the models.

Notes for 1960

Summary of the engine modifications made during 1960 model year.
H12014 onwards – Crankshaft timing side bearing fitted with locking device comprising a small plate located by a screw.
H12107 onwards – New type engine sprocket fitted, incorporating drillings for an extractor.
H12313 onwards – First T100A with primary chain tensioner.
H13115 onwards – First 5TA with primary chain tensioner.
H18392 onwards – First 3TA with primary chain tensioner.
Police machines become identifiable within the build records as the engines are to a different specification, and are recorded as such.

Production

1960 model year production started 1st October 1959 with a batch of 3TAs (H11512-H11545) destined for the USA. There was no Earls Court Show that year, so no show machines, but 5TA H12614 was a USA show machine.
H11962 – First 5TA for 1960 (sent to Uganda).
H12313 – First production T100A , built 16th October 1959, and sent to Johnson Motors 22nd October.
H12331 – First UK production T100A, sent to Pat Keebles, Leiston. Most early production of the T100A was for export, and they can still be found in Borneo, Cyprus, Australia and Venezuela, as well as the USA.
H18611 – 3TA, and 1960 model year production ended 2nd September 1960. The bike was despatched to Nigeria.

Speed Twin – a QD rear wheel was now on the options list.

Casting mark for 1960: another means of dating a C range twin.

Oil filler cap for 1960.

Roy Peplow's trials Tiger 100, built by Henry Vale in the competition shop, carried the registration 612 BFD, a Dudley registration from July 1960. It became a well known machine, and is pictured in Don Morley's book *Classic British Trials Bikes*. Roy later told Justin Harvey-James that he bought the machine cheaply near his home, secondhand, and that the factory helped to convert it for trials use. It eventually became uncompetitive against the lighter Cubs and later two-strokes.

Not surprisingly, the T100A was soon pressed into service on track. The Tri-Cor Monthly Hints and Tips Service Department Bulletin for January 1960 indicated that nine T100As were entered in the 100 Mile Class C amateur race at Daytona Beach (7th-13th March), and that there were six expert riders on new Triumphs in the 200 Mile National. These race machines were likely to have been numbered between H13749 and H13840, as this group of T100As was despatched to the USA in late December 1959. Bob Burnett (T100A) finished fourth in the Amateur Race. Meanwhile, in 1960, at the Bonneville Salt Flats, Danny Macias took a modified 3TA to a new class C speed record of 116.42mph. The machine survives and appears in a YouTube video at www.YouTube.com/watch?v=L699Ry3MvRs. Danny later became Triumph's Racing Manager.

1961

Models covered: Triumph 3TA, T90, 5TA, T100A, TR5AR, TR5AC

Production:

3TA	2995
T90	1 (prototype, H21442)
5TA	1477
5TA Police	18
T100A	1006
TR5AR	462
TR5AC	669
Engine/frame numbers:	H18612-H25251
Prices:	
3TA	£234/0s/3d
5TA	£243/13s/3d
T100	£250/18s/0d

> ### What the press said
> T100A – *Motorcycling*, 10th March 1960
> Remember how Triumph asked Alan Baker to go easy on the first T21 on test, as it had covered only 100 miles? Meriden let *Motorcycling* loose on the first T100A when it had just two miles showing. Not only that, but the bike was left with the magazine over the winter of 1959/60 for staff members to use as an office hack. It was either naivety, or a complete faith in the product.
>
> The bike (148 AUE) was the prototype T100A (H9480), a converted 5TA built in 1959, so it's probable that the engine had been rebuilt after its factory test mileage. Interestingly, the road test photos show (if you look closely enough) some interesting details – the rocker covers are fitted the wrong way round, and the cylinder barrels are black instead of silver.
>
> Being mechanically sympathetic, the *Motorcycling* men did keep speeds down on their low-mileage engine for the first 500 miles, but once that was out the way headed for the newly-built M1 motorway to see what it would do. The T100A would cruise in the eighties and creep over 90mph on downhill stretches. For a definitive answer on top speed they took it to MIRA, the Motor Industry Research Association test track in Warwickshire, and managed 94.6mph with the help of "a very stiff wind." Heading back into the wind, the bike could manage 76.7mph in third gear, and was slower in top!
>
> They still liked it, though, especially the better high speed stability thanks to the slightly longer trail, plus the way it stood up to 1000 winter miles and that the extra performance came in the same compact and easy to handle package as the 3TA.

The C range continued to blossom, taking over more variants from the pre-unit 500s while a prototype sports 350 – the Tiger 90 – was under development. The latest bikes were the TR5AC and TR5AR, which took over from the pre-unit TR5 and were export only, with most destined for the USA.

The TR5AC was intended for off-road racing, which was increasingly popular in the States, and would inspire a whole raft of 'desert sleds' from the British factories. Desert racing arguably also inspired the later trend towards street scramblers and trail bikes. The AC featured a small rubber-mounted competition fuel tank, Trials Universal tyres (3.25-19 front 4.00-18 rear), wide-ratio gears, direct lighting, Energy Transfer ignition without battery,

They weren't far wrong, Triumph really did offer a wide range of bikes, from 100cc to 650cc.

A touched-up brochure shot (actually from 1959) illustrating a Triumph rally in the Netherlands – North America hadn't quite taken off yet.

detachable headlamp, and siamesed exhaust system terminating into a slightly upswept silencer. On early batch bikes the small tank was held in place by a rubber band strap which was later replaced by the four shouldered bolts and rubber bushes seen on all later tanks.

The TR5AR was road oriented, so it had the standard larger tank, ET ignition (though with a battery, and would later revert to standard ignition), a standard gearbox, twin low-level exhausts, and 19in front wheel with ribbed tyre and an 18in Universal rear.

Both TR5s were the most naked C range bikes yet, with no bathtub and a separate headlight (chromed on the AR) in place of the nacelle. The pancake air filter, with its familiar drilled chrome cover, made its first appearance – this became so synonymous with '60s Triumphs that Triumph used a similar styling feature on the 21st century Bonneville. With no nacelle to mount the ignition/lighting switch, this was moved to just under the nose of the seat, on the left – the switch was the same Lucas PRS8 as the bathtub bikes, and is shown in the 1961 Lucas brochure. Neither TR5 was fitted with a left-hand side panel, and both had the unusual looped rear mudguard stays which would feature on the 1962 home market T100SS. Both were significant in signifying Triumph's gradual move away from the bathtub look to a more traditional sporting look which would personify 1960s Triumph

Year by Year: 1957-1974

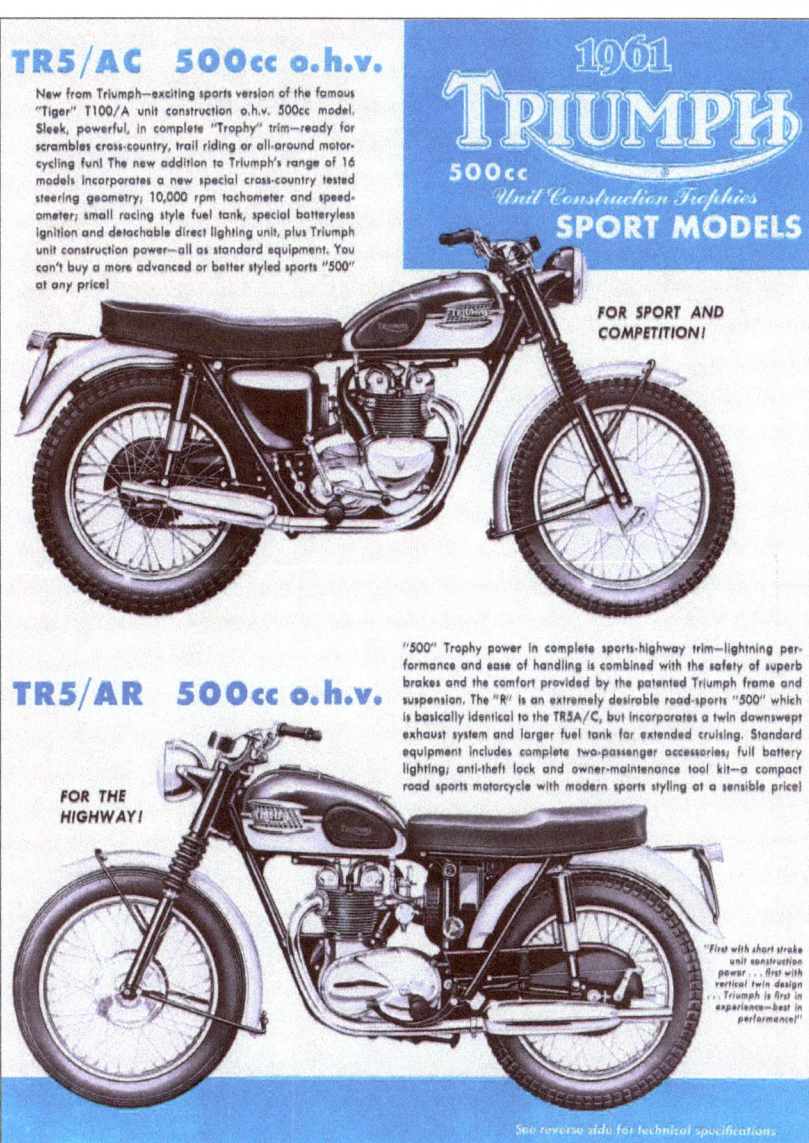

twins, not to mention its association with off-road racing, which went down well with American customers.

Bud Ekins, the legendary off-road racer, was given the first TR5AC received by Johnson Motors to test, as detailed in Lindsay Brooke and David Gaylin's *Triumph Motorcycles in America* (see bibliography). He didn't like the way the badly mounted tank bounced around so much it was leaking after 20 miles off-road, but thought a little tuning would make the unit twin more responsive, and he loved the handling. Both AR and AC TR5s would last for only a year, but they fathered a whole line of sporting 500s, on-road and off.

Note that the engine numbers show TR5R or TR5C rather than the code TR5AR or AC.

To confirm the specification refer to the Supplement to Parts Book No: 4 as this details the sports models, which have four versions for 1961-62. This important document is essential for restorers of these USA models.

Other changes

All models featured a new steering head angle (from H4849), introduced to cater for the sports models, and this gave a slightly increased trail. The frame still had brackets associated with pannier fittings, usually hidden under the bathtub but visible on the TR5s.

Brakes were still single-leading-shoe, but now redesigned 'Floating Shoe' type, with a hardened steel slipper between the light alloy shoe and the fixed spindle. The chromed hub remained relatively plain as before. Pre-'61 brake shoes will not fit the new assembly, but later shoes will fit the earlier one. In the forks,

Americans demanded their own, more sporting 500s, and got them.

Triumph 350/500 Unit Construction Twins Bible 1957-1974

T100A lasted only two years, and even kept its first-year colour for '61.

new aluminium spacer sleeves replaced the rolled steel components previously used.

The T100A received a power boost from new high-performance camshafts and a slightly larger 1in Amal Monobloc carb (now a 376/273). It retained the less restrictive absorption-type silencers (E4157.8) with removeable mutes. Later versions of the Parts Catalogue show differences in clutch components between sports and road models – it's likely that, as for 1960, '61 T100As had the multi-plate clutch with components to match.

The T100A (and the 5TA) were given slightly lower overall gearing, via a 19-tooth gearbox sprocket, to improve acceleration. All 500s, except the 5TA, also gained a Torrington needle-roller bearing on the gearbox layshaft. This was the same bearing as used on the 650s, and was fitted only to the inner end. It can be fitted to earlier C range twins if the layshaft gears are replaced with the 1961 type. Part numbers are: T1650 18T (standard ratio), and T1616 17T (wide ratio).

The T100A's Energy Transfer ignition hadn't endeared itself to everyday road riders, so this reverted to the standard coil system as on the 5TA from H22430. Information in the Tri-Cor Bulletin 60/11 indicated that this change to coil ignition happened at H20000, but this does not match with T100A production. Lucas also supplied a conversion kit (Part Number 54006033) to convert ET ignitions to coil.

There was no change to the 3TA, 5TA and T100A 17in wheels on Dunlop WM2 rims, though all models in the range now had full-width front hubs in black, and the home market bikes came with 3.5in rear tyres; an increase in size for the 3TA.

All road models had the fore and aft fitting stressed petrol tank with screwed-on knee grips, a parcel rack, and the centre seam covered with a chrome trim. The TR5AC's new tank was smaller (2⅜ gallon), with smaller Tiger Cub knee rubbers to suit, had no parcel grid, and was attached to strips attached by specialised brackets on the frame using rubber buffers. The TR5AC was also the first Triumph to feature an additional bracing strut running from the headset to near the seat. This became common to the range after 1965.

The nacelle continued for home market bikes, still incorporating the ignition/lighting switch, ammeter, Smiths speedometer and the steering damper. Distributor ignition still featured, though with the distributor optimised internally for each model.

The 3TA, 5TA and T100A kept their bathtubs and full mudguards for now, while US versions featured painted sports guards

Front drum for 1961, with concentric circles on the hub plate.

Later rear number plate attachment to bathtub.

Year by Year: 1957-1974

1961 Speed Twin, still in Aramanth Red, with distributor ignition and the full bathtub.

and higher bars, with appropriately longer cables. British manufacturers had, by this time, standardised on 7/8in handlebars with controls to match, but Triumph used a variety of bars and spacers on the various models in its range. The picture of the Paris Show TR5AR (H18612) seemed to show ball-ended levers, but these don't appear to have been fitted in production.

A Lucas HF1950 horn was fitted (look for the Lucas date code on the back), which, on TR5s, was mounted on the bracket for the small forward chain guard – it would stay there on all non-nacelle bikes until sometime during 1964 when the horn was relocated forward.

1961/62 hybrids

Some 1961 bikes were actually converted to '62 specification, according to the factory records. It happened to a number of machines built after H24241, and inclued 73 5TAs and 177 T100As, which were also converted to 3TAs. These machines retained the original T100A frame and engine numbers, although new engines were fitted. If your machine falls within this group it is vital that you consult the factory records held by the VMCC to confirm the model and specification.

It seems like an odd thing to do, until you look at production figures, that is. The 3TA continued to be the most popular C range bike, and by a huge margin – with nearly 3000 built for the '61 model year it outnumbered the T100A by nearly three to one. So it could be that the factory converted some part-completed or in-stock T100As simply to meet demand.

Colours

3TA: Shell Blue Sheen with gloss black frame, hubs and ancillary parts, Silver Sheen cylinder fins.
5TA: Ruby Red overall including hubs, Black number plates, Black cylinder fins.
T100A: Black over Silver Sheen, gloss black frame, forks, hubs and ancillary parts, Silver Sheen cylinder fins.
TR5AR and AC: Kingfisher Blue over Silver Sheen, gloss black frame, hubs and ancillary parts, Silver Sheen cylinder fins.

Optional extras: QD rear wheel at £3/16s/0d, prop stand at 19s/11d, and pillion footrests at 19s/11d.

Parts Book 4 covers machines from H18612 (September 1960) to H32464 (all 1964 machines), but it was printed in December 1961, so needs to be consulted with care. To view the Triumph Parts Books use the link to Classic British Spares (see appendix two).

Notes for 1961

Summary of engine modifications made during 1961 model year, from engine number:
H18638 – Timing gears 'crown shaved' to reduce noise and wear.
H22430 – Battery and coil ignition replaces AC ignition (T100A and TR5AR).

Casting mark for 1961.

H23348 – Low gear bush 'pegged' on all engines.
H25128 – Alternator grommet modified to E4144.
H23394 to H23474 – alternator stud holes were tapped CEI instead of BSF in error!

Consult the Parts Book Supplement to confirm the specification applied to the TR5AR and TR5AC as there were four different engine specifications:
TR5AR with ET ignition up to H21122.
TR5AR with coil ignition from H21123 (Feb 1961).
TR5AC with ET ignition up to H25251 (all 1961 models).
T100SC with ET ignition from H25252 (start of 1962 production).
This fascinating document is essential for restorers and parts identification.

Production

1961 model year production began 1st September 1960 with machines for the Paris and Earls Court Shows (latter was 12th November), with main production starting with TR5ACs and ARs destined for export.

Destinations included Singapore, Malaya, Canada and Australia, though most export bikes went to the USA, to either Johnson Motors or Tri-Cor. The Paris and Earls Court show bikes were as follows:

H18111 5TA for Paris Show, despatched 21st September (and it survives).
H18612 TR5AR for Paris Show, despatched 21st September.
H18613 T100A for Paris Show, despatched 21st September.
H18627 5TA for Earls Court Show, retained in the works showroom, eventually despatched to Aberdeen in May 1963.
H18628 5TA for Earls Court Show, despatched to Ceylon in December.
H18629 T100A for Earls Court Show, eventually re-stamped H26201 (5TA).
H18630 T100A for Earls Court Show, despatched to Hallens of Cambridge after show.
H18631 T100A for Earls Court Show, despatched to Harveys of Lambeth after the show (and it survives).
H18632 3TA for Earls Court Show, despatched in January 1961 but destination not recorded.
H18633 3TA for Earls Court Show, despatched to Decat, Belgium.
H18634 3TA for Earls Court Show, retained by factory and registered 104 CUE, eventually despatched to Hitchcocks of Folkestone in January 1964.
H18635 TR5AC for Earls Court Show, despatched to Tri-Cor.
H18636 TR5AR for Earls Court Show, despatched to Johnson Motors.
H18637 3TA for Earls Court Show despatched to Williams of Worcester.
H18638 5TA for Earls Court Show, despatched to Sid Morams of Slough.
H18639 5TA for Earls Court Show, despatched to JE Clarkson, Carlisle.
H18614 T100A built 1st September 1960 to 1961 specification and may have been sent with the other machines to the Paris Show but its destination and despatch date are not recorded.
H18644 TR5AC, possibly a press/factory bike.
H18807 TR5AR, possibly a press/factory bike. The records indicate that it was dismantled in December 1961.
H21441 a 3TA, H21442 (5TA) and H21443 (T100A) are recorded as being built for the factory showroom.
H21442 became the prototype Tiger 90, eventually despatched to Hitchcocks of Folkestone in November 1962, and obviously sold as a 1963 model Tiger 90.

For images of the factory TR5AR and AC look for the relevant pictures in *Triumph Motorcycles in America*. A picture of the Paris Show machines can be found in Roy Bacon's *Triumph T90 and T100 Unit Twins*, along with

Year by Year: 1957-1974

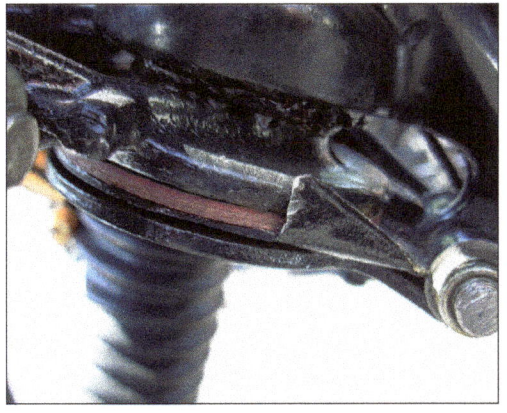

Early steering stop, used up to 1962.

an image of Bill and Ginny Dorresteyn on their TR5ARs.

Some 5TAs were supplied to Republic of Ireland police (H24498-H24505), despatched unassembled in August 1961. These were used as outriders during President Kennedy's visit to Ireland in June 1963, and pictures can be viewed (and purchased) from the Irish Photo Archive at www.irishphotoarchive.ie

Competition

A 1959 Tri-Cor 5TA (H9566) was raced at Daytona in 1961, ridden by Richard Clark, and he finished sixth behind Bart Markel. Clark was a well-known flat-track rider, three times South East Region champion. The bike survived, and, at the time of writing, is undergoing restoration, though its earlier history is unknown.

For 1961 the ISDT (International Six Days Trial) was held at Llandrindod Wells, Wales over 2nd-7th September. The superb site www.speedtracktales.wordpress.com has details, including many previously unpublished photographs. Three Triumph 500s were entered, ridden by Johnny Giles, Roy Peplow and Gordon Blakeway – pictures of Gordon Blakeway's machine are at www.stilltimecollection.co.uk (pictures abe910 and abe911). In the Dutch Silver Vase B team GJ Wassink also rode a 500cc Triumph.

The Motorcycle (21st September 1961) included an article on Johnny Giles' ISDT T100SS (230 CAC), a bike which was converted several times for other purposes. Giles

"... the full-throttle, full-powered OHV Triumph engines make distances shrink ..."

indicated that the bikes were selected from the assembly line then rebuilt by Henry Vale in Meriden's competition shop – the riders were discouraged from tampering with them. Roy would often collect his machine early and then use the additional time to check the machine and to practice repairs. Generally, for the ISDT the smaller capacity machines were considered the short straw! Johnny himself preferred the 650s, while, for trials, the factory favoured the Tiger Cub over the 350/500s.

The ISDT Triumphs (according to factory records):

H18807 TR5AR (119 CAC), Roy Peplow's bike, eventually dismantled and the number deleted.

H18859 T100A (120 CAC), Gordon Blakeway's, despatched to Hughes 4th December 1961.

H18614 T100SS, possibly 230 CAC, Johnny Giles' bike.

1962

Models covered: Triumph 3T, 3TA, T90, 5T, 5TA, T100SS, T100SC, T100SR

Production:

3T	48
3TA	2139
3TAP	23
T90	1
5T	7
5TA	343
T100A	6
T100SS	1470
T100SC	424
T100SR	13
Engine/frame numbers:	H25252-H29732

Prices:

3TA	£241/13s/11d
5TA	£253/19s/4d
T100SS	£258/17s/5d

For 1962, the short-lived T100A and TR5AR/AC were dropped in favour of the T100SS, T100SR and T100SC respectively, all inheriting the performance camshafts and 1in Amal Monobloc from the T100A, though power increased to 34bhp at 7000rpm. The main changes on the SS included new valve sizes, bigger wheels, and a more abbreviated bathtub which soon earned the nickname of the 'bikini.' Triumph was attempting to find a compromise between the original tinwork and the naked look which was increasingly popular – hence the nickname. However, the bikini would be a relatively short-lived affair, and soon the whole C range (3TA and 5TA apart) would adopt the roadster look.

Meanwhile, there was the mystery of the small number of '3T' and '5T' bikes listed as built for 1962. The old pre-unit 3T and 5T were long gone, and there's no indication as to what these actually were – the lack of 'A' in the model code suggests they did without an alternator, but there's no evidence that such a spec existed. The names may have just been a clerical error, and, as becomes clear, Meriden's coding system wasn't always infallible. The workers stamping the codes were human after all.

To suit its sporting pretensions, the T100SS had a smaller gearbox sprocket of 18 teeth (shared with the 3TA), which delivered ratios of 5.33:1, 6.34:1, 9.37:1 and 12.96:1. The gearbox layshaft was supported, as on earlier sports models, with a needle-roller bearing at the inner end and a plain bush within the kickstart pawl. The 3TA and 5TA continued with plain bushes.

Like the TR5s they replaced, the SC and SR were aimed squarely at the American market, and they were described in that year's US brochure as T100S/C Triumph Enduro Trophy and T100S/R Tiger Road Sports. The SC was the more off-road competition oriented

Two-up on a Triumph in the great outdoors – what could be better?

Year by Year: 1957-1974

T100S/C TRIUMPH ENDURO TROPHY
(Supersedes TR5A/C) 30.5 cu. in. (500 c.c.)
New mechanical improvements give this famous Trophy even greater performance and handling ease. For competition riders. *Kingfisher Blue* and *Silver Sheen* with *Black frame.*

T100SC replaced the short-lived TR5 A/C for '62.

bike, with ET ignition, while the SR retained standard coil ignition – Triumph Bulletin 229 gives the ignition timing for the various models in the range fitted with ET ignition. There were differences between the distributors and the ignition advance profiles for each model, detailed in the 1962 Lucas Brochure for Triumphs. SCs were supplied initially with an incorrect alternator rotor; new parts and dealer instructions are described in Triumph Bulletin 227. The T100SC could feature wide ratio gears, and the factory records indicate which machines were supplied as such.

The front end continued much as before, with a black full-width hub containing the SLS floating shoe drum brake. The brake cable stop was attached to the right fork slider, where the lower mudguard stay attached. The fork internals were unchanged from the touring models, but the steering stop arrangement changed to the cadmium-plated extended fasteners used to clamp the fork stanchions. *The Motorcycle* 12th January 1967 carried a detailed fork overhaul article with an excellent illustration. The 3TA and 5TA retain the steering stop arrangement from before.

The 17in wheels used by the full bathtub bikes (3TA and 5TA) were replaced by a 19in front and an 18in rear (both Dunlop WM2) on the SS, SC and SR, with tyres depending on model. Either Avons or Dunlops, these resembled the Avon Speedmaster for the SS and SR, with semi-knobblies for the SC.

All three bikes (T100SS's bikini apart) took their styling cues from the previous TR5s, with separate headlights to replace the nacelle, the housing now supported on the elegant early fork shrouds, while the forks had rubber gaiters. They also inherited 1961's slim front mudguard, supported underneath by a bridge

A sports 500 for the Brits – T100SS with bikini rear end and separate headlight.

Ride your T100 on the beach was the clear message here.

and forward by a single stay wrapping over the painted alloy guard. UK guards had a new, simple, plain curved number plate, attached by two clips.

The rear mudguard had a raised central pressing, and was supported by curved stays inherited from the pre-unit twins, running from the upper shock absorber mounts back and underneath the mudguard, with conventional number plate and rear light support attached to the guard. The rear light on all models, including export versions, was the Lucas 564 type, incorporating a red reflector and clear panel for number plate illumination. Original pressed alloy number plates used in the UK had a distinctive style of script. The exact finish depended on the practice of the dealer – some used adhesive letters, others sign writing, others embossed plates.

The chromed headlamp shell (Lucas SS700P) featured a quick release connector for the wiring, and contained a Lucas lamp unit (look for 'Motorcycle' imprinted in the glass) – different lamp units were supplied depending on the eventual market. A Lucas ammeter (Black/Grey-faced 2AR) was fitted to the shell, but no warning lights or switches. It's thought that the QD wiring connector was replaced on home market machines during the year with the more common connector. Export models continued with the QD arrangement.

The chronometric speedo was a Smiths SC 5301/## 120mph unit, and, if fitted, the rev counter was driven from the right of the exhaust camshaft using a special gearbox fixed to a modified timing cover. The rev counter was generally fitted to machines ordered by Tri-Cor (East Coast USA) while the 1961 illustrations show the drive arrangement fitted to the T100SR model only. The factory records detail most individual machines fitted with the rev counter.

The handlebars for the T100SS and export models were ⅞in diameter, and the fork crown with its steering damper was the same as used on touring models, which featured 1in bars and the nacelle. New for UK bikes was a low sports handlebar – flat, with acute bends – while machines destined for the USA were still fitted with a higher bar. These narrow diameter bars required new brake levers, rubbers and throttle twist grip – the latter featured a new throttle friction clutch, which could not be adjusted on the move. The clutch and brake levers were plain, and featured vertical clamps and sliding 'one finger' adjusters.

The horn switch (Lucas 4A) was on the right, and the dipswitch (Lucas type 99) was on the left, according to the bike tested in *Motorcycle Mechanics* this year. Later batches of machines changed to the Lucas 25SA combined horn/dip switch, attached to the clutch lever by a specialised clamp.

In the USA most riders of the SC models preferred to fit the Tri-Cor accessory handlebar #CD249, and the Tri-Cor Bulletin of 15th August 1962 describes preparing machines for the Jack Pine Enduro. Handlebar rubbers for this period were the Amal type – quite thin – and all

"As modern as the hour" said Jim Alves of the bathtub twins.

Even the footrests became 'Triumph.'

the remaining rubbers (footrest, kickstart, etc) had the Triumph logo (most modern pattern rubbers do not have this detail)! Plug caps were by Lodge.

The exhaust pipes for the SS, SC and SR were siamesed on the right, and terminated concentrically into a silencer supported by the right pillion footrest bracket. Some bikes were fitted with twin pipes and silencers, and, if so, this was recorded in the factory records. A road test T100SS had a small concentric entry silencer, but later machines appear to have had the larger 'Resonator' silencer, seen on 1963 bikes and derived from that fitted to the '62 Thunderbird.

The T100SS single top tube frame retained the fore and aft fixing petrol tank of the other non-competition models, including the internal strengthening beam (visible inside). Triumph was aware that this stressed tank was weak, and, on the T100SC, had already fitted a frame brace and a rubber isolated tank, here in smaller size and without a parcel grid. The stressed tank had a tyre pump fitted to brazed pegs on the right-hand base, with (SCs excepted) the usual chromed parcel grid and central strip covering the tank seam on top. 'Mouth organ' tank badges – which had been introduced in 1957 with the T21 – showed cream lettering and background detail, while chrome styling strips ran forward and back to cover the tank colour separation. Shaped knee grips, with Triumph monogram, were attached by screws.

The T100SS and SR were fitted with the bikini rear fairing, distinctive and new for this year. Consisting of two simple pressings, it enclosed the frame, oil tank and the area under the seat. On the left panel, located under the nose of the seat, was the combined Lucas ignition/lighting switch (PRS8), with the seat release on the right panel and 'Tiger 100' script on both sides. On export (USA) machines, the bikini was sometimes not fitted, and these machines instead have the new left side panel, part number F5559, created from a mirror pressing of the oil tank. Interestingly, it appears that publicity and brochure pictures were sometimes altered to suit different markets, though the results don't always tally. One retouched photograph from the 1962 UK catalogue (featuring four people and a T100SS on a motorway bridge) shows the bike having

Pushrod tubes were changed in an attempt to stem leaks.

no front number plate and the oil tank visible, neither of which was correct for the UK. So, beware of taking brochures as a definitive guide – they weren't always accurate!

All road bikes featured the 'Easylift' main stand, though there are variations with or without extensions to suit the various wheel sizes – the relevant Parts Book has details. Police models can have a special 'Heavy-duty' stand (F4821) which was available as a spare part. Some literature indicates that the footrest hanger brackets were updated – on the earlier models the brackets were free to adjust and could become loose. The later bracket incorporated a peg which locates against the frame fixing preventing the bracket turning – when obtaining new footrests, look for this detail.

The stepped dualseat had a plain grey top with white piping and black sides, and, on all bikes, this had the small skirt previously absent on the TR5AR and AC. The seat hinged, supported with a wire strap, and gave access to the six-volt battery, its carrier and the oil tank, all mounted on metal strips running across the frame, and attached by bushed rubber washers which provided a degree of vibration isolation.

The oil tank had a chromed filler cap with dipstick (Ceandess Ltd, Wolverhampton stamped underneath). The tank featured a frothing tower/breather tube at the top rear, no oil drain plug, but with a simple gauze filter at the base, along with a return pipe arrangement including the T-branch to the rocker feed.

Triumph 350/500 Unit Construction Twins Bible 1957-1974

Unused bracket is a factory fit for pannier frames.

Early rev counter drive from timing cover.

The smaller Lucas multi-plate rectifier (2DS506) also lived under the seat, attached to a frame bracket on the left behind the battery. Sadly, the shaped tool tray of the 3TA/5TA, with each tool in its own socket, was abandoned in favour of a somewhat inadequate kit squeezed into a small leatherette pouch tucked between the battery and oil tank. Attached to the rear mudguard by a bracket was the Lucas MA6 coil, angled to allow the high tension lead to exit to the left – bikes fitted with energy transfer ignition used a Lucas 2ET coil in the same position. The Lucas 8H horn (70163A-B and date stamped appropriately) was tucked behind the left bikini panel. Again, ET ignition bikes used a different item, in this case the HF1950 horn. The horn was held in a Y-shaped bracket sharing the frame attachment for the small front chain guard. The brake light switch was attached to the frame near the main stand and operated by an extended tang on the brake pedal as before. The frame on the T100SS press bike showed the additional brackets for fitting panniers, also featured on the 3TA and 5TAs of the time but hidden behind the bathtub.

Other changes

All bikes now had an O-ring seal on the tell tale button on the crankcase oil pressure relief valve. This useful little feature let the rider know that (in the absence of a warning light) all was well in the oil pressure department. It did have a tendency to leak, though, hence the O-ring.

From engine H26707, cam wheels with three keyway slots replaced the earlier single keyway, and allowed fine adjustment to be made to the valve timing by advancing or retarding the cam wheel positions.

The four-spring clutch continued (with heavier springs on police bikes), now with an altered cable at the gearbox end to allow easier cable changes. However, the cable still ran through the rubber cover for the distributor, which made cable changes tricky.

The 3TA/5TA also featured a new gearbox cover, the removal of the steering damper and the petrol tank styling strips. Siamesed or twin pipes and silencers were fitted as requested. The steering damper hole in the nacelle was plugged with a rubber grommet. Otherwise, the 3TA and 5TA were virtually unchanged for 1962, but did gain the general improvements detailed above. They carried on with 17in wheels, the bathtub, nacelle, and full front mudguard.

Colours

3TA: Shell Blue Sheen with gloss black frame, hubs and ancillary parts, Silver Sheen cylinder fins. From H29617, most in Silver Bronze.
5TA: Ruby Red overall including hubs, black number plates, matt black cylinder fins. Only the 5TA has black cylinder barrel fins – all others are silver.
Tiger 100s: Kingfisher Blue over Silver Sheen, Gold Lining, gloss black frame and forks, Black hubs and Silver Sheen cylinder fins. The stripe on the mudguards extended to the ends but only partially under the seat. Kingfisher Blue

is a translucent finish, and must be applied over Silver Sheen to obtain the correct colour (Triumph Bulletin 235).

Parts Book No: 4 covers all machines from H18612 (September 1960) to H32465 (all 1964 bikes), and needs to be used carefully when trying to confirm the specification for your machine.

Notes for 1962

From 1962 sales of the C range into the USA increased, especially with the introduction of the better-looking and versatile sports models, but pinpointing the exact spec of a US bike can be a fraught process. US Triumph experts John Healy (a former dealer) and Don Hutchinson have told Justin Harvey-James that export bikes were routinely modified prior to sale by dealers to suit local tastes and conditions. Some colour schemes were changed, and fuel tanks routinely replaced or stripped of badges and racks, especially on those sold for competition.

Another point which can make the exact spec and appearance uncertain is that machines arrived in crates at the dealers only partially assembled – the correct process for uncrating and final assembly was detailed in various factory bulletins. So often handlebars, levers, footrests, forks, etc, were replaced with alternative items. Johnson Motors and Tri-Cor also produced their own accessories, such as grab rails and screens, and these may turn up. Finally, many machines were damaged in transit, resulting in the need for parts to be substituted before they could be sold. So it is virtually impossible to guarantee the exact specification of any US machine.

Production

Summary of engine modifications made during 1962 model year, from engine number:
H26450 – New toggle clamp for distributor.
H26707 – Cam wheels with three keyways.

1962 production officially began with H25252, though a number of 1961 machines from H24241 were converted to 1962 specification. H25252 was built on 5th September 1961. This number falls within a large batch of 3TAs and other models, production beginning after a break on 14th August 1961 with T100As H24283 to H24497. Many of these T100As were then converted to 3TAs between 5th October and 6th December before being sold in the home market. So with any machine numbered between H24283 and H25502 it is vital to consult the factory records to ascertain the specification.

Tiger 100SS production began on 9th September 1961 with a batch of 402 machines starting with H25502, a UK-spec machine featuring coil ignition and a 19-tooth gearbox sprocket, despatched to Wragg of Sheffield. Much of the early production was actually destined for the Americas, and was equipped to suit. Major UK production and delivery began with H25760. Unusually, there do not appear to be any pre-production T100SSs. Many early T100SSs (H25502 to H25903) had converted engines taken from T100As from late 1961 production. Note that the T100SSs destined for the USA may not feature the bikini fairing, and may be to 1961 TR5AR specification.

H25861 (UK registration 931 CAC) and H25900 (a T100SC) appear to be the UK test bikes. H25900 was retained at Triumph in the drawing office and works showroom, though both machines were eventually sent to Elite Motors of Tooting.

H26567 to H26666 were factory converted T100As, and during this period more T100As were converted to 1962 specification 3TA and 5TAs. In total, 3131 T100As were built.

Men of action chose Triumph in 1962.

Triumph 350/500 Unit Construction Twins Bible 1957-1974

'WR' stamped just behind the gear indicator denotes a wide ratio box.

Production of the 1962 T100SS ended in July 1962 with H29103.

The 1962 US Brochure illustrates only the T100SC and T100SR, though many SS models were sent there according to the despatch records.

The factory records are very confusing for this period, and machines recorded in the build books often show a different model designation than that shown in the despatch book, and may differ again from the model code actually stamped on the engine and frame. For example, one T100SC (H25900) mentioned above was shown in the corresponding build book as a T100SS. In addition, machines made sequentially on the same day and sent to the same customer (Tri-Cor) show differing order numbers, which may imply a different specification. In short, it may be almost impossible to confirm the original specification for these machines unless you have original photographs to work from.

The April 1962 copy of *Motorcycle Mechanics* had an excellent colour front cover and road test of T100SS 931 CAC (H25861). This bike was featured in many period photographs, and an image of it was used for the art cover of the 1963 brochure. Mortons Archives has a photograph of this machine, from the same set of negatives from *Motorcycle Mechanics* – the image number is 3839918250.

Competition

For the 1962 ISDT, held at Garmish-Partenkirchen in Austria, Gordon Blakeway

'We don't want no Limey bathtubs.' Naked roadsters were more the American style.

Photographer Bill Greene on his '62 T100SC at Kelso Dunes in California.

and Roy Peplow were mounted on Tiger 90s, while Johnny Giles, Roy Smith (on H28967), Dick Clayton and Rohard Rolf were riding 500s. Gordon Blakeway's bike, H26228 (106 CWD), shows in the build record as a Tiger 90, but in 1964 it was converted to 500cc. Roy Peplow's H27606 (105 CWD) is recorded as a T100SS.

Both these machines were registered in April 1962 and pictured later in *The Motorcycle* of 24th February 1966, in an article on Roy Peplow. Both of them survive to this day but, as is usual with competition machines, they show several later features.

Gordon Blakeway told Justin Harvey-Jones how he was forced to retire from the ISDT as his machine was down on power, with the clutch eventually failing. It was later fitted with engine H29984 (T90). Roy and Gordon briefly swapped mounts at the ISDT to prove the difference between the bikes to Vic Fiddler, who was not amused! Roy eventually went on to win a Gold Medal, which he still has.

In the USA, Don Burnett won the 1962 Daytona 200, the first win for Triumph at this event, and there was a nice article in the *Daytona Beach Morning Journal* of 5th March 1962. Other articles are accessible via the AMA website at www.americanmotorcyclist.com

By 1962 Tri-Cor was supplying a racing kit for fitment to the 500cc machines, along with a wide variety of camshafts and parts. Consult the 1962 Tri-Cor Brochure for detailed information. Both Tri-Cor and Johnson Motors rebuilt a small number of engines to race specification for selected customers, and these were stamped T100/RR.

1963

Models covered: Triumph 3TA, T90, T90SC, 5TA, T100SS, T100SC, T100SR.

Production:

3TA	357
3TA Police	47
T90	841
T90SC	25
5TA	237
5TA Police	104
T100SS	366
T100SC	394
T100SR	357
Engine/frame numbers:	H29733-H32464 (H32362)

Prices:

3TA	£261/0s/0d
5TA	£274/4s/0d
T90	£274/4s/0d
T100	£279/0s/0d

A motorcycle for the motorway age? Well, possibly.

New for 1963 was the Tiger 90, the sports version of the 3TA, which, like the Speed Twin and Tiger 100, revived a name from Triumph's prewar past, though the original 1930s Tiger 90 was a 500cc single. In the 1960s, a sports 350 made sense – the class was still a popular one, offering lower insurance costs than the 500s.

The new Tiger 90 was a genuine smaller alternative to the T100SS, with much the same state of tune and the same semi-sports styling. With larger inlet valves than the 3TA, and a 9:1 compression ratio, it offered 27bhp at 7500rpm, the same power as the touring 5TA, though with less torque. The T90 still gave good performance, and its top speed justified the '90' tag. Finished all over in Alaskan White, and with a black frame, it looked distinct from the T100SS (despite most of its components being the same), and had a striking appearance.

The cylinder head also had modified bolts fitted to all of the C range from H29151 – these had longer heads which poked above the fins, rather than being recessed as previously, allowing the use of standard spanners rather than a socket. At the time Triumph cylinder heads were cast by High Duty Alloys of Buckingham Avenue, Slough – look for the letters HDA to confirm this. A former employee of High Duty Alloys remembered that the stampings on the cylinder heads were used to trace the alloy to a particular batch and furnace so that any poor quality castings could be isolated and recycled.

The Tiger 90 used an Amal 376/300 (though not always on early machines) with button or lever type manual choke. Some carbs had a date stamp. As ever, the carbs for each model in the range differed, and care needs to be taken to confirm that the parts are correct for your machine. The offset pancake air filter with chrome cover was used on both the UK T90 and T100 – the body fitted into a chromed-edge recess within the rear bikini bodywork.

A major engine change, launched with the T90 and shared with the Tiger 100, was the replacement of the distributor with Lucas 4CA (47606B) points and condensers (two sets of each) mounted on the end of the exhaust camshaft and accessible behind a chrome cover on the timing case. Twin Lucas MA6 coils were on rubber mountings and spacers attached to the frame rail under the fuel tank. Early Tiger 90s up to H30593 were fitted with an incorrectly operating advance cam, which was rectified under warranty (see notes below). The 1963 3TA and 5TA continued with distributor ignition, while T90s and T100s carried a blanking plate in place of the distributor. Triumph did supply a kit to allow owners to convert distributor

Bikini tinwork was a curious halfway house between bathtub and going naked.

All-white Tiger 90 had a distinctive look about it.

machines to points, and this was detailed in Triumph Performance Bulletin 13 – copies are available through Andover Norton.

Other changes

From engine H29520, Loctite was used to retain the flywheel bolts, while those after H30790 had E1771 timing pinions which were ground to reduce noise. The 1963 engine did not have the TDC removable plug behind the cylinders – this enabled a special tool to be dropped into a corresponding hole in the crankshaft, which would denote top dead centre. Some bikes do appear to have it, but they may have had the left crankcase changed to a later one. The company regularly kept some engines aside for warranty or exchange repairs, which is another cause of anomalies.

All C range bikes had a new three-spring clutch, while the clutch release mechanism on early machines (before H30038) had a quick acting screw instead of the later three-ball ramp mechanism, though that was not advertised until 1964. The clutch cable entry was slightly angled on 1963 machines. From 1st July 1963 (H31736), T100SS models destined for the USA were fitted with a different clutch plate (part number T1885). Within the gearbox, the layshaft featured a bronze bush and a single needle-roller bearing, while the 3TA and 5TA of the period continued with sintered bronze bushes.

The internal gearbox ratios for the Tiger 90 were shared with the T100SS and differed from other models and later machines. Brochures and the workshop manual show the later ratios, which are incorrect. In the 1962 specifications the rear sprockets across the range were 43 teeth, but for 1963 the brochure indicated that there were now two sizes available – 43 for 3TA/5TA and 46 for T90/T100SS. There is no guarantee that the advertised information matches reality!

On all bikes the rocker box caps gained small spring clips to help to prevent the caps coming loose and falling off, a common problem. Look carefully at the caps, as the serrated edge should be well formed to allow the spring clip to engage to prevent the cap from turning. These clips can be retrofitted to all earlier machines. From H31253 an oil feed pipe was provided for the rear chain.

The T90 and T100SS had siamesed exhaust pipes, fitting via a kinked pipe into the elongated 'Resonator' silencer on the right-hand side, its bracket also mounting the right pillion footrest. But this doesn't mean that all these bikes were supplied new with siamesed systems. At least three T90s (H31452, H31520 and H31559) were fitted with twin exhausts at the factory, which would have been at the request of the customer or dealer. Other machines may have been dealer modified prior to sale. As before, the 3TA and 5TA were supplied either with twin silencers or a siamesed system, and details were recorded in the factory records.

For export bikes the situation is more confused, especially as so few original photographs survive. A US press machine for 1963 shows twin, low-level silencers, though one original photograph of a US 1963 SC shows high-level exhausts.

For 1963 Triumph began supplying and fitting some Police and Export 3TA and 5TA machines with a pancake air filter kit detailed

Clips helped prevent those tappet covers from flying away (but didn't guarantee it).

Anti-clockwise rev counter was an option.

in Triumph Bulletin 242, which had the filter attached externally on the left of the carburettor.

Suspension, wheels, electrics

The forks were unchanged, with gaiters and flat chrome top nuts for the T90/T100, and shrouded on the 3TA/5TA. The rear shocks featured enclosed 145lb springs and three-position adjustable pre-load, while the wheels now had grease retaining seals inboard of the wheel bearings. The front hub was silver on the Tiger 90/100 while the rear hub remained black.

A quickly detachable rear wheel was an option, and many buyers chose it. On the T90 and T100SS both hubs were laced with 18in Dunlop WM2 rims shod with 3.25 front and 3.50 rear tyres. Other bikes in the range had different wheel sizes to suit their intended market: the T100SC had a 19in front wheel and tyres suited for off-road use.

The ignition and lighting switches (88SA) for the six-volt electrical system were located side-by-side and forward on the left-hand bikini bodywork, with chrome trim surrounds. The light switch (Lucas 54330934), on the outside of the ignition had unequal length tags and a non-chromed centrepiece. The ignition key was the 'sardine can' type, with an emergency start position in case of a flat battery. Chrome script (Tiger 90, Tiger 100, etc) appeared on both sides of the bodywork, attached by press fit non-release tags.

The headlight shell had a Lucas (SS700P) lamp unit with Lucas ammeter (Black/Grey faced 2AR), but, as in '62, no warning lights or switches were fitted. US competition machines had the smaller Lucas MCH66 pack and equipment to suit – listed in the 1963 Lucas spares list for Triumph.

The 120mph speedo continued from 1962, and, if the optional rev counter was fitted, it was driven from the left-hand end of the exhaust camshaft, though without the 90-degree drive box fitted from 1966. Pre-'63 bikes drive the rev counter from the timing cover using a special gearbox, and the crankcase does not have the screwed plug to suit. No Tiger 90s

Ignition and light switch on left-hand side of the bikini.

Bikini or bathtub – which had the better bragging rights in 1963?

before H32372 were fitted with a rev counter on assembly, though some had one fitted prior to despatch; others may have been fitted later at the dealers.

The horn attached to a frame bracket fitted behind the left skirt, an early type Lucas 8H unit (70163) with all screw construction and a central acorn nut. Usually a date stamp will be visible on the reverse showing the month and year of manufacture (ie 663 for June '63) but it's rare for the original horn to survive. The 8H was a common fitment to British bikes at the time, also used by the Royal Enfield Clipper and Continental, Ariel Arrow and BSA C15. Different serial numbers were used (70166 and 70169) to indicate the fitting bracket supplied and its relation to the electrical connections. The finish was silver (cadmium plate), and poor copies are available! Competition models used the HF1950 horn and 4A horn push – refer to the Lucas Spares list for details. Others used a Lucas combined dip and horn switch (31563D) with grey wiring, mounted next to the clutch lever clamp.

The rear brake adjuster had four 'ears,' and the brake light clip was the early scroll type, a rare part but nicely illustrated in the Parts Book. The brake light switch changed to the later 22B (31383) type mounted on the chain guard, operation relying on the internal spring within the switch. Modern Lucas pattern switches used on pre-'66 machines with the original arrangement will have been incorrectly assembled.

Tinwork

The new twin coil mounting necessitated a new fuel tank to make room, the underside shaped with space for the coils. The new tank retained the internal strengthening beam and still acted as a stressed member. As such, it often fractured, repairs usually being carried out under warranty. Triumph would fit a frame brace and four-bolt tank mounting to 1965 bikes, allowing the tank to 'float' on the frame, almost stress-free. Some earlier bikes have been modified to suit this later style tank.

American and export T100SC and some T100SRs destined for the West Coast had a smaller tank with four-point fixing and frame brace, these parts taken from the earlier TR5AC which used the frame brace in 1961. The small export tank seems to show no or only minimal

space for the coils, and had two fuel taps, one acting as the reserve. The brackets for this tank were for 1963 only and are very hard to find as a spare part. As ever, Triumph assumed that American off-road riders wouldn't be carrying parcels, so the tank-top grid was not fitted. Either that, or the factory had acknowledged that the grid could cause serious (and eye watering ...) injury in the event of a crash. The tapped holes for the grid were plugged with rubber bungs. This design of the small tank seemed to stabilise from this point on, and appeared on many later machines. Factory records show that a batch of T100SRs sent to Johnson Motors (H30467 to H30500) were fitted with smaller fuel tanks.

The bikini bodywork fitted to the T90 and T100SS for 1963 differed in detail to the '62 version, featuring side mouldings and added decorative strips wrapping around the seat base. These are fragile and rarely survive. In any case, many 1963 machines had the bodywork removed as more and more riders hankered after the sports look, and, in any case, some export bikes were not fitted with the bikini at the factory. The specification for USA models is difficult to confirm as changes were introduced during the year, and very few contemporary images survive.

For those who thought the bikini (let alone the bathtub) was just too staid, Triumph now offered the left-hand side panel F5559 as a part, which hid the battery if the bodywork was discarded. It would be standard on '64-on bikes when Triumph finally gave up on its smoother tinwork.

T100: "... for the sporting rider who demands the highest performance with light weight and ease of handling ..."

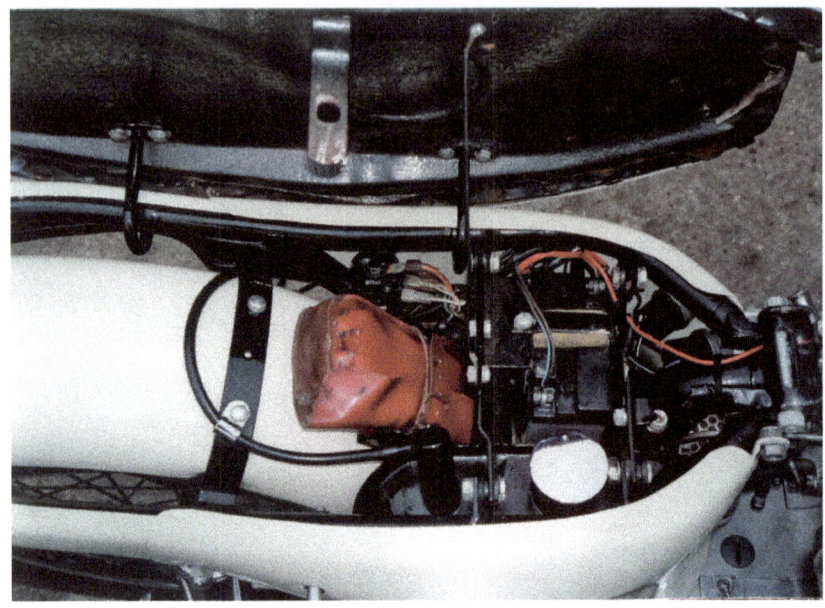

Under seat arrangement in 1963 – the tool tray had given way to a common or garden bag.

Extended cylinder head bolt heads allowed the use of standard spanners.

The aluminium front mudguard was supported by a brace underneath, between the forks, and a single stay to the front, while the rear mudguard continued to show a distinctive raised centre moulding and had an attractive sweep at the rear.

The rear mudguard forward bridge support was brazed or welded to the mudguard and painted in the overall colour scheme, while at the rear a new support loop replaced the earlier arrangement. It is likely the pattern of the mudguard changed during 1963 to the later form without the moulding. Both mudguards had sharp edges at each end, while the fasteners used were slightly domed (¼in dsv7). Original Triumph fasteners were quite specialised, the bolts generally slightly domed, and Simmons-type nuts were regularly used, with cadmium plating used extensively.

The pillion footrest and exhaust mounting brackets were now the triangular form, which replaced the tubular type. Sometimes, the left pillion footrest had a drilled hole between the fixings, but with no apparent purpose! Meanwhile, the Parts Book shows a very different pillion footrest bracket from the earlier 3TA.

The control levers were still plain, not ball-ended, with the brake and the clutch adjusters a sliding fit, the clamps vertical, attached to a flat and narrow ⅞in handlebar with acute bends. Machines destined for export, especially the USA, continued to have higher bars and extended control cables, while the bathtub 3TA/5TA are thought to have retained their 1in bars and controls to suit.

American dealers were encouraged to sell a rubber-mounted handlebar kit (#CD306) which included a new top lug with bonded rubber mounts and special eyebolts, similar in design to that fitted as standard in 1967.

A black steering damper control with the Triumph logo was mounted centrally, and the grips were the thin Amal pattern. As for '62, the stepped dualseat had a plain grey top with white piping and black sides, while US models show a seat strap fitted. Under the seat, the battery carrier had distinctive folded triangular bracing. On early machines the tools were tucked between the battery and oil tank, while later machines featured a simple open tool ('fag packet') box bolted to the rear mudguard. From June 1963, Avon Fairings made by Mitchenall became available for all Triumphs (*Motorcycle Sport*, June 1963).

Colours

3TA: Blue Sheen or Silver Bronze – the colour is usually in the factory records.

Tiger 90: Alaskan White overall with mudguard stripes gold lined in black. The stripe does not extend under the seat but does extend to the ends of the guards; it should be no wider than the front number plate mounts. Frame and ancillaries in black.

5TA: Ruby Red as for '62 though one source now refers to the colour as Cherry Red.

Tiger 100SS: Regal Purple over Silver with black pin-striping

All bikes except the 5TA had silver cylinder barrel fins to complement the lightly polished engine cases. The cycle parts were gloss black enamel, and the mouth organ tank badge had letters picked out in gold, and featured chromed styling strips running fore and aft on all bikes except the 3TA and 5TA.

American differences

For the 1963 Tiger 100 there were detail differences depending on the model – SS, SC or SR – and the original destination of the machine will help to confirm the specification. The 1963 US brochure shows detail differences between the US and UK machines, but it's worth studying the Parts Book carefully.

T100SCs generally had energy transfer ignition, with those sent to Tri-Cor fitted with wide-ratio gearboxes, though this is something of a generalisation. The off-road models also had crankcase under shields, Universal tyres, and no pillion footrests or main stand.

The 1963 USA (West Coast) brochure describes the T100 as either the Speed Tiger (Road) or Sports Tiger (Competition), with specification differences to suit.

USA T100SC and T100SRs built after H31735 in July 1963 may have featured several detail differences to the earlier models, including larger wheel sizes. A Johnson Motors supplementary parts list details all the new parts fitted, and is available in the VMCC library.

Production

Summary of engine modifications made during 1963 model year, from engine number:
H29151 – Longer cylinder head bolts to ease access.
H30593 – T90, first engine fitted with 14-degree auto advance.
H30790 – T90, first engine fitted with E1771 pinions (8th January 1963).
H31212 – T100SS, oil drip feed to rear chain (25th April 1963).
H31736 – T100SS, T1885 clutch plate for USA models (1st July 1963).
H32209 – 3TA, Loctite on all alternator nuts (29th August 1963).

The 1963 model year production began with a Tiger 90 on 24th September 1962 (H29733, which survives), and ended on 7th August 1963 (H32463). Eight hundred and sixty-three Tiger 90s were built that year in total, and the final two were specials for the experimental department, with wide-ratio gearboxes, 3TA pistons, cylinder heads and clutches.

T100SS home market production started with H30083 (actually destined for the Paris Show), and was 332 machines in total, mostly in small batches. This very low production makes the 1963 T100SS rare – by comparison, 1470 T100SSs were built for the previous model year. Even rarer was the T90SC variant. A batch of 25 was supplied to Johnson Motors, and it's assumed that JoMo made a special order for SC off-road spec bikes with the 350cc T90 engine and special modifications, including broached pistons, ET ignition, and a 17-tooth gearbox sprocket. One of these rare bikes survives today.

Overall C range production figures were down substantially on '62, with just 2728 bikes built in total, against 4470 in the previous model year. But production was more evenly spread across the variants – in 1962 the 3TA and T100SS had made up the lion's share – with the Tiger 90 the best seller. This sharp drop in production was probably down to a number of factors. The home market was certainly going through a bad patch, and exports were falling as well, which affected the entire British motorcycle industry, production plummeting from over 140,000 for 1961 to less than 100,000 in 1962 (both calendar years). Triumph may also have been giving priority to the new unit construction 650s, launched for the 1963 model year – these were now bigger sellers than the C range, especially in the USA.

Bikes built for the Paris show were Tiger 90 H29752 and Tiger 100SS H30083. For the Earls Court Show the pre-production

CB points now moved to the timing cover.

Early rev counter drive later changed to a neater arrangement.

Tiger 90 (H21442) was displayed. It had been converted from a 1961 5TA taken from the works showroom, and was eventually sent to Hitchcocks of Folkestone on 3rd November 1962. Other show bikes were as follows:

H30201 – T100SR sent to Johnson Motors on 29th November 1962.

H30236 – T100SC sent to Tri-Cor on 15th November 1962.

H30286 – 3TA for Earls Court Show, Silver Bronze, despatched to Elite of Tooting on 7th December 1962.

H30287 – Tiger 90 for Earls Court, then despatched to Decat Belgium for the Brussels Show on 18th December 1962.

H30288 – Tiger 90 for Earls Court, then despatched to Hughes Wallington on 4th December 1962.

H30289 – 5TA for Earls Court.

H30290 – T100SS for Earls Court Show, then despatched to Stokvis (The Netherlands) on 13th December 1963.

Triumph also had a stand at the Blackpool Show held at the Winter Gardens in July 1963, but the show bikes have yet to be identified.

Notes for 1963

Towards the end of model year 1963 production batches of 3TAs and 5TAs were produced, some of them Police models. Most were for export, and the factory records detail the colour schemes applied to each machine. If you have a machine with an engine/frame number between H31916 and H32361, consult the factory records at the VMCC library to identify the correct specification.

Tiger 90s from H32362 to H32461 were mostly sent to Pride and Clarke of London. These were the final C range machines for 1963, built in early August, and the records confirm that they were built to 1963 specification – at least five of these machines survive.

The 1963 sales brochure listed such extras as pillion footrests, prop stand, QD rear wheel, rev counter and steering lock.

For Tiger 90 photographs and information look for the road tests in *Motorcycling* (7th November 1962) and *The Motorcycle* (23rd May 1963), while other earlier editions of *The Motorcycle* also show the same press bike. *The Motorcycle* 25th October 1962 and *Motorcycling* 24th October 1962 give some Triumph range detail, with the excellent cover photo showing a different machine. The Tiger 90 illustrated on the cover of *The Motorcycle* October 1962 carried the same registration number as a 1962 T100SS pictured on 7th October 1961. This well known machine was used in several publicity shots, and one is the basis for the cover illustration of the 1963 brochure.

Mortons www.mortonsarchive.com has an excellent set of glass plate negatives of a press bike (H29935) in the archives. This machine later became Johnny Giles' ISDT mount, and the engine survives. Tiger 90 H29984 was used as a donor machine to repair Gordon Blakeway's earlier ISDT bike H26228.

A leather jacket, a brand new Triumph and high summer – the world was his ...

Oil pressure relief valve lost its plunger.

The VMCC in its photo archive also has an excellent photograph of one of the two Earls Court Show Tiger 90s, possibly the pre-production bike. Johnny Giles' machine is beautifully pictured and documented in Don Morley's *Classic British Trials Bikes* and *Classic British Scramblers*, both published by Osprey (see bibliography for details). Both these books are out of print, but secondhand copies do come up for sale online.

For the US Tiger 100 look for the image on page 17 of the March 1963 edition of *American Motorcyclist* via the AMA website (www.americanmotorcyclist.com). It is a particularly good shot of a US spec T100SR, and the rider is Robert Brandt, husband of film-star Janet Leigh. Another advert image can be found in the April '63 copy of *American Motorcyclist*, this time with possibly the same machine being ridden by Gil Stratton, film-star and sports reporter, who was employed by Triumph at the time. There may have been clever marketing going on, as the adverts also appear in *Sports Illustrated* for the same period. It's not clear if the bike is to East Coast or West Coast specification, but the small tank suggests it was supplied to California-based Johnson Motors.

There is evidence of two pre-production Tiger 90s built for competition, though one is referred to in the factory records as 'T100SS 350cc.' These were registered by the factory in May 1962, several months before production officially began. H26228 and H27606 were destined to become famous as 105 and 106 CWD, the ISDT Tiger 90s (see below).

Racing

In the Bemsee 1000 (km) race held on 19th May 1963 at Oulton Park, the 350cc Class was won by M Low and DF Peacock on a Tiger 90, with A Dugdale and T Fearns second on another Tiger 90. These are likely to have been H31540 and H31541, both built on 8th May and despatched on 15th May. They were later converted to T100SS spec for the Thruxton 500 race. The class-winning machine (H31451) was ridden by Brian Davis and Bill Scott, and featured in *Motorcycle Mechanics* September 1963. It was quite extensively modified, with rear set footrests, 8in front brake, low bars, alloy levers, and other modifications.

The Thruxton race entries and press reports for the period make interesting reading – see *Motorcycle Sport* August 1963 for a detailed report and list of entrants. In total 13 Triumphs were entered at Thruxton, of which five were Tiger 100s or converted Tiger 90s. Two other Thruxton bikes have been identified in the factory records: T100SS (H31734), built on 28th May 1963 and supplied to Dugdales in Thruxton specification; and T100SS (H31735) built the same day to the same spec and supplied to Keebles of Leiston.

Johnny Giles won the Pirbright 100 Mile Scramble on his Tiger 100, which may have been his reworked ISDT machine – see *Motorcycle Sport* August 1963 for an excellent photo.

The 1963 ISDT was held in Czechoslovakia at Špindlerův Mlýn in the first week of September. Roy Peplow and Scott Ellis were on 350s – Roy on 105 CWD and Scott on

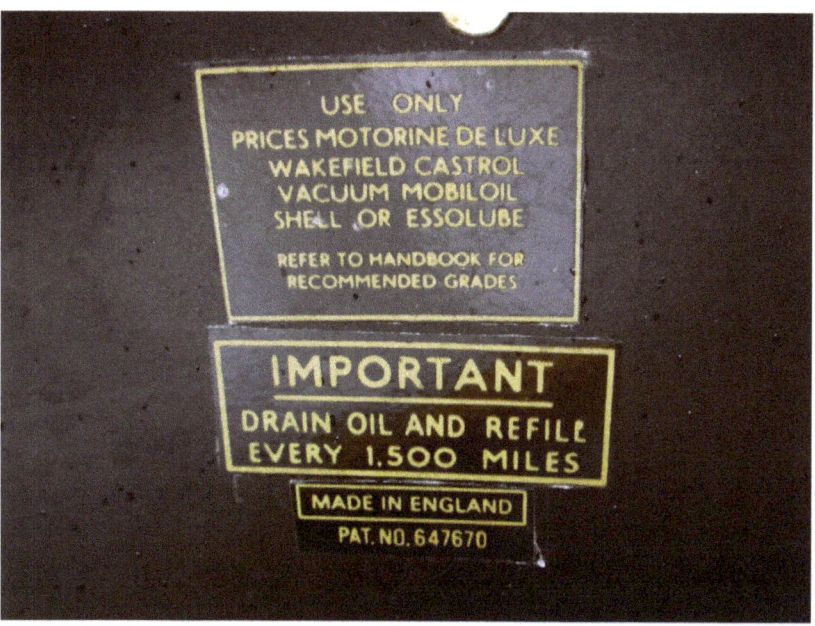

Clear instructions on the oil tank.

106 CWD. Roy Smith, Johnny Giles and Dick Clayton were riding 500s, while Bud Ekins, Eric Chilton and Ken Heanes took 650s – Ken's was 929 FNX, an early unit construction Bonneville (T120 DU 1557). For more on the ISDT look at the excellent website www.speedtracktales.wordpress.com Johnny Giles' ISDT bike was loaned later in the year to Gunnar Johannson to compete in an event in Sweden, the two-day Novemberkasen. A picture of the bike can be seen in *Motor Cycling* November 6th 1963.

Although the Tiger 90 was Triumph's most popular C range bike for the '63 model year, with over 800 produced, very few of them were exported – just 60 in all (to Europe, the Far East and USA), and that included the special batch of 25 T90SCs for Johnson Motors.

UK registration numbers

UK registration extra letters denoting year of registration are actually only a guide to the date. The letter 'A' is 1963 but was only used in registration areas where three letters and numbers had run out (London, for example). Rural areas continued with the old system until 1964 or even later! Some machines were not registered for several months, and can, therefore, appear to be later machines. Even if the letter suffix does reflect when a bike was first registered, this doesn't show the date it was built – that information is (at the risk of repeating ourselves) in the factory records.

'Tiger 90 Itis'

John R Nelson described the warranty problems suffered by the early Tiger 90s – they were so specific to the bike that the service department and dealers took to tagging it as 'Tiger 90 Itis.'

"We had desperate phone calls from all over the country telling us that once started, and on the road, the bikes would become sluggish, misfire, and in many cases, just not pull the bike along. Marvellous! The trick was to tell 'em to remove the centre rectifier wire from the terminal, and bingo! Performance restored. The problem actually was an extra spark as the contact breaker points closed, firing the incoming mixture, and was cured by a redesigned contact breaker cam. Funnily enough, the problem only commenced following a low battery at start-up, when it became fully charged. Then you had to run the bike until the battery ran down, reconnect until the battery was charged up again, when it all began again. At least it got you home until we could supply a modified CB cam."

1964

Models covered: Triumph 3TA, T90, 5TA, T100SS, T100SC, T100SR
Production:

3TA	779
3TA Police	41
T90	574
5TA	375
5TA Police	28
5TA Military	30
T100SS	476
T100SC	717 (Trophy/Jack Pine model)
T100SR	489
Engine/frame numbers:	H32465-H35986

Farewell tinwork, and the Tiger 90 turned into a mini Bonnie.

Year by Year: 1957-1974

Tiger 100 also went for the mini Bonnie look.

Prices:
3TA	£261/0s/0d
5TA	£274/4s/0d
T90	£274/4s/0d
T100	£279/4s/0d

Following the introduction of the T100SS and variants for 1962, and the Tiger 90 for '63, there were no new models for 1964, though the C range did see some changes, notably new forks, cams and pushrod tubes, while the T90 and T100 finally said goodbye to their extra tinwork.

New pushrod cover tubes and seals were fitted in a further attempt to stem leaks – they were featured in the 1964 brochure, and described in Performance Tech Bulletin No 13. The tubes had improved seals, and were a simpler shape: a single diameter throughout their length. There were new camshafts, too,

Straight pushrod tubes with improved sealing.

and the clutch operation was officially now the three-ball type (though the change had actually been made in the '63 model year, see above). The clutch cable attachment was made more accessible, to allow cable changes without requiring removal of the gearbox outer cover.

The gearbox gained a second needle-roller bearing within the kickstart spindle, while the selector cam plate was induction hardened, and a bridging strap added to prevent the plate spreading in use.

One source refers to a larger gauze and drain plug in the sump for 1964, and a wider and deeper chainguard. All bikes were now listed as having the 46-tooth rear sprocket, but with various gearbox sprockets according to model.

The T90, T100SS and T100SR now had twin exhausts in place of the two-into-one siamesed systems. On the Tiger 90 these had a distinct 'shoulder,' and a change in diameter at both the cylinder head and the silencer end (1¼in, only fitted to Tiger 90), though it had the standard C range silencers.

The lighting and ignition switches were now placed one above the other (lighting above ignition), and the lighting switch changed slightly to two smaller unequal tangs and a chromed centre detail. 3TA/5TA kept the combined lighting/ignition switch in the nacelle, but adopted the same handlebar diameter and controls as other models. During 1964 the horn/dipswitch moved to the handlebars, attached by screws with a rubber insulation support. US brochure and press pictures do show bikes with ball-ended clutch and brake levers. With the bikini rear end gone on some bikes (see

Triumph 350/500 Unit Construction Twins Bible 1957-1974

Tiger 90: "... A 350 with power 'plus' performance to match superb road holding ..."

below) the oil tank was now exposed – it also gained a drain plug near the lower front corner. An oil level transfer on the tank replaced the integral dipstick – cheaper, but less accurate. Clips for the tyre pump were now mounted near the right-hand rear stay. Triumph literature mentions a new design of rear shock giving greater tyre clearance.

Suspension, tinwork

The T90s and T100s had new forks with external springs (8¾in), double-acting oil seals, plus new gaiters held in place with zinc-plated turnbuckle straps. The fork sliders and spindle caps retained the 1963 form on early machines, but later '64 bikes feature an improved fork with shorter lower sliders and longer, 9¾in springs. The early sliders were steel tubes with brazed-on fork ends, while later sliders were extruded from solid billet steel. Some factory literature stated that internal damper kits were available for all models from 1964. The design of the fork top nut changed – not obvious from the outside, but the underneath did not feature the recess and securing pin holes of the 1963 version. The 3TA and 5TA forks were also modified, but kept their shrouds. During 1964 the front brake cable stop moved from the fork to the brake plate, probably in association with the later fork slider change.

There were big visual changes, too, as Edward Turner's tinwork continued its retreat in the face of buyers lusting after naked roadsters. The non-USA T90 and T100s lost their bikini rear ends in favour of the naked look American export bikes already had. Meanwhile, the 3TA and 5TA finally said goodbye to the full bathtub, which had been such a distinctive trademark

3TA and 5TA lost their bathtub.

52

Year by Year: 1957-1974

of the C range since the very first T21 in 1957. In its place, they inherited the bikini panelling along with the pancake air filter, but kept the voluminous 'Roman helmet' front mudguard, headlight nacelle and shrouded forks. Some T90s and T100s made between H33843 and H34021 and supplied via United Engineering to Malaya and Singapore (order numbers 7474A and 7377A) were fitted with the nacelle.

T90/T100 mudguards changed, the front now in steel, while the rear lost its raised centre moulding and the sweep became somewhat plainer. Two front mudguard stays replaced the brace and single stay of 1963.

Magnetic instruments were fitted, the speedo an SSM 5001/00A or 00B 1600 item, and the anti-clockwise rev counter an RSM 3001/02. As before, the rev counter was an optional extra, with a straight drive, not the later 90-degree drive box. The speedometer drive used a 19/10 ratio gearbox (unserviceable, fragile and now rare). A rubber sleeve was reportedly added to the steering damper to prevent it coming loose. The horn is sometimes illustrated located beneath the tank forward of the engine but other illustrations and photographs don't show it here. It was a Lucas 70163 8H, the riveted type which retained the Acorn centre nut.

As in previous years, the Lucas 700 headlight and shell should have 'Motorcycle' moulded into the glass if it's the original. Competition bikes used the smaller 575 package, which has 'Motorcycle Light Weight' in the glass. Original headlights rarely survive and should be carefully preserved.

Most 1964 machines had the four-point fixing type of fuel tank, and the bolted-on frame

brace not officially fitted until 1965. Factory illustrations all show the stressed tank, and early 1964 bikes examined by Justin Harvey-James are the same. The 3TA and 5TA continued with the stressed tank. The seat was the same for all models: grey top and fringe, black sides, with no Triumph logo at the rear, something confirmed by period photos.

Colours

3TA: Silver Bronze.
T90: Lacquered Gold over Alaskan White with Black pin striping, though the striping detail is something that has been very difficult to prove. Original pictures from 1964 seem to show Black. The gold covering the tank top swept down below the knee grips to follow the lower edge of the tank. Only the front chrome styling strips were fitted, though the badge retained the locations for the rear strips. The mudguard stripes were gold, lined in black as before. Note that Tiger 90s were sometimes referred to as the Baby Bonnie because they shared colour schemes with the T120.
5TA: Gloss Black over Silver Sheen.
T100: Hi-Fi Scarlet over Silver with Gold striping. The US brochure describes the colour scheme as Flamboyant Scarlet over Silver. The tank colour sweeps below the knee grips as on the T90.

Battery cover and substantial strap.

Parts Book No: 5

Triumph 350/500 Unit Construction Twins Bible 1957-1974

In the small print, the US market T100S/R was "the Daytona Model," but its twin-carb namesake was still three years away.

American differences

Export bikes differed significantly in specification from UK machines, and there appear to have been further differences between models supplied to Johnson Motors and Tri-Cor.

The T100SC (also known as the Tiger 100 Competition Trophy or Jack Pine in the USA) also had several changes over the T100SR road bike. These included a smaller fuel tank without parcel grid, featuring two petrol taps, locations for the coils, and finished with Tiger Cub badges and knee grips. There was also the bolted-in frame brace, QD headlamp package, polished alloy mudguards, siamesed exhausts exiting left, raised bars, and off-road tyres.

According to factory records the SC was made in a number of batches through the production year, the batches show differing order numbers which indicated differing specification. For example, order number 7303, applied to approximately 150 machines sent to JoMo early in 1964. If you have an early 1964 production SC (H33017 to H33644), contact www.triumph-tiger-90.com.

One useful document for owners of US bikes is the USA Owners Manual for the 500cc machines. This details the differences in specification between the T100SR and SC – a copy of this, which includes machine pictures and specifications, can be obtained from the VMCC library.

Tri-Cor Service Bulletin #3 (8th July 1964) indicates that all US models of the T100SR and T100SC were fitted with 19in front wheels, while rears could be 17 or 18in!

Notes for 1964

Summary of engine modifications made during 1964 model year, from engine number:

Two-tone tanks in Flamboyant Scarlet and Silver made the US bikes flamboyant indeed.

H33687 T100SC, Lucas 54021079 alternator fitted (17th Jan 64).
H35647 3TA, Old type engine sprocket E4141 fitted from here to H35753 (29th June 1964).

1964 production began in batches on 9th September 1963 with H32465 (a T100SS), and ended on 6th July 1964 (a 5TA). T90 production began on 20th September (H32572), and ended on 2nd July 1964 (H35867), with a total of 574 for the year. 29 machines were exported to destinations as varied as Malaya, Mexico, Denmark and Germany.

T100s H34372-4 were modified and supplied to Dugdales for the 1964 Thruxton 500. Paris Show machines shown in the factory records for 1964 are: T90 H32572, 3TA H32622, and T100SSs H32547 and H32548. 3TAs H35132 and H35133 and 5TAs H35134 and H35135 were supplied to Morris Greenberg of Israel for the Tel Aviv Show.

For videos of a 1964 Tiger 90 look for Tiger Jim's Channel on You Tube – https://www.YouTube.com/watch?v=IlP0B8kGGwk.

For pictures of 1964 bikes, *Motor Cycling* 15th January 1964 had an excellent set of photographs of a 5TA road test machine (registration 675 JNX, H32982).

Roy Bacon's book *Triumph Twin Restoration* has some excellent factory images of a 3TA – see page 147 in particular. *Motor Cycling* (30th October 1963) or *The Motorcycle* (31st October 1963) had details of the Triumph range of 1964. Justin Harvey-James has original pictures of a 1964 Tiger 90 being collected from the factory, being raced, and seen later after a crash.

Optional extras for 1964: Pillion footrests, prop stand, QD rear wheel, rev counter.

New frame brace bolted to the headstock.

Competition

The 1964 ISDT was held in Zeilort Erfurt in the DDR (East Germany), 7th-12th September. Entrants on Triumphs were:
Roy Peplow, Tiger 90 (105 CWD, H27606).
Bud Ekins, Dave Ekins, JF Steen and Ray Sayer were on Tiger 100s (Ray on Tiger 90 106 CWD, H29984, converted to 500cc).

Ray's bike was the same Tiger 90 from the 1962 ISDT, and it survives in the Dick Shepherd collection. Bud Ekins' Tiger 100SC was H35403, and Dave Ekins' was likely to have been H357401.

Steve McQueen, Johnny Giles, Cliff Coleman, and Ken Heanes rode 650s in the ISDT, Johnny on 117 LAC (6T DU 9331), and Ken on 929 FNX (T120 DU 1557). Ace Classics (www.aceclassics.co.uk) has more recently built a replica of McQueen's bike, but the original also survives.

Ray Sayer and his wife Carol have fond memories of the ISDT, where they remember a party atmosphere prevailing, with drink flowing freely. Interestingly, the ISDT 'Gold' medals (of which Ray had three when Justin Harvey-James interviewed him) were not actually made of gold, and were manufactured by the Birmingham Medal and Badge Company, of 95 Albion Street Birmingham.

The British Team ISDT Triumphs were used in other events, such as the Army Three Day trial, and were usually retained and serviced by the factory, only being released to the riders a short time before each event. Roy Peplow lived near Meriden, so would collect his machine personally and practice the various service/repair jobs (puncture repair, cable replacement, etc) until he was confident. Roy, Ray, Gordon and Johnny Giles later indicated that they were discouraged from modifying the machines themselves.

The 1964 US Team ISDT machines were modified production bikes, not works machines. The story of the 1964 ISDT is well documented in the book *40 Summers Ago* by Rin Tanaka and Sean Kelly: a brilliant photographic record of the competition, and features many rarely seen images. For information and photographs of Bud and Dave Ekins have a look at this excellent site www.budanddaveekins.com For details on the ISDT go to www.speedtracktales.wordpress.com

Triumph 350/500 Unit Construction Twins Bible 1957-1974

Kelso Dunes in Mojave National Preserve was a popular spot for sand riding. It's 1965, and photographer Bill Greene has brought his 1962 T100SC along, together with his wife and Bill Jnr.

In the US, Bill Baird was the most successful enduro rider using Triumphs, and two of his famous machines survive. One is displayed at the AMA Museum in Pinkerton, Ohio, while his earlier machine is in a private collection.

In the 1964 Thruxton 500 there were several teams using Triumphs. *Motorcycle Sport* (August 1964) and other magazines have the results, and the following three C range bikes probably took part. They are recorded as being built in May and early June 1964, with a batch of T100SRS built for Tri-Cor:

H34372 despatched to Dugdales, Greenbank Garage, Alvanley, Cheshire.

H34373 despatched to Mr RA King.

H35374 despatched to Kilbourn Motorcycles, Mead Lane, Chertsey, Surrey.

1965

Models covered: Triumph 3TA, T90, T90SC, 5TA, T100, T100SS, T100SC, T100SR
Production:

3TA	620
3TA Police	82
T90	801
T90SC	2
5TA	336
5TA Police	79
5TA Military	1
T100 Police	21
T100SS	571
T100SC	1180
T100SR	827
T50 Military	17
Engine/frame numbers:	H35987-H40527

Prices:

3TA	£279/9s/8d
5TA	£283/1s/5d
T90	£283/1s/5d
T100	£286/13s/0d

Since the first T21 of 1957, Triumph had used the same basic frame for C range bikes, in which the fuel tank was a semi-stressed member. Although adequate for the touring 350, it began to show up handling deficiencies in the faster 500s, and the fuel tank could even split and fracture on a hard-ridden bike, as it was twisted along with the frame. The flaws were most obvious on competition bikes, and US off-road machines had already been fitted with an extra top tube to brace the frame, and a different mounting for the smaller fuel tank.

For 1965, the extra brace finally found its way onto the whole range, with a bolted-in strut to stiffen the frame, and the 3.5-gallon tank changing to a four-point fixing. Using special bolts located through rubber buffers, mounted on steel strips across the frame (themselves

Tiger 90 for 1965 – Triumph had discovered the advantage of annual colour changes.

attached by U-bolts) this allowed the tank to 'float' on the frame, removing it as a stressed element. The T100SC continued to have a smaller tank and had shorter nuts.

The C range had also been criticised for harsh, short travel forks, and this was addressed on the T90 and T100 with longer, lower rate springs, plus longer stanchions, outer members and inner damping sleeves to suit. The T100SC used harder springs (originally intended for sidecar use) and a damper kit. The fork sliders and spindle caps on T90/T100 changed, and were now the simpler semi-circular form again seen on some 1964 machines. Meanwhile, the 3TA and 5TA lost their steering damper, and retained significant differences from the rest of the range – the top lugs and headset stems differ and are not interchangeable, while the fork stop was different from the extended nuts fitted to the T90/100, though these are not accurately illustrated in the Parts Book!

Finding Top Dead Centre for accurate ignition timing could be a challenge, and this was eased by a new milled slot incorporated in the flywheel. Removing a threaded plug on top of the crankcase allowed a special tool to be screwed in, which dropped into the flywheel slot at exactly TDC. It had been seen earlier but not officially fitted. Also on the flywheel, the three bolts lost their washers, and were instead secured with Loctite, though this is also referred to in the 1963 records.

The long-running oil pressure tell-tale button was dropped. In theory this gave the rider instant reassurance that all was well, poking out when under pressure. In practice it was a source of leaks, and Triumph covered the hole with a domed nut. From Tiger 90 engines H39194 to H39205, the drive side main bearing was described as a 'Three Spot Bearing.'

Felt washers were added to the gearbox output oil sleeve (only to be deleted again the following year), and to the right-hand side of the rear wheel hub, while the QD hub was redesigned to accept ball journal bearings instead of the previous taper-roller bearing. In the clutch, there were new friction segments.

The 3TA and 5TA continued with the earlier gearbox layshaft arrangement of plain bushes, while the T90 and T100 used Torrington needle-roller bearings at both ends of the layshaft. The layshaft, its gears and the kickstart spindles are not interchangeable between these two types.

Tiger 90, now looking near-identical to its big brother 500.

Triumph 350/500 Unit Construction Twins Bible 1957-1974

Another wide US range for 1965, but the Tiger 90 didn't get a look-in ...

The Lucas 70163 8H horn was now all-riveted, located under the tank, and there were corresponding changes to the frame brackets beneath the tank to suit. After H37635 new alternators were fitted across the range (54021079).

Triumph decided to fit a 'chain oiler' from July 1965, which was nothing more sophisticated than a pin hole drilled into the circular cover plate behind the clutch, allowing oil from the primary drive to (hopefully) dribble on to the chain below. However, owners complained of oil leaks, so the hole was deleted from H41568, early in the 1966 model year. Triumph service bulletins advised peening over this hole to cure the problem.

The 3TA and Tiger 90 shared exhaust pipes, but these differed from those of the 500s. On the 350s the pipes exited the head and then reduced in diameter until reaching the silencer, where the diameter increased again. All machines featured the standard silencer for the period, and the Parts Book showed mutes available for all models.

Brakes, controls & tinwork

The front brake cable stop moved onto the brake plate as part of the fixed shoe location – late '64 machines also showed this change. The brake and clutch levers had horizontal clamps, and ball-ended levers were available as an alternative to the standard plain levers – it is likely that ball-ended levers were fitted to all export machines, certainly those destined for the USA.

The seat remained as they were on the earlier machines, though the US brochure again shows a grab strap. Under the seat the toolbox was partially closed off, but was still attached to the rear mudguard.

Tinwork continued to shrink, with the 3TA/5TA dropping the generous 'Roman helmet' front mudguard in favour of slimmer guards with a raised central rib, similar to those used on the T90/T100 for 1963 – part numbers were H1901 and F5963, and the front number plate lost its chromed beading. The Parts Books and brochures show styling strips associated with the tank badges, but these didn't appear to have been fitted in practice. The rear number plate was changed slightly to allow room for seven characters, and the rear light changed to a Lucas 679 type (53972B) on export bikes, as shown in the period Lucas brochure for Triumphs.

If the 350 wasn't fast enough, Triumph service bulletin number 240 of July 1965 detailed the parts available to convert a 3TA and Tiger 90 to 'High-performance Specification.'

Colours

3TA: Silver Bronze

Tiger 90: Pacific Blue over Silver with Gold pinstriping, though one source states Light Pacific Blue over Alaskan White.

5TA: Black over Silver Sheen – it also stuck with black cylinder barrel fins, whereas all other bikes were silver.

Tiger 100: Burnished Gold over White. Interestingly the colour image on the cover of

T100SS with non-standard paintwork, two-into-one pipes and megaphone.

Motorcycle Mechanics shows the pinstriping in Blue, while other sources say Black!
A world speed record holder transfer was added to the tank opposite the filler cap, and the Triumph lettering was picked out in deep red or light gold, as shown in the brochure. This clearly varied from time to time – H36979's badge shows gold while H37631 is red!
All bikes had silver front hubs.

Parts book No 6. Several of the illustrations in the Parts Book, such as that for the frame, do not accurately represent the parts fitted for 1965.
Optional extras: pillion footrests, prop stand, QD rear wheel, rev counter.

The '67x70' 500

By 1965, Triumph already had a possible replacement on the stocks for its 500cc twin, though not a radical one. In 1994, Doug Hele told American journalist Lindsay Brooke that plans were "quite far advanced" for a new twin using a bore of 67mm and stroke of 70mm. It appears to have been more of a rationalisation than any great leap forward – the group's 250cc single and 750cc triple (the latter now in prototype form) used the same 67x70 dimensions, so from a production point of view standardising these across the range made a lot of sense.

According to Hele, the twin-cylinder version would have included some very useful updates including a narrower valve angle, beefier crankshaft with roller main-bearing on the timing side and tappet adjustment by eccentric spindle. The idea was to make 200 of these to homologate the new engine for the Daytona 200, but there wasn't enough time, and Hele's team decided to concentrate on maximising performance from the existing engine.

Notes for 1965

Summary of engine modifications for 1965, from engine number:
H35987 3TA, modified contact breaker bolt (9th September 1964).
H36039 3TA, 18T gearbox sprocket fitted as standard (10th September 1964).
H37636 All models, Lucas 54021079 alternators (14th January 1965).
H37722 T100SC T1614 layshaft bearing fitted together with blanking disc (18th Jan '65).
H38411 T100SC, Two thin clutch plates fitted (11th March 1965).
H39194-H39205 T90, drive side bearing, 'Three Spot Bearing' (25th March 1965).
H39378 3TA, E6120 camshaft fitted (24th May 1965).

Earls Court Show bikes and their eventual customers:
H36715 3TA, despatched to Chapmans of Norwich on 8th December 1964.
H36716 5TA, despatched to Dene of Newcastle, 10th December 1964.
H36717 T90, despatched to Arbour of Leicester, 22nd December 1964.
H36718 T100SS, despatched to Steiner, Switzerland, 12th February 1965.
H36718 T100SS, despatched to Arbour of Leicester, 18th December 1964.

Rubber mounting for the four-point floating fuel tank; no longer a stressed item.

Triumph 350/500 Unit Construction Twins Bible 1957-1974

What the press said
Tiger Trio – *Motorcycle Mechanics*, June 1965

As the title suggested, this test by *Motorcycle Mechanics* wasn't of one Tiger, but three – the Tiger Cub, 90 and 100. The Cub impressed with its short wheelbase agility, steering and fuel consumption, but a wide ratio gap between second and third meant working the little 200cc single hard to make good progress. Oh, and the electrics were judged "fairly adequate" – make of that what you will ... Top speed: 75mph. Fuel consumption: 95mpg.

The Tiger 90 test began with a quote from Triumph's super salesman Neil Shilton: "Dig into the box and find the revs," were his parting words to the tester who rode away from Meriden on the T90, "and then you'll find the power coming in." And that set the tone of what was a very brief test – that is, that a Tiger 90 only really delivered the performance goods at high revs. According to the writer, "sluggishly the needle climbs to 5000rpm," but power then came in with a vengeance, right up to 8000. The technique (not surprisingly) was to hold on to lower gears for as long as possible, so as not to land in the engine's pancake zone of 4-5000rpm. Top speed: 91mph. Fuel consumption: 75mpg.

The Tiger 100 had a more glowing write up, despite not quite managing the 100mph suggested by its name. After 1000 miles, the testers proclaimed it to be "the best all-round bike" they had handled for a long time. Top speed: 98mph. Fuel consumption: 65mpg.

Other machines (H36067 T90 and H36068-H36071 T100SSs) were sent to Reinhardt, Denmark for show duties.

In January 1965 BSA Group bought a controlling share of Johnson Motors (Triumph's highly successful West Coast distributor) and shortly afterwards purchased Hap Alzina Inc which had been handling the sales of BSAs into the Western USA. From now on all sales and marketing of both BSAs and Triumphs into the USA was owned and arranged through the BSA Group in England. As detailed in Lindsay Brooke and David Gaylin's book *Triumph in America*, this news was not welcomed with open arms by Triumph dealers and enthusiasts in the USA. BSA had bought Triumph back in 1951, but a low-level rivalry between the two names and factories in Britain carried on for years afterwards. In the USA, this BSA vs Triumph rivalry became quite serious, echoing the dogged and traditional tribalism of Indian vs Harley-Davidson. The truth was that Triumph's cohesive band of dealers and loyal riders did not want their distributors taken over by the BSA group, but that is what happened.

Production
Production for the 1965 model year began on 9th September 1964 with a 3TA, and ended on 12th July 1965 (T100SS). T90 production was in batches, and the first of these began rolling down the line on 11th September 1964 (H36143), and the last ended on 30th March 1965 (H39375), with a total of 803 built, 18 of which were exported. Japan, Canada and British Guiana were some of the destinations. T100SS production began with H36586, but early production figures were low, and only 549 of these were built for '65. Reflecting the increasing importance of North America, the best selling C range bike was the T100SC, followed by the T100SR. The T90 was selling a reliable 800 a year, and the 3TA, while well down from its glory days of 3-4000 a year, was still managing nearly 700. The 5TA always sold fewer than its little brother, with only 336 for 1965 – the market was moving away from these soft tourers, and perhaps those who simply wanted easygoing, economical transport were content with the 3TA's performance rather than pay extra for a 500. Either way, both these bikes were nearing the end of production – 1965 was their penultimate year.

Road tests and features
The June 1965 issue of *Motorcycle Mechanics* had a 'Triple Test Feature' covering the Tiger Cub, Tiger 90 and Tiger 100 (see below). The

Small fuel tank with four-point mounting clearly visible.

test bikes were registered on 1st April 1965, and the T90 (H39276) survives.

The 1965 Triumph Range Supplement in *The Motorcycle* of 8th October 1964 detailed changes for the year, and had an excellent engine detail photograph. Other images of this bike are in Roy Bacon's *Triumph Restoration Guide*. Note the colours given for the finish in the Range Supplement do not correspond with the 1965 Triumph brochure. In *Cycle* (USA) of February 1965 the Triumph range was featured, with a superb colour cover shot of one of the 650s. In its September issue, the same magazine ran a road test of a T100SC. Though published in September 1965, after 1966 production had begun, the test bike was a '65 model, with the later export rear lamp, high bars, siamesed pipes, alloy mudguards, etc.

The Motorcycle (4th February 1965) had an article on ISDT modifications undertaken by Henry Vale and Vic Fiddler. *Motor Cycling* (17th April 1965) had an excellent side view of Roy Peplow's bike, showing the new silencer for 1965 fitted to the ISDT machines. *Motorcycle Sport* (December 1965) had a superb article with pictures of Ray Sayer's ISDT Tiger 90.

Competition

The 1965 ISDT was held on the Isle of Man, 20th-25th September. Dale Richards rode in several ISDTs (the '65 event being his first) and would usually collect his bike from Ken Heanes or Cheneys. Dale was a well known enduro rider in his home state of Idaho, and winner of

Tigers three ... *Motorcycle Mechanics* tested Triumph's 200, 350 and 500 in June 1965.

Cheney-framed Triumphs were bred for off-road competition, and were highly effective.

Triumph 350/500 Unit Construction Twins Bible 1957-1974

1965 (right) and '66 (left) Tiger 90s.

Go modern? 12-volt electrics were a step in the right direction, but Triumph's artist still had a thing for cravats.

the Paul Bunyan Run in 1963. He featured in a well-known 1965 ISDT photograph showing Ken Heanes on Sky Hill – copies are available from Mortons Media Archive. As ever, www.speedtracktales.wordpress.com has details of ISDTs year by year.

In the Army Three Day Trial for that year, Ray Sayer crashed his T90 heavily on the third day, losing consciousness briefly and wrecking the bike when entering a dried up stream bed that was deeper than expected. He had actually been well ahead of his time allowance at the point. The bike was likely to have been 105 CWD (H27606), as this has since been fitted with a later frame. *Motor Cycling* (24th July 1965) carried a report on the event, including pictures of Roy Peplow's and Ken Heanes' machines.

1966

Models covered: Triumph 3TA, T90, 5TA, T100, T100SS, T100SC, T100SR

Production:

3TA	680
3TA Police	289
3TA Military (T35WD)	1
T90	913
T90SR	4
5TA	235
5TA Police	255
5TA Military (T50WD)	1
T100SS	1066
T100C	1977
T100SC	721 (including 341 Mercuries for South African Army)
T100SR	1150
Engine/frame numbers:	H40528-H48728

Prices:

3TA	£279/9s/8d
5TA	£283/1s/5d
T90	£286/13s/0d
T100	£291/8s/7d

This year saw big changes for the C range (with more to come for '67) and, as the model list above shows, it was an increasingly complex line-up of bikes, which, in turn, makes the task of identifying exact specifications more complicated. During the year the SC and SR designations in the factory records were replaced by C and R models, a move which seems to have been made in November 1965 – this T100R, incidentally, was not to be confused with the following year's T100R Daytona. There were also several changes to specification during production across the range this year, and great care needs to be taken identifying which model you have and when it was made.

It was the last year (apart from a final military order for 3TAs) for the 3TA and 5TA, originators of the C range, and whose touring demeanour had been overtaken (sometimes literally) by rortier roadsters that '60s riders wanted for weekend fun. In a sign of the times, they lost their bikini tinwork, retaining just the nacelle as a final link to Edward Turner's original dream of a clean and elegant motorcycle. As

for the man himself, although officially retired, he would soon begin work on a new double overhead cam 350cc twin intended to replace the C range. Although fast, it was flawed and was completely redesigned by Doug Hele's team as the Bandit/Fury (see page 111).

It's worth noting that many of these late TAs were supplied to the police, and these bikes often have specifications and parts that differ from the other production models, such as side panels without switches, unusual seats, early type mudguards, different switchgear, and other parts that are generally unobtainable as spares and not usually illustrated in the Parts Books. These bikes can be difficult to return to factory specification, as very few survive in original condition and information is scarce. Even standard UK 5TAs in the final year of production are now rare, as not many were made.

Engine

There were some detail engine changes for 1966. From engine H47024 (a T90 built late in the model year), the removable cover over the sludge trap was deleted – engines were sometimes installed in bikes out of sequence, so engine H46840 for example, doesn't have the cover, while H47638, H47736 and H48561, ostensibly built after it was deleted, do have it!

From H44000 bikes had two warning lights in the headlight shell (green for ignition, red for high beam), though this was only used for the T90, T100SS and T100R. The 3TA/5TA still had a nacelle, and this wasn't modified for the warning lights. It was also planned to fit an oil pressure warning light (though this didn't actually happen until the '69 model year) but late '66 model year bikes did have changes to the crankcase adjacent to the oil pressure relief valve in preparation for this.

According to the Parts Book the T90 and T100 were fitted with a crankcase chain protector, and there was a tapped hole on the crankcase to accept the fastening. This distinctive hole is visible on all post-1966 crankcases – the fastener fits with the nut visible on the top. The 3TA and 5TA used a rubber plug to blank off the hole.

T90 and T100 now featured aluminium bronze valve guides, and the carb showed a date code (possibly week/year) stamped on the nearside flange. 5TA, T90 and T100 used the same camshafts, but inlet manifolds differed between the models – refer to the Parts Book for details.

The oil tank was larger (now six pints), and incorporated a chain oiler, frothing tower, and changes to the rocker feed takeoff, drain plug location and breathing pipe. The mountings changed to more effective rubber isolated spigots shared with the new battery carrier, with changes to the frame brackets to suit. This design of oil tank only applied for 1966. The left side panel was modified slightly to incorporate a chain oil feed pipe exit in addition to the brake light wiring. Some bikes have the chain oiler routed through a hole in the crankcase over the engine sprocket, but the Parts Book shows a crankcase protection bracket fixed here, certainly fitted to the T100C models destined for America. The crankcase protection blade was officially fitted from H42963, but Justin Harvey-James' own machine (H42001) has the threaded hole for the attachment bolt.

Electrics

The big news here was the change to 12-volt electrics, with a Zener diode on a simple aluminium heatsink behind the side panel.

This couple has braved sand dunes on a T100SR – note that the parcel grid has gone from this US bike.

Not only did this mean better lights, but it was simpler and more reliable than the six-volt system, removing the need for the complicated PRS8 lighting switch and multiple wires to the alternator.

Early machines used two six-volt batteries with carrier and parts to suit, but after H45511 a single Lucas PUZ5A 12-volt battery was provided. A shallow plastic tool tray (light grey and very rare, but pattern ones are now available), was mounted on welded brackets across the frame behind the battery.

The early Zener diode heatsink (F6900) had the earth lead to the diode incorrectly fitted, causing overheating of the unit – after H43714 the heatsink was the F7237 type, with the earth terminal relocated to the rear. The battery carrier was modified to suit, and had two holes on the left to mount the heatsink. After H42328 the rectifier was located centrally behind the battery (or batteries), instead of to the left as before, and the wiring was modified to suit. The headlamp shell now carried a red ignition warning light, while the ignition switch became a barrel type (Wilmot-Breeden Union) lock. A Lucas SS5 (35601) kill switch was fitted to the right-hand handlebar (very rare indeed, but good quality patterns are now available), with period photos showing black wiring, while that for the dipswitch was grey. Factory data stated that the HT cables were suppressed internally.

Frame, brakes, tyres

The bolted-in frame strut was now welded in place, though the frame retained the bolt mountings. A steering lock body was attached to the headstock (the 'Neiman' lock mechanism detaches when not in use) and pillion footrests fixings were simplified to bolts instead of studs and nuts as previously used.

The non-QD rear brake drum (Qualcast) was attached to the hub with distinctive headed bolts and locknuts, and gained a separate sprocket (46-tooth, attached with distinctive fastenings) instead of being integral – it remained integral on the optional QD rear wheel. A new form of rear brake adjuster had two instead of four ears. The brake light clip was simplified to a plain strip drilled to accept the tension spring. Note that neither the adjuster nor clip changes are shown in the Parts Book. Some original unrestored machines have the

The top frame strut was now welded, not bolted, into place – a more permanent solution.

brake light switch standing off the chainguard on additional nuts, again not shown in the Parts Book! This feature was introduced on some models from September, but may not have been universal.

TA wheel sizes increased to 18in at both ends, to match the rest of the range. T100Cs supplied to Tri-Cor were supplied with either Trials Universal tyres or Sports tyres, with the details sometimes recorded in the factory records.

Tinwork

For their last civilian year the 3TA and 5TA lost the bikini, and most tinwork parts were now common to the rest of the range except for the nacelle. All UK C range bikes had a new fuel tank on slightly changed mountings, and the new 'Eyebrow' tank badges were fitted to all models, the lettering of which was black on the Alaskan White background. This simpler badge replaced the long-running 'mouth organ' type badge which had been used since the start of production. The 'eyebrow,' although it seems so familiar on mid and late 1960s Triumphs, was itself replaced after just a few years. The knee grips on UK bikes were now glued on rather than screwed (so the tank lost its threaded holes), while the smaller-tanked export machines continued with screw-on grips attaching to welded brackets. See the 1966 US brochure and Parts Book for confirmation.

From H44000 (January 1966), T100Rs and T100Cs shipped to the USA were fitted with the 1966 B range (ie 650cc) style 2.5-gallon tank.

Year by Year: 1957-1974

Justin Harvey-James' 1966 Tiger 90 on tour – backdrop is the Grand Canyon.

These are not actually the same as the 650cc version, as both tank and frame mountings are different, so they are not interchangeable.

The chrome plate on the front hub changed to a plainer, slightly more dished design.

The front mudguard lower support, which swings down to become a stand, now appears in two versions; wide and narrow. Both types have been fitted to original machines, though the narrow version is rare and may only have been fitted to the 3TA and 5TA for a short time before being superseded.

Although 1966 mudguards appeared similar to the previous year, the rear guard did now feature a cut away area to allow the enlarged oil tank to fit. Some '66 machines have a small rolled bead, but this is unusual and is probably signifies a '67 guard. The 3TA and 5TA had a new type of front mudguard attachment and amended forks.

By 1966 Triumph was not making its own mudguards, these being supplied by several companies in Birmingham, to slightly varying designs, so the actual design details would be very difficult to verify. Jim Lee (former Meriden employee) remembered that due to industrial action at the usual suppliers, Triumph was obliged to obtain mudguards wherever it could, in order to continue production. This could account for the several variations of mudguard seen on original bikes from 1966 onwards.

T100Cs had a taller centre stand – note extra loops welded to the bottom of the legs.

The USA T100C had differences between the East and West coast versions, and one period photo shows the bike without a left-hand side panel and with the smaller QD headlight. As ever, consult the Parts Book and supplementary update carefully if you are restoring a T100C.

Instruments, controls

T100Cs were now fitted with the VDO 'Enduro' speedometer, while the other bikes continued with magnetic instruments. Police machines in the UK continued to use chronometric speedometers, as these could be calibrated for accuracy. A rev counter was still optional,

Triumph 350/500 Unit Construction Twins Bible 1957-1974

Kill switch for 1966, one of the less significant electrical changes for that year.

but, if fitted, now used the neater 90-degree drive unit, while the instrument itself was the clockwise version (RSM 3003/01). The cable ran at a quarter engine speed.

Clutch and brake levers are difficult to verify – several UK period photographs show the same plain levers with horizontal clamps as fitted in 1965, while others show ball-ended levers, as does the T100R in the 1966 US brochure.

A plainer open-ended kickstart rubber was fitted, without the Triumph logo. The end of the earlier closed-end rubber had a tendency to the break off, something which can even be spotted in road test pictures!

Handlebar grips were white, perhaps not the best choice given the dirt and dust of life on the streets. Fitted to most Triumphs for 1966, these were universally disliked at the time, but now, at the time of writing, white grips are obtainable from Jeff Hunter (email Jeffalanhunter@aol.com). The left grip was sometimes cut away to allow the dipswitch to operate.

Colours

3TA: Pacific Blue over White with Gold lining, Silver cylinder fins.
5TA: Black over Silver Sheen.
Tiger 90: Grenadier Red (Tangerine) over Alaskan White, Gold lining.
Tiger 100: Polychromatic Sherborne Green over Alaskan White, Gold lining. The works manual indicates that Sherborne Green is a metallic (which it wasn't).
Export bikes: Colours are difficult to verify as original colour images are rare. The 1966 US brochure shows the T100SC in a single colour with the usual polished alloy mudguards and off-road fitments.

For all two-colour tanks, the top colour sweeps below the knee grips, following the curve of the tank badge. The rear mudguard stripe does not extend under the seat.

John Nelson has described the process of selecting colour schemes for the forthcoming year. "We would be called to Edward Turner's office," he remembered, "where he would then say, "Come in gentleman, these are the colour schemes we have agreed upon!"

Carrs of Birmingham was one of the paint suppliers to Triumph, and would provide Mr Turner with a set of colour swatches. He, then, would select the shades and the design. The paint shop would then produce samples of tanks and mudguards, before these were shown to the staff, including representatives from Johnson Motors and Triumph Corporation USA, for approval. The only colour not well received by the American buyers was the

T100SS in Sherborne Green ... with grid.

66

Quiff, denims and a '66 T90 – this is Brian Trull back in the day.

1966 Tangerine scheme – see the relevant US brochure for images.

Parts Book No: 7

Notes for 1966

1966 model year production began at H40528 with a batch of 341 T100SCs. These were the famed Mercury model, and were destined for the South African Army. Supplied to Keep Brothers SA, they were finished overall in Brunswick Green and to export T100SC specification, with small tanks, pre-66 knee grips, QD headlight, and with the addition of panniers and crashbars. At least five of these rare machines survive. The VMCC archive has a publicity shot of a 1967 Mercury and a small brochure on the 1968 model, advertised as being available in both 350 and 500cc versions. The factory records did not differentiate the Mercury specification from standard machines, and it could be that machines supplied in groups to foreign governments were, in fact, classed as Mercuries.

The factory records for 1966 and 1967 do mention T100WDs, but the numbers are small.

Any UK machines from the first batches made in September 1965 will sometimes have a C registration, making them appear to be 1965 machines, even though they were to '66 specification.

The illustrated 1966 Parts Book is useful in identifying the differences in specification between the standard models, but some parts shown weren't actually fitted – the front mudguard bottom stay H1482 is an example. The Parts Book also shows differences between the US East Coast and US West Coast T100s.

The last 3TA ever (Dutch military versions apart) was H46082 (sent to the MOD in Beirut, 23rd June 1966), and the final 5TA was H46431. About 20,000 3TAs and T21s were built in total, plus around 8500 5TAs. The 3TA, in particular, had done Meriden proud, and, given its export

US spec T100SR, now with 2.5-gallon tank. The advert details a competition for which the first prize was a trip for two to the Daytona 200 – the lucky winners would have seen Triumph's milestone victory.

success, the bathtub bikes are still to be found all over the world, with 3TAs surviving in Pakistan, Malaya, Nigeria, New Zealand and Nepal.

1966 Tiger 90 production began on 3rd September 1965 with H41923, and finished on 6th June 1966 with H47063, a total of 912 being made. The T90 was overwhelmingly a home market bike, with just 94 being exported this year, to (amongst other places) Guam, Nicaragua, Tahiti and Formosa! One ex-Formosa machine survives, and is now back in the UK. Two of the 25 bikes which went to Guam have since been sent on to the USA. Guam was a small but useful export market for Triumph, no doubt thanks to the US naval and air force bases located there.

The first T100SS for 1966 was built on 1st September 1965 (H41719), and 1066 machines would be built in all. Unlike the T90 many were for export, though a large batch of home market machines was made late in 1966 production. The last of these was H48728, despatched to David Paul Motorcycles, Camborne, Cornwall.

A workshop manual for the C range, designed and instigated by John Nelson to replace the earlier owner's handbook, was available from February 1966.

Road tests & features

The Motorcycle, 22nd September 1966, featured a test of a late batch 1966 T90 (H46806) with a wealth of detail. A few weeks later (13th October), the same magazine ran a Tiger 90 information article. Also look for the Tiger 100 test in *The Motorcycle*, 18th August 1966, and the range information in the same title two weeks later (2nd September 1965), detailing changes for 1966.

The single sheet US brochure had two re-touched photographs showing an early production TR6R and the T100SR/R (Speed Tiger), both images showing a wealth of detail not seen in the UK brochure illustrations. The original image of the T100SR/R which was used in the 1966 US brochure is available in the VMCC's collection. The photograph seems to have been taken at Warwick University in the UK, then a new building taking the place of an American campus! For more period photos, look for bcgreeniev on Flickr, which has colour images from California, taken in the '60s by photographer Bill Greene, who owned a Triumph and loved riding the Kelso Dunes, now part of the Mojave National Preserve.

Competition

The 1966 ISDT is held in Villingsberg Sweden, and the factory entered several machines:
HUE 252D (H44954), ridden by Ray Sayer.
HUE 253D (H45023), Sammy Miller.
HUE 254D (H45117), Johnny Brittain, and used as the scouting machine.
HUE 255D (H45140), Ken Heanes.
HUE 256D (H45150), Gordon Farley.
HUE 258D (possibly H45126).
105 CWD H27606 (Tiger 90), Johnny Giles.

This is how they took 'studio' shots in 1966 – backdrop is a white sheet.

106 CWD H26228 (500cc), Roy Peplow. There were several other privateer entrants on Triumphs but these were the factory bikes.

Ray Sayer's 1966 ISDT Tiger 100 survives, and is still regularly used. It features in a famous photograph with Johnny Giles astride the machine in conversation with Vic Fiddler. One of the ISDT machines (HUE 254D) is pictured in scrambles trim for the Farleigh Castle event of 1966 in Don Morley's book *Classic British Scramblers*. This excellent but rare book contains a wealth of technical information on the engine development process for the factory machines.

One of these developments was the small batch of alloy cylinder barrels produced for the ISDT bikes. Fifteen were cast in all, at Small Heath, in varying capacities (including at least one of 504cc) as the ISDT rules demanded a presence in each class. Unfortunately, several of these highly desirable components were stolen while in transit from the BSA machine shop to Triumph's competition department. It is thought that just eight made it to Meriden, an epic journey of 11 miles, but some of the barrels which 'disappeared' en route have since turned up!

In addition to the usual medals, the winners were presented with rather attractive engraved crystal vases featuring a Viking longboat design on the front, with 'ISDT Sverige 1966' engraved at the base on the back – keep an eye out for these rare items of memorabilia.

Other machines show up in the records, and 17 bikes (H45491-H45507) were taken from the production line and passed to the experimental department.

In 1966 a team of four Triumph-mounted riders led by Bud Ekins set out to ride along the Baja California peninsula from Tijuana to La Paz, and set a new record in the process – this was the year before the famous Baja desert race began. Bud and his brother Dave had previously done the trip on Hondas in 1962, setting a record of just over 39 hours. The four Triumphs (two TR5s and two TR6s) were ex-USA team ISDT bikes, and made the trip in 40 hours and 3 minutes, having suffered various crashes, punctures and breakdowns. Read Dave Ekins' account of the ride at http://www.budanddaveekins.com/baja-by-triumph/

A race-prepared Tiger 90 competed at Oulton Park (and at Snetterton and Brands Hatch in 1967). Built by Bill Chuck of Nelson & Ford (Basildon), it was either H46535 or H46907, and a number of articles on this machine appeared in *Motorcycle Sport*.

The biggest race story for Triumph in 1966, though, was, of course, the Daytona 200 in Florida, USA. This was a flagship event, and victory here could pay dividends in what was now Triumph's biggest and most lucrative market. For years the race had been dominated by Harley-Davidson, apart from a string of Norton wins in 1949-52, while Don Burnett had taken the flag on a Tri-Cor sponsored T100 in 1961. For '66 Triumph decided on a major factory backed team, and six race-prepared T100s were shipped over from Meriden. All of them (H44111 to H44116), were made on the production line on 13th January 1966, then thoroughly reworked by Doug Hele and his talented team at Meriden.

Although based on production bikes, the changes were extensive, with a new lower frame in Reynolds 531 tubing (though using standard frame lugs) with extra bracing. A new cylinder head with narrower valve angle and larger inlet valves was fitted, along with twin Amal GP carbs plus megaphone exhausts, boosting power to 46.5bhp at 8200rpm.

In February 1966 five of the bikes were shipped to Tri-Cor and tested at the Marlboro, Maryland Circuit by Gary Nixon, under the watchful eyes of Tri-Cor's Rod Coates as well as Doug Hele. After Gary Nixon had selected H44114 as his mount the remaining machines were divided between JoMo and Tri-Cor.

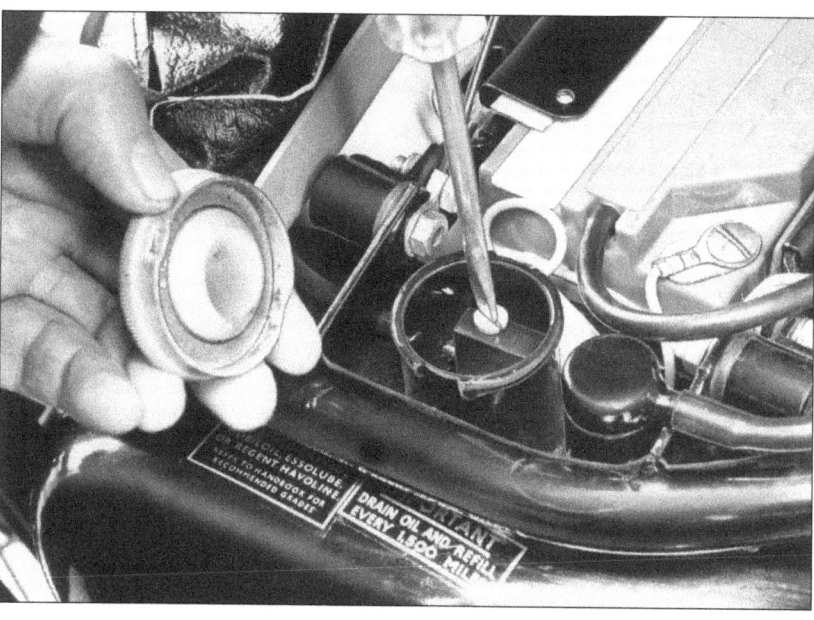

The oil tank now supplied a drip-feed to the chain – this is the adjustment.

Triumph 350/500 Unit Construction Twins Bible 1957-1974

Oil tank delivery/return pipes, without rocker feed T-piece.

Speed Twin in its final year, now naked apart from the nacelle.

What the press said

Tiger 100 – *The Motorcycle*, 18th August 1966

This test, printed just weeks before the 1967 bikes were announced, could say little new about the Tiger 100, now in production for several years and very familiar to most magazine readers of the time.

In the way of magazine tests back then, it said lots of nice things about the bike, and criticism was either focused on minor items (the size of the toolbox and span of the brake and clutch levers) or veiled. The new 12-volt headlight was merely deemed 'adequate' (albeit up to the 70mph limit), and cruising at 70mph "made one aware of high frequency vibration through handlebar and footrests." Though the writer added that, "On short trips this was not too annoying." So that was all right then.

But the tester was genuinely impressed with the Tiger's brakes and handling, plus the way it combined tractable low speed manners with a "smooth spread of power up to the peak 7000rpm ... If you are looking for a machine with an ancestry that will stamp you as a discerning rider, give you performance plus fun when riding, take a passenger if you wish and leave your budget in a reasonably healthy state as well, it's time you talked Tiger 100 with your Triumph dealer."

For an account of the race, see Lindsay Brooke's and David Gaylin's *Triumph Motorcycles in America*, but briefly, the Meriden race bikes proved more fragile than more stock machines tuned in the USA, though last minute rebuilds saw them all start, and Buddy Elmore's factory bike won at 96.38mph – replicas of this bike have been built over the years. A number of these Daytona racers survive, and Dick Shepherd, who has one of the most extensive private collections of Triumphs, owns one of them, which was displayed as Buddy Elmore's winning machine at the Earls Court Show – it is currently on display at Triumph's Visitor Centre in Hinckley.

Race bikes for the 1966 Daytona (though some details conflict with other sources):

H44111 Prepared by Johnson Motors.

H44112 Prepared by Johnson Motors. Later rumoured to go to Triumph of Long Beach and raced by Ralph White and Don Castro.

H44113 Later sold by Tri-Cor to Elmer Morra, Pittsburgh.

H44114 Entered for Gary Nixon, who in the event decided to ride 5TA H7924R, an earlier motor.

H44115 The motor blew in practice and was replaced by Herb Rieber's H2152 (a converted 3TA engine).

1967

Models covered: Triumph 3TA WD, T90, T90P, T100SS, T100C, T100CP, T100SC, T100R, T100T, T100P, T100WD T100R (Daytona race)

Production:

3TA WD	1104 (Dutch Army)
T90	200
T90P	178 (Police machines)
T100SS	216
T100C	2637 (Sports Tiger)
T100CP	53 (Mercuries)
T100SC	56 (Mercuries)
T100R	3341 (Daytona Super Sports US)
T100T	421 (Tiger Dayona Sports UK)
T100P	73 (Police machines)
T100WD	10 (Royal Navy)
T100R	8 (Daytona race bikes)

Engine/frame numbers: H48729-H57082

Prices:

T90	£291/6s/4d
T100	£296/3s/5d
T100T	£331/7s/6d

Year by Year: 1957-1974

1967 was one of the peak years for C range production, with 8297 bikes leaving the factory. This was largely thanks to sales continuing to rocket in North America, which the previous year's Daytona race win had done nothing to discourage. Just four years earlier, Triumph had sold 6300 machines across the USA, but the official order for the 1967 model year was 28,700 – it had just about quadrupled. The Americans loved Triumph's 650 twins, and that year ordered over 20,000 of them, more than half of which were T120 Bonnevilles. But the T100R and T100C still sold in useful numbers, with nearly 5000 finding homes in the USA, while Triumph also sold 2700 T20M Mountain Cubs.

But this was also an increasingly complex market, with East and West Coast USA taking different specifications of the same model. Then there were all the police and military variants, plus the fact that, as ever, home market bikes differed from those for export. So, when restoring a C range Triumph, it is vital to identify its original destination and model, and, at the risk of repeating ourselves, that is something offered by the Meriden factory records.

Once you know the model type and original destination, the Parts Book (No: 8 for 1967 model year), can be used to confirm the specification. But even this isn't infallible – the Parts Book does have several inaccuracies, and does not cover the Military or Police models. Triumph Corporation recognised this, and produced Parts Bulletins (in yellow) 67-5P and 67-6P, to identify all the parts not applicable to the US models, as well as errors in part numbers, but even this had to make clear that no assumptions could be made about was or was not fitted to a particular bike for a particular market in a particular year, as this statement underlines: "Where it is stated in our correction bulletins that an item is 'not fitted to US Models,' this means only that the part is not fitted at the factory to that particular range as supplied that year to the Eastern United States. These same parts may very well be fitted to other Triumph ranges or may be available from our parts stock."

The big news was a new model, the twin-carburettor Daytona, inspired by that race win at Florida in 1966, and timed just right to take advantage of increasing Stateside demand for Triumph twins. Labelled the T100R for export

This is the prototype Daytona, probably in early summer 1966.

Twin carbs gave Daytona owners something to shout about.

markets, and T100T at home, it followed the development of the race bikes in a milder form. The Daytona didn't have their magnesium crankcases, and changes were focused on the top end of the engine – the cylinder head was new but the bottom end little changed. The biggest new items (and selling points) were the twin Amal Monobloc carburettors, backed up by bigger $1^{17}/_{32}$ inlet valves and higher spec exhaust valves (using a more heat-resistant material) with a narrower valve angle in a shallower combustion chamber. Another good selling point (and a real plus for Triumph enthusiasts) was the adoption of Bonneville spec cams with the E3134 profile, with larger radius tappet feet ($1^{1}/_{8}$in) to minimise wear. Compression ratio increased to 9.75:1 (though one source has it remaining at 9.0:1), and the Daytona produced substantially more power than the single-carb Tiger 100, 39bhp at 7400rpm – one source states it as 41bhp,

Triumph 350/500 Unit Construction Twins Bible 1957-1974

The Daytona was a huge success for Triumph, capitalising on that famous race win.

Later type frame. Careful development turned the Triumph 350/500s into fine handling bikes.

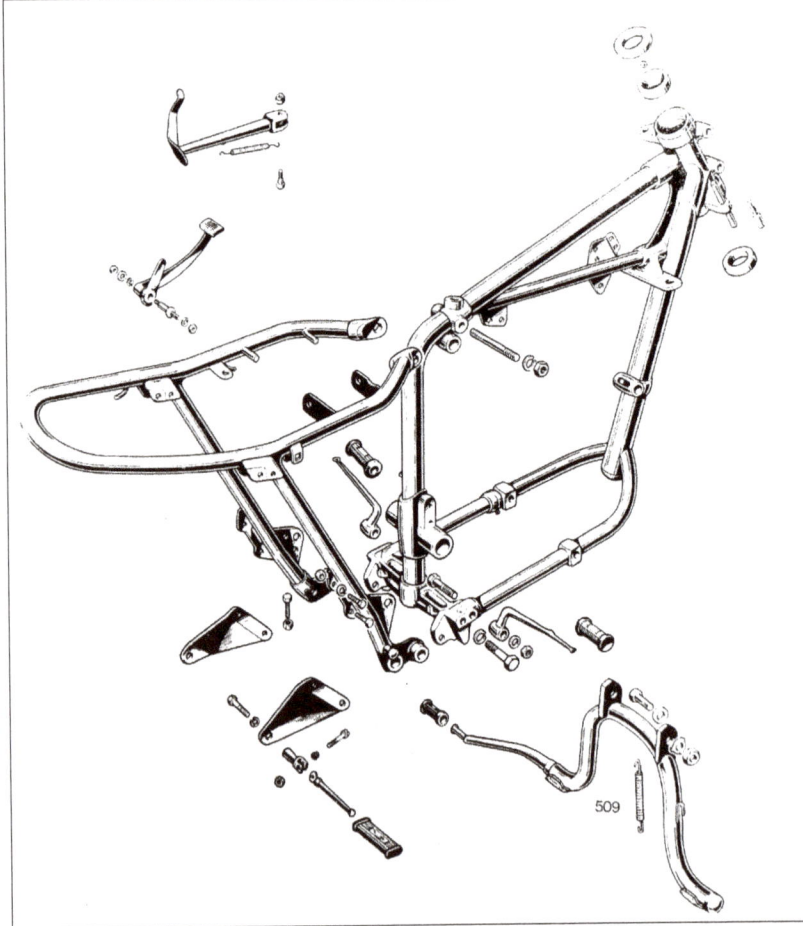

but it was certainly a boost. Either way, it was significantly quicker, with one road test recording a top speed of 113mph. For some reason, the twin Amals had no choke fitted.

The frame was new, based on that of the racers (though not of Reynolds 531, this being a mass production bike which had to sell on price), with a stronger top tube and thicker front downtube. The top tube was also shortened, to lower the overall frame height, and bring the engine down by half an inch. These changes sound small, but Doug Hele and his team had discovered that weight distribution was crucial to stable high speed handling, and lowering the whole mass of the bike helped to achieve this. The steering head was also stiffened, and fully triangulated. At the back, the swinging arm spindle mount was strengthened by two triangular support brackets, while the swinging arm was made stiffer and wider. At the same time, the spindle grease nipple was moved from the underside of the swinging arm to a far more accessible position on the end of the spindle – the theory was that a more easily accessible grease point would receive more regular attention, which was probably true!

Back to the C range in general (and indeed all Triumphs for 1967), and thread forms began to change from Cycle to UNF. This change happened gradually, and was not fully documented. The changes are particularly noticeable on the fork components, but officially, UNF threads do not appear on the forks until 1968. Tri-Cor Bulletin 67-12P gives detailed information on Unified Thread forms and part numbers applicable from 1966.

Engine

According to confidential factory correspondence, a batch of bikes had crankshafts which had been incorrectly hardened, and suffered from rapid wear. It only affected engines prior to H55204, but 50 years on, it's doubtful that this will still be a problem today! Another batch used the incorrect type of Loctite on the cranks (AV instead of Hydroseal).

Tappet blocks on all bikes gained additional O-rings to combat leaks, initially just the exhaust block but soon the inlet block followed suit. The engine of the T90 featured a new cylinder head, Hepolite pistons from H49837, and alloy con-rods (H-section RR.56 Hiduminium alloy).

Year by Year: 1957-1974

Traditionalist brochure artwork for 1967 – it might have been the Summer of Love in LA, but no one had told Meriden.

Oil pressure relief valve now included a casting for an oil pressure switch (actually brought in late in the '66 model year).

Oil tank delivery and return lines, with T-piece on the return to supply the rockers.

All models gained a larger scavenge section of oil pump to improve scavenging at high speed, increased from 0.437in to 0.487in. From H50445 a dowel was added to the timing cover/crankcase and, from H51016, the exhaust adaptors featured holes instead of slots – this is a particularly distinctive feature to look for when searching for cylinder heads: easy to spot and a good indication of the date of particular cylinder head.

Some engine changes that had begun to trickle in with late 1966 model year bikes were now in place for good. So the removable cover over the crankshaft sludge trap behind the right cylinder was now deleted and blanked off. An oil pressure switch casting was added under the oil pressure relief valve (something else seen on some late '66 machines) – no switch as yet, just a blanking plug, but it was otherwise ready to go.

Early 1967 road bikes had issues with an extra spark being produced by the Lucas coils when the points closed, due to an incorrect points cam being fitted (Lucas part no: 54441729). From engine H51616 this was superseded by a new auto advance unit that cured the problem (160-degree contact breaker cam 54041118 – Bulletin 67/3). Shortly afterwards (from H51717), the alternator stator was encapsulated, and a longer engine breather pipe fitted.

The oil tank was changed again, and, from H51726, reverted to a T-piece to take oil from the return line to the rockers, but retained the adjustable chain oil feed. From H53963 the oil tank was etch primed instead of phosphated as previously.

The clutch was now secured with a self-locking nut instead of the tab washer of earlier machines, with an extended threaded section to suit. This made the clutch hub more secure on the mainshaft, and less likely to come loose. These changes were made in conjunction with the move to UNF threads, which the mainshaft adopted. These gearbox parts are not interchangeable with earlier models.

Frame

Triumph twins of the 1960s have a reputation for superb handling, but this was only fully deserved after the changes wrought by Doug Hele and his team in 1965-67, latterly thanks to experience with the race bikes at Daytona. It was all good news for '67, with the whole range gaining the same new frame as the

All 1967 bikes shared the Doug Hele-developed frame, with thicker top tube and reinforcing strut below.

New steering lock was easier to use than the old headstock item.

T100R/T100T Daytona. Percy Tait's factory race bike, very similar to the Daytona and another beneficiary of the Hele developments is on display at the National Motorcycle Museum just outside Birmingham.

The revised steering head now had a barrel-type lock (Wilmot-Breeden Union), fairing mountings, revised steering stops, head steady location, and steering damper. The Parts Book (No 8) has several inaccuracies. On page 53, the top lug (H2100) and the associated bushes for rubber-mounting the handlebars were not factory fitted, but were available as spares. The same is true of the stanchion covers (H1696) – not fitted on the production line but available from dealers. Refer to the Parts Book for details of the forks fitted to home market and USA models. The mudguard bottom stay (H1678) illustration is incorrect, as there is only one mounting tab. Stay H1482 was not fitted to the US models. All have spring clips for the fork gaiters, introduced in late 1966.

Tinwork

A new fuel tank had three-point mounting rather than four, retaining the two front mounts but with a single rubber mount at the rear, attaching the centre of the tank to the frame top tube. Home market machines had a three-gallon tank while all US bikes used a 2.5-gallon version, and fittings as shown in the Parts Book No 8 pages 64-65. Early tanks of the new type had incorrectly welded rear brackets.

3TAs supplied to the Dutch Army (see below for details) featured a special tank which did not show the tapped holes for the badges or parcel rack, but did include a snorkel from the air filter to the front of the tank, for when crossing deep water. This tank also shows different fittings to the 1966 or 1967 versions.

The design of C range mudguards changed again, now featuring a small rolled bead at the leading/trailing edge to reduce the sharpness of the ends. The front mudguard stay/wheel stand was now a simpler curved type, which wrapped around the mudguard and had two fastenings replacing the single specialised nut of earlier machines. The US brochure shows the Daytona (T) and Sports Tiger (C) fitted with polished alloy or stainless steel mudguards.

Wheels & brakes

Both T100C and T100R featured 19in front wheels, and the Parts Book also showed differing fork and headset components for those

Rubber-mounted handlebars for '67.

Year by Year: 1957-1974

T100C exhaust guard, nicknamed the 'chip pan' for obvious reasons (if you're British).

1967 under seat, showing tool tray and single 12-volt battery. Note the single rear mount for the fuel tank.

USA bikes. US bikes were also not factory fitted with the QD rear wheel, though the parts were available from dealers.

The new Daytona, whether UK T100T or US T100R, had the 8in single-leading-shoe front brake and hub from the larger B range 650s. Interestingly, none of the brochure images or Parts Books for 1967 show this, and only one of two road test machines had the 8in brake, though it is indicated in the works manual specification for the T100T. With demand running high for 650s, was there a shortage of 8in brakes, so very early Daytonas had to make do with the standard 7in item? Maybe it was just for brochure shots, but it seems highly unlikely that a road test bike would be sent out with a lower spec brake. Either way, this is speculation.

The rear brake rod changed to run outboard of the shock absorber, while the rear brake arm was cranked to meet the brake rod, and a chain oiling pipe was added to the rear brake torque stay.

On the rear shock absorber upper mounting the original smaller-headed bolts are marked 'Bradfield,' with Nyloc type nuts which became an increasingly common fitment, especially on the mudguards.

Controls, instruments, seat

The lighting switch (light grey or black with two equal tangs), was now located centrally on the headlight, below the ammeter, which, in turn, was flanked by two hexagonal warning lamps: green for ignition on the right; red for high beam on the left. One road test stated that these were the other way round!

The horn was back under the tank again (now Clearhooter 27899), moved from the 1966 location. With the lighting switched moved, the left-hand side panel now just housed the ignition switch, high up near the seat, and lost the hole for the chain oiling pipe.

All UK models had new handlebars (H1871), which were actually the same bars used on the 3TA and 5TA in 1966, which had a slightly raised profile. US models continued with higher bars, H1519 for the T100C and H1873 for T100R.

The Parts Book shows differences in the handlebar mounting arrangements between US and home market bikes; the US machines continuing with the previous rigid arrangement of split washers, clamps and bolts, while those for the UK had the new rubber isolated eyebolts. Were American riders more immune to vibration? Either way, as mentioned earlier, the rubber mounting parts were available from US dealers.

UK and American models featured differing levers, nicely illustrated in Parts Book No 8. The handlebar grips were the new 'balloon' type, the padding intended to absorb vibrations, with the left one cut away to allow operation of the dipswitch.

The VDO Enduro speedometer, fitted to the T100C for 1966, was replaced by the standard Smiths magnetic fitted to everything else except police bikes, though it was still available at dealer or customer request. Police machines still usually featured the chronometric speedometer, favoured for its accuracy.

A new 'Quiltop' dualseat marked 1967 bikes: slightly longer than before, overhanging

Triumph 350/500 Unit Construction Twins Bible 1957-1974

Part of the T100C's appeal (in Pacific Blue for '67) were those sinuous down pipes, just visible here.

the rear frame loop, and with a ribbed top in grey plus black Vynide sides and white piping. A gold embossed Triumph logo graced the rear of the seat, and very nice it was, too, though it seems not all bikes necessarily had one. (A logo that is, they all had seats.)

Colours

Identifying the exact specification and colour schemes of the various models for 1967 is a minefield! We do know that all cylinder barrel fins and front hubs were in Silver. Anyway, here is a basic guide ...

Tiger 90: Hi-Fi Scarlet over Alaskan White. Note the Scarlet sweeps over the top of the kneegrips, not underneath as previously, while the rider's view of the tank shows a pronounced Vee at the front. Surviving police Tiger 90s have been seen in overall Gloss Black.

T100SS (UK): Pacific Blue over Alaskan White, 3-gallon tank with rack, painted mudguards, Lucas 564 rear light.

T100T Daytona (UK): Pacific Blue over Alaskan White, 3-gallon tank with rack, painted mudguards, Lucas 564 rear light.

T100R Daytona (US): Pacific Blue over Alaskan White, 2.5-gallon tank with no rack, polished alloy mudguards, Lucas 679 rear light.

T100C (US): Pacific Blue over Alaskan White to 1966 pattern, 2.5-gallon tank with no rack, off-road equipment, Lucas 679 rear light.

Put like that, it all looks straightforward, but over the years several bikes have come to light with original paint schemes that do not follow the official pattern for that year. From 1967 Triumph became inconsistent in following one scheme throughout the year, and later production machines especially may not correspond with the published materials, adverts or road tests. For example, some Tiger 90s have mudguards in Hi-Fi Scarlet as the main colour, with Alaskan White as the stripe (lined in Gold), or the other way round. Other C range bikes for '67 don't have a stripe at all. Brochure and road test pictures can show this up. Incidentally, the Tiger 90 was now officially listed as the 'Tiger Cub (T90)'!

Parts Book 8 – covers the 1967 model year bikes from H49833 (but not the Dutch military machines).

Notes for 1967

The BSA group won a Queens Award for Industry, and in the previous three years Triumph had exported 82 per cent of its total production, with BSA exporting 68 per cent. It's sobering to think that from these dizzy heights, which would see C range production reach a peak of nearly 10,000 in 1970, BSA-Triumph's fall from grace was extraordinarily rapid – big losses and a production disaster came the following year.

The Dutch army bikes

Just when the 3TA was nearing the end of its life, Triumph bagged a major fleet order for the bike from the Royal Netherlands Army. It had been on the cards for some time, as, back in early 1963, the Dutch military began testing 200cc bikes. These were a Triumph (presumably a Tiger Cub), BSA, Puch, Maico and Zundapp. The Cub did quite well under test, topping the riding and construction categories, but the Dutch concluded that none of the five small bikes was up to the rigours of military use. The Maico and Zundapp soon dropped out of the test, while the Cub, Puch and BSA all had serious piston problems within 5000 miles. The idea of a lightweight army bike was abandoned.

Two years later, the Dutch decided to try again with 350s, and this time the candidates were the BSA B40, Matchless G3, and the 3TA.

They were tested over a gruelling 7500 miles, 3000 miles of which were off-road, and the Triumph came out the clear winner. The Dutch liked its lighter weight than the other two, its greater ground clearance, smoother twin-cylinder power unit, and durability. Their only real complaints were that the full chaincase tended to clog up with mud when off-road, and, with a top speed of 118km/h (74mph), it didn't quite meet the army spec of 140km/h (88mph), though it was the fastest of the three.

The military 3TA had several changes from the civilian bikes, though it kept the elegant nacelle, which looked a little incongruous in military context! A Solex carburettor replaced the Amal, and there was a different air filter and a high-level air intake, as described above. A wide-ratio gearbox (still four-speed, of course) was fitted to improve off-road performance. The bikes (H48739 to H49832) employed many 1966 features as well as parts unique to the model. Different alternator wiring, for example, meant detail changes to the crankcase. There was a two-into-one exhaust, leather panniers, and, of course, the bike was finished in a shade of khaki. There were lots of other detail differences, including grease nipples for the control cables.

On 14th December 1965 an order was placed with the Dutch Triumph importer, and the first bikes arrived in November 1966. Initial testing, however, showed them to be well down on top speed, at 63-64mph. More testing ensued, of 16 bikes, with the same result. Engines were torn down, compression ratios measured, but it seems they never really got to the bottom of it – averaged out, none these 3TAs could crack 70mph.

Young men, national service, motorcycles ... the rest is inevitable.

But it wasn't just top speed. According to the excellent Dutch website http://www.triumph3ta.nl/ (which provided much of the information for this section), a lack of production capacity at Meriden meant that sub-assemblies were stored outside before they were needed, covered by a tarpaulin to keep off the autumnal elements. As a result, they needed some rework on arrival and frequent maintenance was the order of the day. Not that they were being treated with kid gloves. According to Harry Meijer, who ran one of the maintenance departments, bikes were sometimes dragged over rough ground, breaking the aluminium oil pipes. But overall, despite the problems, the 3TAs were thought to have "performed pretty well."

In 1988, the Dutch military decided to sell them on to the public. Unfortunately, many were stored outside before sale, and some were described as "wrecks." Many went in lots to the highest bidder, and non-runners were scrapped in a blast furnace, with lots of parts like tanks and mudguards ditched. What a shame. Still, many of the Dutch 3TAs have survived, and there is a strong following for them in the Netherlands.

Kees van der Linden (despatch rider)

"In November 1978 I was drafted, and the only thing I knew was that I would get motorcycle training. After a few days we were shown our mounts: a few rows of Triumph 3TAs in Army

Hundreds of Dutch military 3TAs were sold off in the 1980s, but suffered from being left outdoors.

Military bikes had several special features, which didn't extend to the full-width front hub on this bike.

Kees van der Linden has fond memories of his army issue 3TA.

Green, all on their centre stands in a tray filled with sand to catch the occasional oil drip. Very impressive.

"The first two months were filled with theory and driving lessons; our extra gear over the normal soldier's stuff consisted of a helmet with kind of fish bowl visor, black gauntlets, a heavy, wide leather support belt (to keep your kidneys in place ...), a heavy canvas DR overall, and black fur-lined boots.

"This was for me the first time to drive a motorcycle, so everything was new, but those who already were experienced riders had problems changing gears on the wrong side! We were also trained to do 'circus tricks,' like standing on the bike, on the knees, etc.

"During my stay in Germany I did convoy duty; sometimes very scary, when you had to pass at full speed heavy vehicles on narrow, slippery roads, and sometimes, during the night, without lights. And as a DR, you had to be available 24/7, which meant that you were exempted from the normal chores and guard duty, but could sleep whenever you were not required.

"The German DR has a kind of two-stroke, very good off-road; the Triumphs were less easy in the terrain. But on the road the Triumphs were much more comfortable.

"We could do only first-line maintenance, like oil change, chain tensioning, etc; the more complicated maintenance should be done by qualified motorcycle mechanics, and there were not enough of them, so we had often to do it ourselves. Not a problem, because we loved our bikes and took care of them.

"While on reserve duty in 1982 I expected the new Moto Guzzis, but fortunately, the faithful 3TAs were waiting for us!"

Production

1967 production began (H48729-H49832) with the batch of 1104 Military 3TAs for the Dutch Army. The first Dutch bike was, in fact, H45509, a 1966 model year bike provided for Neale Shilton (Triumph Sales Manager) for the Amsterdam Show, and was featured in *Motorcycle Sport* April 1966 as well as in Neale Shilton's excellent book *A Million Miles Ago*.

1967 T90 production was in two batches, starting on 15th October 1966 (H51045) and ending on 15th March 1967 (H55203), totalling 378 machines. A lot of these – 109 in all – were actually police versions (H51665-H51715 and H55077-H55134). Most of the first group went to New Zealand, with the second group destined for locations in Burma (now Myanmar) and around the Arabian Gulf. There are surviving 1967 police Tiger 90s in New Zealand, Tenerife and Myanmar.

Britain's police also used Tiger 90s, and five were supplied to the Chief Constable of Buckinghamshire, of which two survive, while others went to Dorset and Middlesbrough.

Seventy-one Tiger 90s went to British Guiana, possibly Mercurys or police spec bikes, and one survives in Holland!

A high proportion of civilian T90s were also exported that year – 200 of them, with destinations including Portugal, Jamaica, Formosa and Australia, as well as those mentioned above. As a result, UK '67 T90s are

Tiger 90 continued as the Daytona hoovered up all the glory – it had one more year to go.

Year by Year: 1957-1974

Multi-coloured Triumphs for the Americans in '67. From the top: Burgundy Red, Grenadier Red, Mist Green and Pacific Blue.

quite rare. If looking at one of these, don't forget that the UK registration letter system changed at this time, from January-January to August-August, so the 'E' registration was only used from January until August '67.

T100 production was even more export orientated, with most bikes heading overseas, and the first Daytona T100R (H49833) went to Johnson Motors. In fact, the majority were shipped to the USA, though other locations included Canada, Mexico, Puerto Rico and Denmark. H49833 to H52108 were earmarked for motorcycle shows at Duarte (USA), Paris, Cologne, Earls Court and Daytona, together with batches of Mercurys and other machines for special purposes. Production figures for this period are very interesting, and any machine made during early 1967 needs to be checked carefully against the factory records to identify the original customer and destination.

A few examples:
H49833 – T100R sent to Johnson Motors 6th September 1966.

T100C in its element: out in the woods.

1967 Daytona front end, looking identical to its single-carb equivalents.

H49834 – T100C sent to Johnson Motors on the same day.

H49835 (T100T) and H49836 (T100SS) both sent to CGCIM, France for the Paris Show.

H52101 to H52106 were the Daytona race bikes (see below) ridden by Dick Hammer, Larry Palmgren, Buddy Elmore, Gary Nixon, Gene Romero and Eddy Mulder. As in the previous year, they were shipped to Baltimore first for testing and selection. According to Bill Milburn, the bikes and riders ended up as follows:

H52101 – Dick Hammer. This bike survives at the AMA Museum in Columbus Ohio (though the engine is unnumbered).

H52102 – Larry Palmgren.

H52103 – Buddy Elmore.

H52104 – Gary Nixon (bike under restoration in USA, at the time of writing).

H52105 – Gene Romero.

H52106 – Eddie Mulder.

H52107 – Percy Tait's bike, retained and raced in the UK – for details, see Claudio Sintich's *Road Racing History of the Triumph 500 Unit Twin*, which also covers most of the race machines and races in detail.

Road tests & features

The Motorcycle got in early with a '67 model year test, featuring a T100T Daytona (KNX 809D) on 3rd November 1966 – the same issue detailed the Triumph range for 1967, with extra pictures of the Daytona. Another T100T (KUE 533D) featured in the November 1967 *Motorcycle Sport* – both these machines were early '67s, registered between October and December 1966 in Warwickshire, though only the second one had the 8in front brake!

A series of articles appeared in *The Motorcycle* in early 1967 which covered development of race bikes. On 6th April it ran a feature about a race-prepared T100, based around a Ken Sprayson frame, tuned Daytona engine, and developed by Geoff Duke. David Nixon was third in the 500cc Production TT that year, at 85.11mph – Ray Knight would win the same event the following year on a T100 sponsored by Hughes, at 90.09mph.

In *Motorcycle Sport* March 1967 the single-carb T100 test had good pictures, useful for restorers today. The same machine (an early '67 press bike registered in October '66) was featured again in a clutch strip article in *Motorcycle Mechanics* July 1967.

Although a lot of press attention was focused on the Daytona, the single-carb bikes hadn't been forgotten, and *The Motorcycle* 13th July 1967 featured a road test of an export specification T100C showing many of the details of this model. Articles in *Cycle* and *Cycle World* (see Appendix V – Magazine Articles, page 151) are also worth searching out for US-spec bikes.

Competition

For the 1967 Daytona 200, Triumph was keen to bag another win, but didn't want a repeat of the mechanical troubles which led to so many rebuilds. So, rather than aim for ultimate power increases, the factory concentrated on reliability and useable mid-range power. The connecting rods (a weak spot the previous year) were strengthened, the valve gear was lightened, and new freer-breathing cylinder heads featured squish bands, with peak power now up to 48.5bhp at 7000rpm.

To back this up, there was a close-ratio gearbox, 210mm double-sided (ie four shoes) Fontana front drum brake, new fork internals, and a new exhaust system which improved engine access while retaining ground clearance. Notably there were no major changes to the frames, which spoke volumes for Doug Hele's development work the previous year.

Year by Year: 1957-1974

> ## What the press said
> T100T Daytona – *The Motorcycle*, 3rd November 1966
> History does not record exactly who was first to give the Daytona the title of mini-Bonneville, but it was probably *The Motorcycle*, kicking off the Triumph section of its BSA Group supplement. "A Meriden Mini-Bonnie! True enough, brand new from Triumphs for 1967 comes a searing sportster in five-hundred form, with twin carburettors."

Win on Sunday, sell on Monday? That was the clear message of victories in Daytona and the ISDT.

Meriden prepared six race bikes to this specification, shipped them across the Atlantic, and the company was rewarded with a far less stressful event. There were no pre-race mechanical dramas during practice, all six bikes finished, and Gary Nixon took the top spot at a new record of 98.22mph. As icing on the cake, Buddy Elmore, last year's winner, took the runner-up spot, giving Triumph a 1-2.

As for the ISDT there was no factory supported team, as Triumph concentrated on the broader appeal of Daytona, but Ken Heanes, Roy Peplow, Johnny Giles and Gordon Farley (who was sponsored by Triumph dealer Comerfords), all rode on private entry Triumphs. *Motorcycling* (9th and 16th August 1967) carried pictures and details. Johnny Giles and Gordon Farley did well, but British riders in general suffered many retirements – it looked like the glory days of British wins at the ISDT were over.

1968

Models covered: Tiger 90, Tiger 100S, Tiger 100SS, Tiger 100C, Tiger 100R, Tiger 100T, Tiger 100P

Production:

Tiger 90	675
	(345 standard,
	330 Police)
Tiger 100S	578
Tiger 100SS	260
Tiger 100C	3400
Tiger 100R (Daytona Super Sports US)	2808
Tiger T100T (Tiger Daytona Sports UK)	540
Tiger 100P	207
Engine/frame numbers:	H57083-H65572
Prices:	
T100S	£332/17/2
T100T	£372/5/0

T100C's two-into-two left-side exhaust left, the right side bare.

"When the new Triumph Military and Police Mercury model was unveiled at the Brussels Motor Show last month, they immediately attracted orders totalling £20,000. Customers include the Irish Army and Garda (Police) and the Belgian Police." So said the February 1968 issue of corporate magazine *Triumph World*

Triumph 350/500 Unit Construction Twins Bible 1957-1974

> "It's here. The swingingest, scorchingest group of motorcycles ever assembled under one roof."

Wide. As for the bikes, the 1968 model year saw no radical changes, but a continuing refinement of the C range aimed at improving reliability, practicality and ease of maintenance.

All bikes received the new Amal Concentric carburettor to replace the Monobloc. To this day, the debate continues as to whether this was a real improvement, though at the time, the all-in-one Concentric, with its integral float chamber, was no doubt cheaper to make. Interestingly, when Amal was developing the new carburettor in 1967, it offered riders a free carb swap so that they could try it – perhaps a means of getting some real world testing done by willing guinea pigs! Whoever tested it, the new carb came with cap bolts for the inlet manifold.

The T100S now shared the Daytona's 39-degree valve angle, and larger, 1^{17}⁄$_{32}$in inlet valve, though, of course, it was still single carb. The official literature also refers to stellite-tipped valves. From H57100 the rocker boxes increased in thickness, and, from H63307, the oil feed to the pushrods changed, and the drillings through the rocker arms were deleted,

Concentric, the new carburettor for 1968.

now relying on splash lubrication. The pushrod tubes also lost their lower cup. In a bid to prevent leaks from the cylinder barrel base, the nuts were now 12-point items (from H58798), that were more accessible and gave more purchase for tightening with a ring spanner. These are only available in UNF threads, so require a change of stud and crankcase thread to suit. Correspondence between Triumph engineers

Frank Baker and John Nelson indicated these were being considered for production back in August 1967.

The tappet guide blocks now had O-rings where they fitted into the barrel casting (also mentioned during the previous model year), and the Zener diode moved from under the seat to a distinctive finned heatsink underneath the headlamp – it was something of a styling feature in its own right.

Meanwhile, there were big changes to the ignition system. Getting the correct ignition timing could be a fraught process on any Triumph twin, often needing to be a compromise between the two cylinders. For 1968, a new removeable cover in the primary chaincase allowed stroboscopic timing, though the pointer to align with marks on the alternator rotor wasn't introduced until engine H65011, and a separate timing plate (D2014) was offered as a service part. You might expect that this relatively advanced feature meant the end of the TDC plug in the crankcase, but some factory information shows it still there.

The other ignition change was a move to Lucas 6CA contact breakers. These moved the condensers (previously squeezed in with the points) to their own mounting under the fuel tank, greatly improving accessibility to the points. Not only that, but each set of points could be adjusted independently, allowing more accurate timing for each cylinder, rather than a compromise between the two. Early production bikes (the first 1500) had incorrect machining (by Lucas) on the new set, so the plate was turned 180 degrees to compensate, and engines H57083 to H63307 had no lubricating wicks. In the 21st Century, many C range bikes have been converted to electronic ignition, so all of this is irrelevant, but if your machine still uses points, the Lucas 6CA set remains a great improvement.

1968 Tiger 90 in Riviera Blue, on Brighton seafront.

All bikes had the new primary drive access plate for stroboscopic timing – Triumph logo should be black, not white.

Threads and running gear

BSA/Triumph was moving over to UNF threads (noted in the new cylinder barrel nuts) and this obviously has implications when ordering parts. For 1968 the C range gearbox mainshaft threads changed from Cycle threads ($9/16$ 20tpi) to UNF ($9/16$ 18tpi). The front forks went UNF as well (now 28tpi) as part of a major redesign developed by Ernest Rodgers as well as Doug Hele and Percy Tait. They now had floating shuttle valves in the base of the tubes to give two-way damping. The valves, screwed into the bottom of the stanchions, were simple but effective, stiffening the recoil damping to reduce pitching on bumpy bends.

Condensers now moved from the contact breakers to under the fuel tank.

Instruments for 1968, still with just two warning lights (ignition and high beam) plus the ammeter.

Some owners fitted their own oil pressure switches.

The new finned Zener diode was a pleasing thing in itself, quite apart from the electrical benefits.

Other new parts included different seal holders, top covers with slots for headlamp mounting, and the ignition switch was moved to the left-hand top cover (easier to see and reach than the previous mounting on the left-hand side cover). The lighting switch also migrated away from the side cover, now a toggle switch on top of the headlight – again, easier to reach than before, especially on the move. Moving both switches had the side benefit of allowing the side panel to be quickly detachable and act as a toolbox.

The oil tank was also new, still six pints and rubber-mounted, now with an oil feed pipe plumbed from the return pipe to the rocker feed. It also had a dipstick attached to the cap – officially, this wasn't fitted until H65573 (1969 model year), but it does appear on earlier bikes. The oil tank breather changed, too, now running under the rear mudguard to end at its lower edge – the breather pipe is often left off now, unless a bike has been meticulously restored.

All handlebars were now rubber-mounted, with the balloon type grips which were supposed to combat vibration. Air filters on the Daytonas were now of cloth and gauze, and the main fuse rating was reduced to 20 amps. As ever, exact wheel size and brake specifications depended on model, destination and date, but the T100R and C had a 19in front wheel, with the C having a wider, 3.5in, rim instead of the standard 3.25in. The Daytona was also fitted with the 8in brake taken from the 650 twins, with its distinctive larger spoke flange. This wasn't introduced at the beginning of the model year, something which goes for many of these changes, which filtered in over the year – see below for engine numbers of each change. Either way, the bigger brake was a welcome move, but may also have been expedient for Triumph – the big twins had moved on to a twin-leading-shoe drum, and there may have been some spare stocks of the 8in brake there for the using!

There were stronger braces for the exhaust pipes; these now bolted to the front engine mounts.

Tinwork

The chainguard changed, and the kneegrips were now thicker, glued-on items, with a spaced herringbone pattern, though the eyebrow tank badge remained. The steering damper was

Engine breather vented to the end of the rear mudguard.

deleted (was Triumph trying suggest that the much improved chassis no longer needed one?) while the metal script on the side panels gave way to simple transfers in gold. UK bikes may also have a Queens Award for Exports transfer – the company had been given this title for the many thousands of bikes it was shipping across the Atlantic now.

As ever, the T100C had a few different parts, notably the high-level exhaust system, with both pipes exiting on the left, plus a sumpguard and folding footrests. Plain gearlever and kickstart rubbers replaced those with the Triumph logo, and the front mudguard lower stay was now of a simple hoop design rather than having distinctive 'feet.'

US bikes had round Lucas RER 14 reflectors fitted under the front of the fuel tank, and official literature also refers to a longer rear brake lever and new three-hole number plate mounting. The T100C and R seats had a black quilted top, grey on Home and General Export bikes. All seats now had new hinges, using pressings and pins welded in place.

Specification summary

Once again the specification for the various T100s is a minefield in which many an unwary restorer has fallen, even the professionals! Detail differences between the models abound, and the literature cannot be relied upon to give an accurate answer, but these are the general details:

T100T (UK Daytona): twin carbs, low-level exhausts, 3-gallon fuel tank with rack, in 1966 colour scheme, painted mudguards, Lucas 564 rear light.

T100SS (UK): single carb, low-level exhausts, 3-gallon tank with rack, in 1968 colour scheme, painted mudguards, Lucas 564 rear light.

T100R (US Daytona): twin carbs, low-level exhausts, 2-gallon tank with no rack, in 1968 scheme, painted mudguards, Lucas 679 rear light.

T100C (US): single carb, high-level exhausts on left, 2-gallon tank with no rack, colour sides/contrasting stripe, polished alloy mudguards, off-road equipment, Lucas 679 rear light.

Colours

Colour schemes this year did not follow a consistent form – study various original machines, brochures, photographs and road tests and you'll find several variations. If restoring an original machine pay special attention and record what you have before setting out to repaint.

Often traces of the original colour, unfaded by sunlight or contaminated with dirt, will survive beneath the tank badges and knee grips. These 'chips' can be used by your auto shop to produce a close match in modern paints.

Some compromise is necessary, and even during original production there would have been subtle changes in shades and hues between batches of machines. There is no such thing as 'the exact original colour,' especially for light metallic finishes, where atmospheric conditions such as temperature and humidity affect the 'lay' of the aluminium flakes during drying. Modern paints will give more consistent and resistant finishes, and are also more environmentally friendly, plus they will give you a bike that looks good for a long time.

Tiger 90: Riviera Blue over Silver Sheen (the official range information incorrectly says White!), Gold lining, 'Tiger 90' transfer opposite the filler cap. Note that, on the Tiger 90 and Tiger 100S, the blue paintwork does not extend below the kneegrip, but instead sweeps above and to the back as in the '67 style. Again the pronounced Vee pattern of paintwork is displayed on the front of the tank.

Tiger 100: Aquamarine over Silver Sheen with White lining, and the 1968 US and UK brochures feature a clear colour photograph of a US T100R showing good detail. Note that only on the T100S does the colour pattern follow that of the T90 – the T100R has the same

Triumph 350/500 Unit Construction Twins Bible 1957-1974

Overshadowed by the Daytona perhaps, but the single-carb T100SS still sold in reasonable numbers.

1968 T100SS with left-hand side panel removed – tools were now stored in the panel.

style as the 1966 bikes, while the T100C is single colour with a contrasting central stripe on the tank. But to show how things varied, one original photograph of a brand new UK spec T100T (registered in February/March 1968) shows the tank in a single colour. The T100C was the only model with polished mudguards – all others were painted.

Parts Book: No 9
To view the Triumph Parts Books use this link to Classic British Spares www.classicbritishspares.com and use the Parts Book library Tag.

Notes for 1968

Summary of modifications for 1968, from engine number:
H58191 Permatex 300 gasket sealing compound used from here.
H58797 TDC timing location holes in flywheel amended to $^{15}/_{64}$in diameter.
H58797 Dunlop K70 tyres fitted to Tri-Cor USA bikes.
H58797 Holes and grooves deleted from the oil pump plungers (interim condition).
H58798 12-point cylinder base nuts fitted.
H60232 Revised rubber mix used for knee grips.
H60232 US models supplied with seat grabrails, though limited supplies mean rails are not actually fitted at the factory but shipped at a later date.
H60570 Holes and grooves deleted from the oil pump plungers (final condition).
H60620 Grab rail factory-fitted for Johnson Motors' bikes.
H60832 Grab rail factory-fitted for Tri-Cor bikes.
H63307 Front petrol tank mountings change to 'Cleveloc' nuts.
H63307 Steel oil tank filter and crankcase filter.
H63307 Rocker oil system changed to splash lubrication.
H63307 $^{1}/_{16}$in diameter hole drilled in swinging arm oil seal to allow air to escape when greasing.
H63307 'Stat-o-Seal' washer for petrol tap sealing.
H63307 Cylinder head bolt torque now 18lb/ft.
H63307 Front mudguard lengthened (not polished guard).
H63307 Coupled upswept exhaust pipes (T100C).
H63307 Stronger connecting-rods.
H63307 Felt lubricating wicks added to 6CA contact breaker, exhaust camshaft taper amended.
H63370 Thicker-walled cylinder barrels gradually introduced.

Production

1968 production began with a small batch of ten T100SS machines destined for the BBC and supplied by Harvey Owen, the well-known London dealer (H57083-H57092).

T90 production began on 2nd January 1968 (H62186) and ended on 13th May 1968 (H65570) with the total for the year being 675,

300 of which were exported to Africa, Denmark and the Far East, and some of these may have been to 'Mercury' specification (see 1966 Notes). A small batch of Tiger 90s was built in 1969 for the Garda (Irish Police), and these were likely to have been classed as Mercury bikes – at least one survives. Two Tiger 90s (H65385 and H65404) were supplied with reinforced frames, both bought by dealer Sid Morams of Slough.

1968 was the final year for the Tiger 90, the 'baby Bonnie,' and the last bike – H65570 – survived (at the time of writing is undergoing restoration in the USA). The records indicate that it was exported to France, but it was, in fact, bought by a US Forces pilot based in Italy, and eventually sent to California on his retirement. Total Tiger 90 production of all years was 4204, with a small number of engines each year exported or retained for service exchange.

One major change at the factory during 1968 was the move to testing each bike on a rolling road before dispatching it, rather than taking it out onto the roads of Warwickshire. Real road testing might have been thorough, but in the winter bikes could come back filthy, and unless they were thoroughly cleaned before crating, could arrive at American dealers rusty, thanks to the salt used to treat the winter roads around Meriden.

However, the rolling road system wasn't perfect. In that first year a batch of bikes was dispatched without piston rings, something not picked up by the new testing regime, as former tester Jim Lee explains: "We would start the rollers, select second and drop the clutch to start the engine, working the engine through the gears and testing everything. The exhausts were attached to an extraction system so we never realised that the engines were smoking heavily – only on arrival at the dealers was the problem found!"

In fact, bikes could turn up in the USA damaged as well as rusty, and in January 1968 the standard shipping cases were modified in an attempt to eliminate 'In Transit Damage,' to give it the official term. Research into company records reveals that quite considerable numbers of machines were damaged in some way during shipping and delivery to the dealer. T100C H58369 for example, was delivered with a damaged frame and oil tank, while H60751 (another T100C) had a bent exhaust and mudguard. One shows some 70 machines damaged in transit, and this was just the C range bikes for 1968. This new information needs to be included when assessing the specification of any Triumph.

The T100C was ostensibly a US-only model, but, according to *Motorcycling* on 11th October 1967, some of these sold into the UK through Comerfords, the well known dealer in Thames Ditton, Surrey. These were to full US specification including the US tail light and tank reflectors.

George Best, the highly talented football superstar of the early 1970s, appears to have been given a T100R by Triumph on 23rd March 1972 – the bike was H57708, which makes it a '68 model, so it may have been on display in the factory showroom for some time. Being a T100R also made it a US model. At the time of writing, this bike has not been heard of since, so we don't know whether it survived.

A number of 1968 machines were supplied to the UK Police forces – Glasgow, Dublin, Liverpool, Buckinghamshire, Dorset, etc numbered (T90P H******), all fitted and finished appropriately for their duties. Each police force could specify the bikes to suit their particular requirements.

T100T H61427 was one of the press machines, registered PAC 520F, and it survives. From the same batch, T100T H61527 was

Twelve-point cylinder barrel nuts enabled tighter torquing.

another press bike, featuring in the Haynes workshop manual.

The Motorcycle 8th November 1967 carried the range information for '68 Triumphs, and the August '68 issue of *Motorcyclist Illustrated* included a brief test on the Tiger 100 – the same test bike (H61944, registered PAC 521F) appeared in print elsewhere. *Cycle* magazine, in the same month, carried a good road test of a T100C – it's worth seeking this one out, as it has excellent pictures, including a colour shot.

We've already mentioned how Triumph was able to offer bikes tax-free to overseas citizens, who would pay the sales tax on the bike once they had shipped it home. T100R H60173 (PNX 896F) was one of these, bought by a Mr Daniel R Pike under what was known as the Personal Export Scheme. Mr Pike was given a parking ticket in Bullstrode Street, London W1 during 1968 and failed to pay it, leading to correspondence between Triumph and the Metropolitan police; the company having to explain that it wasn't the bike's owner.

A similar case was that of Wayne Burke, of Gainesville, USA. He bought a Bonneville, which was later seen speeding and being ridden recklessly near Edinburgh. The police followed it up, thought Triumph was the owner, and received the following reply from Meriden:

"Dear Sir,

"Further to your notice of intended prosecution dated 30th May 1968 we wish to inform you that the Motorcycle registration number PUE 905F does not belong to us.

"The Machine was sold to an American visitor under the Personal Export Scheme for Motor Vehicles and the transfer took place on the 9th May 1968. The owner is a Mr Wayne Michael Burke of the United States.

"Yours Faithfully,

"Triumph Engineering Company."

Competition

If Triumph was hoping to repeat its '66 and '67 Daytona 200 wins in 1968 – which of course it was – then it was disappointed. Johnson Motors and Tri-Cor had retained the 1967 Daytona racers and fielded these, though fitted with Sonicweld swinging-arms. Two of these bikes – H52101 and H52105, both prepared by Woody Leone – were the fastest Triumph 500s in practice. The factory-built race bikes for 1968 had a new frame, which the riders criticised for being less stable than the '67. Front-mounted oil tanks and oil coolers, also part of the '68 race specification, were quickly ditched ...

H63301 to H63306 were the new factory bikes, and three of these were entered for the race, along with five '67 machines, as follows (information kindly supplied by Bill Milburn):

1967 bikes
H52101 – ridden by Van Leeuwen, prepared by Woody Leone
H52102 – Bob Sholly for Tri-Cor
H52103 – Buddy Elmore for Tri-Cor
H52105 – Jim Odom for Johnson Motors
H52106 – Tim Coopey for Deeley's

1968 bikes
H63302 – Dusty Coppage (Johnson Motors)
H63303 – Chuck Palmgren (Tri-Cor, now on display at the AMA Museum)
H63305 – Gary Nixon (Tri-Cor)

None of this worked, though, as Cal Rayborn won the Daytona on a Harley (as he would in '69) followed by Yvon Duhamel on a Yamaha 350, the first time a two-stroke had reached the Daytona podium. Triumph and BSA would soon see success at Daytona again, but with the 750cc triples, and the short run of C range glory at the track was over.

Triumph 500s were successful elsewhere, however. As noted above, Ray Knight won the 500cc Production TT in 1968, and David Dixon and Peter Butler took top spot at the Thruxton 500 on 12th May 1968 – their bike was a T100R supplied by Boyer of Bromley, and it survives. *The Motorcycle* (15th and 29th May 1968) covered the Thruxton win.

1969

Models covered: Tiger T90P, Tiger T100S, Tiger T100C, Tiger T100R, Tiger T100T, Tiger T100P, Tiger T100C SP

Production:

Tiger 90	28 (police machines)
Tiger 100S	1336
Tiger 100SS	15
Tiger 100C (Trophy 500)	3230
Tiger 100R (Tiger Daytona Super Sports US)	2388

Year by Year: 1957-1974

Look closely: this 1969 bike has the earlier Amal Monobloc carb and plain primary drive cover.

Tiger 100T (Tiger Daytona Sports UK)	501
Tiger 100P	352 (police machines)
Tiger T100C SP	11
Engine/frame numbers:	NC100-JC23789

Development does not always result in a better motorcycle, but, for the Triumph C range, things definitely improved in the late 1960s. For 1969, the engine was beefed up all round, with a more substantial bottom end, thicker cylinder barrel, stronger RR56 con-rods, and yet another pushrod tube oil seal arrangement – the previous bottom end, with its plain bush timing side main bearing, had been adequate for the 5TA, but could wilt under the extra stress of the harder-revving, higher-powered Daytona. It's widely thought that the 1969/70 650s are amongst the best, most sorted Triumph big twins, and the same is true of the 1969/70 C range.

Taking the bottom end first, a ball-bearing journal replaced the plain timing side bush, with oil supplied to the big-ends via the timing cover – previously, it had been fed through the bush, with a loss in pressure if this was worn. As well as being stronger, the ball-race gave positive location for crankshaft end float. On the drive side, the previous ball-bearing was replaced by a roller, and two small lumps on the front and rear of the triangular timing case are the identifying marks for this new bottom end. For the time being, it retained the previous breathing arrangement, but this would change in May 1969. The big changes meant new crankcases to suit, and Triumph took the opportunity to equip them with wider joint faces, where possible, to reduce oil leaks.

The twin carburettor T100R and T100T were given stronger con-rods of RR56 aluminium alloy, fitted with Vandervell VP3 big-end shells. They also had nitrided camshafts, in response to rapid wear of the cams – this was a benefit from development of the 650cc twins, whose cams had the same heat treatment. The T100R/T100T still had E3134 camshafts, while the single-carb T100S and T100C used the softer E3325s. They also continued to use bigger-radius cam followers (1⅛in on the T100T/R, ¾in on the T100S/C).

As part of these major changes, the move to UNF threads continued (now used for the crank, amongst many other parts). By now, almost all threads in the engine and gearbox were Unified, although across the machine this was a gradual process, and didn't affect all parts in the same year. As can be imagined, this can make identifying the correct parts an exacting process! An example is the new oil pressure switch, which now moved into the timing cover

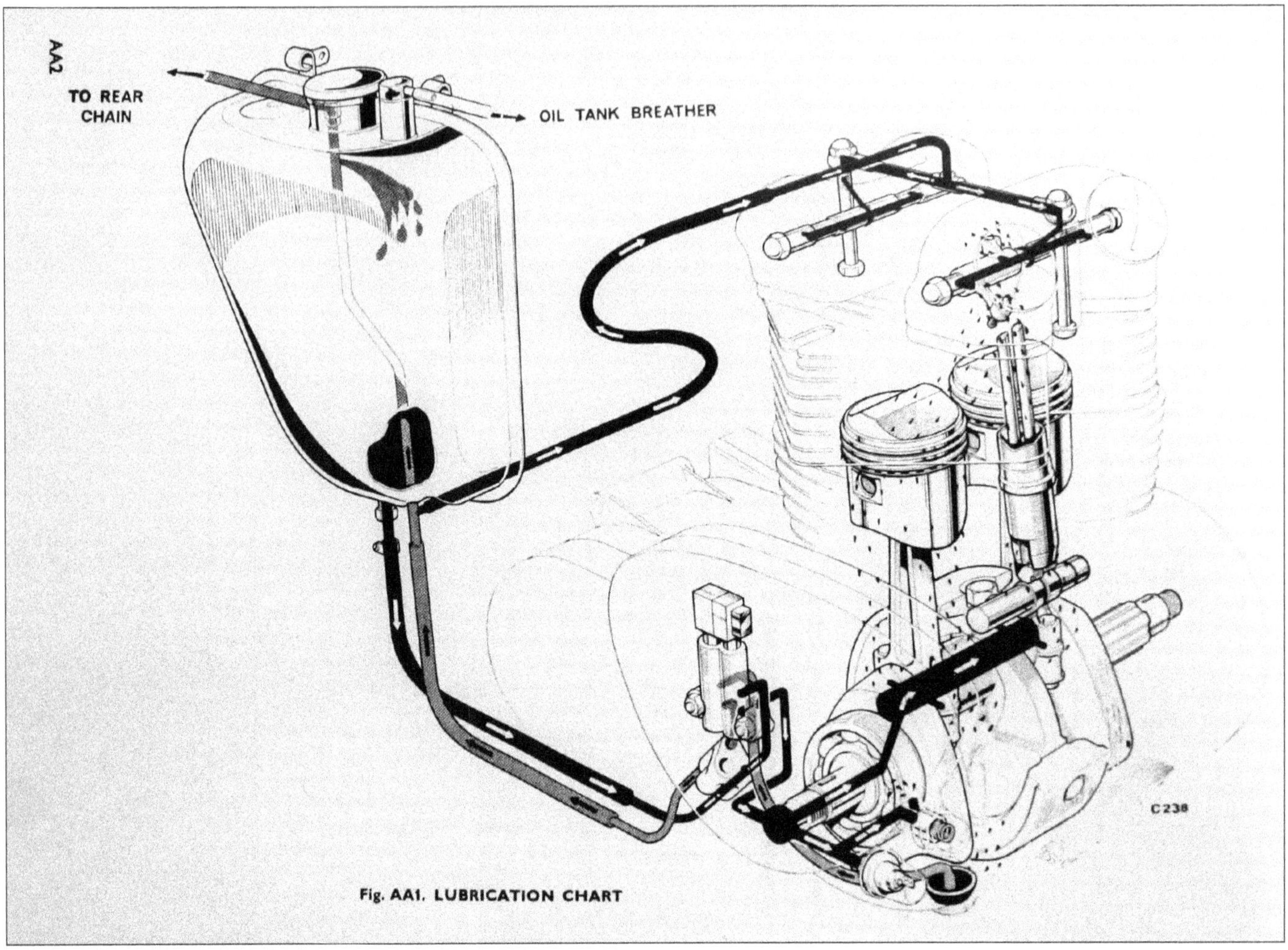

Triumph 350/500 Unit Construction Twins Bible 1957-1974

Fig. AA1. LUBRICATION CHART

TO REAR CHAIN

OIL TANK BREATHER

Later lubrication system with ball-race timing side main bearing.

T100T: a Daytona for the Brits.

as part of the new oil feed arrangement. The switch was recorded as being UNF, but, in practice, the thread used was either ⅛in NPT (National Pipe Tapered) Smiths Part 5307/05, Triumph D1943, BSA 19-6504) or ⅛in NPS (National Pipe Straight) Smiths Part 5330/1/03, Triumph 60-3719). The actual thread form shares some dimensions with Unified threads,

Year by Year: 1957-1974

Single carb T100S outsold the UK market Daytona by three to one in 1969.

for example, 60-degree included angle, but both NPs are 27 threads per inch, and have a major diameter of 0.405in. It is thought that all early 1969 bikes had a tapered thread in the timing cover, later changing to a straight thread around the introduction of the new engine number codes (see the next section). Check carefully, as fitting a straight threaded oil pressure switch into the tapered hole will damage the timing cover.

At the same time, the switch was connected to an oil pressure warning light in the headlight, which also acted as an ignition light. It was set to go out once the engine had started and pressure rose above 7psi. Some sources stated that the light, which seemed such a modern convenience, simply caused needless worry among riders if it lit up when oil pressure was fine, which could happen.

Cylinder barrels with thicker walls were applied to all bikes from late 1968 (engine number H63370) – still cast iron, of course, and painted silver, as most C range barrels had always been. The T100C now had cast iron valve guides, while all others carried on with Hidural 5 bronze guides. From early 1969 the Amal Concentrics had new needles, needle jets and jet holders, details being re-cored in Tri-Cor Bulletin No: 69/3 (20th February 1969).

The perennial problem of oil leaks from the pushrod tubes was addressed (again), this time with O-rings both for the tappet blocks and inside the pushrod tubes. The tubes themselves now had 'fingers' or castellations, at the top, whose job it was to guide oil towards the centre of the tube. Another annoyance was the rev counter drive coming in loose over time, and this now had a left-hand thread to keep it tight. Finally, a Lucas RM21 alternator was fitted – it had encapsulated stator windings and two leads instead of three, while the alternator cable exit was moved to above the gearbox, rather than hidden beneath, a distinctive feature of the 1969 model year crankcase.

Gearbox, engine numbers

In the transmission, a new locating plunger and spring were fitted to improve gear changing, while the primary drive cover now carried the Triumph logo on the removeable ignition timing plate. The Parts Book indicates that the East Coast T100C had wide-ratio gears fitted, with close ratios available for other models.

One of the biggest changes during the 1969 model year, certainly from the point of view of a restorer, is that Triumph changed its long running engine/frame numbering system. Instead of the model code, and the prefix 'H,' followed by the engine/frame number, there was now a two-letter prefix, the first showing the month of manufacture and the second the model year – for details, see appendix on engine/frame numbers (page 147). This change affected both the C range and the 650s. In an attempt to make tampering more difficult, the engine number boss was now stamped over with the Triumph logo.

This change didn't happen at the beginning of the 1969 model year, and H65573 to H67331 ('69 model year) were the final C range bikes to the old numbering system. Someone at the Meriden factory, unfamiliar with the new

91

Engine/frame numbering system changed to show month as well as year of assembly – this one's from January 1969.

system, also made an error on 1145 bikes built in January 1969, stamping them with the code 'AD' instead of 'AC' – so AD7780 to AD8884 should be AC7780 to AC8884.

Frame, cycle parts

A new frame front section featuring a new steering lock platform was introduced under a new part number, while the side stand was lengthened and strengthened, and now mounted forward of the lower engine mountings. To allow wider front tyres, the fork stanchions were spaced half an inch further apart (now 6¾in centre-to-centre), and the front wheel spindle was longer to suit. Fork crown, stem and top lug were also new, and now with UNF threads.

The stanchions had two extra holes drilled to improve damping – see Factory Bulletin 69/11 (18th May 1969) for details, and note that earlier stanchions should not be used in these '69-on bikes (see Bulletin 69/13). The gaiters did away with their clips, gripping the seal holder with a labyrinth seal, and at the top by a groove in the abutment (with a corresponding ridge in the gaiter); it was neater than clips.

The rear Girling shocks now had exposed chrome springs instead of shrouds, following the fashion of putting appearance above practicality as the market moved further towards motorcycles as leisure items for the young, rather than cheap all-year round transport. As far as the C range was concerned, it was a trend that started when the bathtub was ditched back in 1965, and it was still going on. UK model shocks were now 145lb/in spring rate, while US riders had softer 100lb/in springs. For solo riding, some still preferred the softer springs for their greater comfort.

All bikes now had the twin-leading-shoe front brake, the 8in version for T100T and T100R and 7in on T100S and T100C, all with a mesh-covered air scoop. A modified bell crank lever enabled a tidier cable run, parallel to the forks. We say all bikes had these front brakes, but early T100Cs for 1969 were shipped with the single-leading-shoe drum. The front hub had new grease retainers fitted, and the chrome plate had concentric ribs instead of the plain finish of the earlier models. The front brake anchor peg was longer on the wider fork (now 1 27/64 instead of 1 19/64in), allowing the use of differing brake plates.

The exhaust pipes on all bikes except the T100C were now connected by a balance pipe

More inconsistencies – a '69 bike with plain primary drive cover and shrouded shocks – non-standard parts are common.

1969 Daytona, showing the balance pipe.

near the cylinder head; originally intended to improve gas flow but now reducing noise. As for the T100C, that gained a connector near the silencers, and had the distinctive and attractive wire mesh 'chip basket' heat shield, which looks better than the nickname suggests. The Parts Book also shows folding footrests and sumpguard fitted to the T100C. Silencers were internally baffled on all bikes except for the US T100R.

Ball-ended brake and clutch levers, which had been available for some time as an option, were now standard across the range. The steering damper was now an option, and when not fitted, a decorative chrome cap nut took its place to improve the appearance of the steering head. The oil tank dipstick gained min and max markings, the difference between them equating to one pint.

Tinwork

The parcel grid was finally gone! However, this wasn't because Triumph riders no longer carried their shopping home by bike. There was at least one well publicised case where a rider was seriously injured when he hit the parcel grid during a crash, and took Triumph to court. Meriden wisely decided to ditch the grid for UK bikes as well as those bound for North America. At least one owner brazed neat little ramps on the back edge of the parcel carrier, to make it less of an obstacle.

Another instant recognition point for '69-on bikes was the new simpler 'picture frame' tank badge, which gave the Triumph logo more prominence. The tank's centre seam trim was now fitted with a hook at the front to reduce stresses that had causing cracking of the earlier version. US bikes had Lucas RAR 25 amber reflectors fitted under the front of the tank, and there were new tank top and side panel transfers, in a simple block script.

The front mudguard stay no longer acted as a front wheel stand, and was now a lighter-duty loop, though still with a single-bolt fixing. The US T100R had chrome front mudguard stays, while those on the T100C were black, still with polished stainless steel guards.

A new clip on the toolbox was designed to prevent the knob loosening over time, and depositing the contents of the toolbox all over the road – part number F11357, and it can be fitted to earlier bikes. The toolbox carried a model transfer, and UK machines could also have a 'Queens Award' transfer, though, as for 1968, neither of these are illustrated in the Parts Book.

All bikes now used the same version of the dualseat, with a black Quiltop cover and chrome rim band. Export bikes had the grab rail that was introduced late in the '68 model year (see 1968 Notes), and the seat knob was now black plastic covered rather than chromed.

Electrics

The C range didn't have such niceties as indicators and a front brake light switch yet, but extra leads were added to the wiring loom to make these much easier to fit. As well as the Lucas RM21 alternator, 6CA points and separate capacitors (Lucas 2CP), the ignition coils were Lucas MA12 on home market bikes, and Siba on the others – the Siba coils used a different 'S' bracket, with suitable spacers to mount to the frame. Plug caps were a bone

Scalloped colours on the tank weren't standard, either.

New Lucas rear light for 1969.

of contention – some road test pictures show metal suppressed caps fitted to a European test bike, while the brochure images show standard black plastic or rubber items.

As previously, the T100C featured the smaller Lucas MCH66 lamp unit, while the others have the larger SS700P unit with ammeter, three-way lighting switch and warning lights. At the rear was either the Lucas 564 or 679 unit with additional red (Lucas RER 24) reflectors, depending on the market the machine was supplied to. For additional information consult the period Lucas brochure CE830/69.

Colours

There was a change of policy with regard to colour schemes, with all bikes using the same basic colours – Lincoln Green (a metallic green) over Silver Sheen with White lining – and the exact style of finish differing between models. As ever, all bikes had painted mudguards, apart from the T100C. As for 1968, there were several variations in the style of the paint finish, but fewer road test pictures to show them. The 1969 Triumph Bonneville shows three different paint schemes for the year, and it's likely that T100s were similarly affected.

US fittings alternatives

High bars
Twin rotor twist grip T100R
Sump plate T100C
Folding footrests T100C
Steering damper T100C

Notes for 1969

With the introduction of the new numbering system the factory records changed in the way machines were recorded. If you are intending to consult these records in the VMCC library, note that the actual books changed from individual model range books to large, fabric-covered, ring-bound ledgers. Each entry shows the engine and frame code and number, the engine build date, machine assembly date, despatch date, invoice number and destination. A separate set of records covers engine assembly, and includes brief notes detailing new parts or assembly methods used.

1969 production recorded in the new books began with T120R Bonnevilles NC100 to NC2034, with C range production starting at PC5516 (30 3TA engines). C range complete bikes came in three distinct batches during the model year: XC6297 to AC9987 (December 1968 to January '69); EC17978 to EC19912 (May '69); and HC24353 to JC24839 (July-August '69). The account books for the period do not survive, so it has not been possible to identify how many of each model were supplied to the differing markets, but most T100R and T100C production was from the first batch. The few T90s built were all to police specification, possibly for the Royal Ulster Constabulary. At least one of these rare bikes survives.

The engine books no longer contain the separate pages of notes detailing the starting engine number for new parts being used. This new system makes deciphering changes much more difficult, hence the lack of a summary of engine number 'milestones' for major changes from this year onwards. Some information is revealed in the Factory Bulletins.

For example, 500cc twins to EC17978 had problems with undersized drive side main bearings (Bulletin 69/14 June 27th 1969), while early T100Cs (prior to AC9210) had the earlier single-leading-shoe brake rather than the twin-leading-shoe version.

Once again, the Personal Export option was an attractive one for overseas buyers living in the UK (usually Americans), so, if looking into the history of a particular bike it is well worth consulting the factory records in the VMCC library.

Parts Book No: 10 is the correct one for 1969 models, published in September 1968, and showing the parts fitted across the range for all markets. Parts now had five-figure numbers, for example Styling Strip F10007. Some parts showed the Unified part numbers (for example 14.0303) that were introduced later.

1970

Models covered: T100S, T100C, T100T, T100P
Production:

Tiger T100S	1497
Tiger T100C (Trophy 500)	4122
Tiger T100R (Daytona Super Sports, US)	3234
Tiger T100T (Tiger Daytona Sports, UK)	380
Tiger T100P (Police)	281
Engine/frame numbers start at:	KD27850

1970 was the peak model year for C range production, with over 9500 leaving the works – the previous best (1967) saw less than 8500, so it was high point. But from here, sadly, it was all downhill, and production slumped to little over half the peak the following year. A lot of that '71 slump was down to BSA/Triumph's disastrous new model launch, which saw badly developed bikes, multiple production hold-ups, and missing a key part of the vital USA selling season.

But there was something else. The extensive changes made for 1969 suggested a manufacturer keen to invest in the range, to keep it fresh, up to date and attractive to buyers. But they would be the final major changes made to the 500 unit twins, which saw no more serious development work until production ended four years later. The smaller twins had always played second fiddle to the 650s, which sold in greater numbers, and probably made more profit per bike into the bargain, so it is possible to understand the corporate logic.

The company, which so recently had won those Queens Awards for Exports, would now slide rapidly into the red, and its priority became the bigger bikes. Also, while a 650cc Bonneville or 750cc Trident were still among the fastest, best handling bikes available, the 500s didn't stand up to the Japanese competition as strongly. They were well developed now, perhaps the best they had ever been, were still reasonably fast and handled very well. However, to a young rider reading the paper specifications – no electric start, a four-speed gearbox, drum front brake, pushrod valves and a mere 39bhp – must have seemed old-fashioned, to say the least. The Triumph 500 twin, well honed though it was, in the early 1970s, was starting to look like yesterday's bike.

Tiger 100 for 1970 – not perfect, but certainly well honed.

The new engine breather system exited from the rear of the primary drive.

Engine/gearbox

All this doesn't mean to say there were no changes at all. The most significant was a complete redesign of the engine breather system, which was applied to all Triumph twins and triples that year. The previous breathing arrangement, a disc fixed to the inlet camshaft, was blanked off. The engine now breathed directly into the primary chaincase, via holes drilled into the left crankcase. This, in turn, vented to the outside world via a large diameter pipe which connected to an elbow outlet at the top rear of the chaincase and stopped at the end of the rear mudguard. It was a simple and effective system, which did reduce oil leaks from the bottom end, and, as a side benefit, did away with the engine sprocket's oil seal. The new breather arrangement was very distinctive, and allows dating of crankcases from 1970 and beyond even in the absence of an engine number.

On the exhaust camshaft the rev counter take-off plug was now solid and screwed in, instead of a pressing – the latter could often fail prematurely, in which case the camshaft had to be removed to replace it. The right-hand crankcase lost its abutment ring for the timing side main bearing, and instead (from engine XC06297), a clamping washer was fitted between the timing pinion and the bearing. The pushrod tubes' sealing arrangements were changed once again, with the 'fingers' deleted (though still illustrated in the Parts Book).

There were minor changes to the transmission, with the clutch's thrust plate modified and the gear finish improved by gas-carburizing treatment – the gears themselves

Factory oil pressure switch was mounted on the timing cover.

were of hardened nickel chrome. These changes were made after an increasing number of gearbox failures occurred on the twin-carb bikes. There was also a new precision-pressed cam plate during the 1970 model year.

Single carburettors on the T100S and T100C were now partially rubber-mounted to reduce frothing, using rubber washers under the retaining nuts and a thicker O-ring in the carburettor flange. All bikes now had a cloth and gauze air filter.

Frame, cycle parts
The frame number was now stamped on a raised plinth (still on the left-hand side of the steering head); initially this was plain but was later partially stamped with the Triumph logo as an anti-tampering feature, as was the engine number.

There were a few changes to the forks, with the stanchions now being hard chromed and ground to a micro finish, to make them harder wearing and to prolong the life of the oil seals. The brake anchor lug was stronger, made from cold drawn steel and welded to the right-hand fork leg. The right-hand fork shroud now had a hole and grommet for control cables to pass through. The rear shocks kept their exposed springs but, to improve weather protection, a collar now covered the adjustment cams.

The steering damper option was deleted, except on the T100C which had a sleeve nut instead of the chromed nut, so it was still easy to fit as an option or from spares. The rear brake torque stay was now made of flat section steel, painted black and attached with Cleveloc nuts, which were becoming common across the bike.

The oil tank was new, still the same 5½ pint capacity, but with a new part number to reflect new production methods. The chain oiler feed and its adjuster were dropped, while the froth breather tower was linked to the main engine breather outlet via a T-piece, and the silver D-shaped plastic pipe then ran to the rear of the rear mudguard, attached by clips along the left-hand side.

The front engine mountings were modified to ease fitting and removal of the engine, the rear wheel changed to UNF threads, and the prop stand now had an adjustable stop added. As in the previous year, all bikes now used the same seat, which, for 1970, had a black pierced 'Ambla' top, though the rear Triumph logo was sometimes missing.

Electrics
Smaller Lucas 17M12 coils were fitted, mounted on a reinforced bracket, and there was another change to the alternator cable exit from the primary drive, now with no grommet, and with the wires exiting directly from the crankcase. Also new for 1970 was the Lucas MC2 ignition capacitor and its distinctive mounting spring, allowing the battery to be removed on competition machines.

Tinwork
The most notable change here was the distinctive chromed rear support rail and lifting handle, incorporating the passenger grab rail.

All bikes now benefitted from the respected twin-leading-shoe front drum.

Year by Year: 1957-1974

Simple machine – timing side of a T100C in Jacaranda Purple.

The front mudguard lost its number plate holes and had two fixing holes for the lower stay. British riders took to mounting the curved front number plate above or below the headlight, until bikes were no longer required to display a front plate. The rear guard acquired holes to accommodate the big breather pipe clip and the new lift handle/grab rail.

The handlebars were now shared with the 650s, and the control levers had holes to allow mirrors to be fitted, if required. As ever, the choke and dip/horn switch were on the bars, and grips were still the padded balloon type.

Colours

As in the previous year, there was just one set of colours, arranged in different styles – the previous year's Sherwood Green gave way to a more flamboyant Jacaranda Purple over Silver Sheen with Gold lining.

The various models show differing paint schemes, and the available period pictures do not necessarily represent the finish that was used throughout the year. The scheme shown in the first adverts for the year does not seem to have lasted for very long in production – it's unlikely that bikes after XD34763 would use this scheme. Note that, on the rear mudguard, the stripe is often absent, especially on UK bikes and General Export machines fitted with the UK number plate.

Twin high-level pipes were the T100C's big statement.

Notes for 1970

The Parts Book (No: 11) was now subdivided into UK and General Export and USA sections – make sure you consult the correct one. Refer to Factory Bulletin #70/3P which is the Corrections for the 1970 Parts Book 99-0903, and is essential for restorers.

The QD rear wheel parts described on page 48 of the USA Parts Book only refer to

Triumph 350/500 Unit Construction Twins Bible 1957-1974

> ### What the press said
> Trophy 500 – *Cycle World*, February 1970
> "How much longer can it endure?" asked *Cycle World* of the T100C Trophy 500, pointing out that its lineage stretched back 32 years. The writers added that in 1970 you could get a 650 or 750 for not much more money.
> Despite all of that, they clearly loved it. "Versatility is what sells it. The Trophy 500 handles as well or better than any production road bike made. Stripped of lights and re-geared it makes an excellent cow-trailer or fire-road machine, good enough to win the national enduro championship for seven straight years."
> It was smooth and flexible in town yet power came in with a rush from 5000rpm up to 7500 and valve float, thanks to the Q-profile inlet camshaft. Sure, it was buzzy at speed compared to a 650 Triumph, but smoother (yes, that word again) with it. *Cycle World* praised the stronger bottom end and crankcase breathing, plus the fact that Daytona twin carburettors could be bolted straight on. Transmission, frame, forks and rear shocks also garnered points for being improved over the years. Good brakes and easy starting were mentioned as well.
> Was there anything they didn't like? Well, they would have liked a five-speed gearbox, and pointed out that the Trophy had gained quite a bit of weight over the years. "We can see its virtues," they concluded, "tangible and intangible. But can the mass market see? They are not as devoted as we are."

bikes AD34763 to AD35762. After AD38465 the 1969 wheel was used.

Production

1970 model year production was in five distinct batches, with production alternating between the larger 650s as orders were prepared and planned delivery dates arranged. Most of the USA machines were built in the autumn and winter of 1969.

Though the model year is indicated as starting with KD24750, two press bikes were built earlier, in July 1969: KD24712 was the show T100T, eventually sent to Andrews of London in February 1971. KD24713 was the show T100S, despatched to John Cooper (the very same John 'Mooneyes' Cooper) of Derby in November 1970.

1971

Models covered: T100C, T100R, T100P
Production:

1971 Triumph Tiger 100C (Trophy 500)	2331
1971 Triumph Tiger 100R (Daytona Super Sports)	2368
1971 Triumph Tiger 100P (police spec)	103
Engine/frame numbers start at:	JE0001

The British motorcycle industry had several nadirs, and one of the worst was over 1970/71. Royal Enfield ceased production, and Velocette went to the wall. Norton's Commando was selling well, but it was intended to be a stopgap, hardly the basis for long-term survival. Meanwhile, BSA/Triumph lost a whopping £8.3 million in '71 (equivalent to £100 million in 2018). It had been a meteoric fall from grace after the record production and Queen's Awards just a year or two earlier. BSA/Triumph already had a long-term illness, but 1971 was the short-term shock that tipped the company into rapid decline. How did this happen?

The launches of the 1971 range on both sides of the Atlantic in 1970 are already the stuff of legend – millions of pounds was spent on lavish hospitality, and it was nothing if not ambitious. In one fell swoop, the company sought to launch a new 50cc three-wheeler (the Ariel Three),

Later type frame number, this one from August 1970, is actually a Bonneville.

Trophy 500, now with indicators, but few other changes.

the new DOHC 350 twin (Triumph Bandit/BSA Fury), and a new oil-in-frame chassis for the 650s. But the following months turned out to be a succession of production and sales nightmares.

The Ariel Three proved to be a sales flop, the new 350 was cancelled (after millions had been spent on tooling) and the oil-in-frame 650s were very late going into production, thanks to the tardy arrival of engineering drawings and, therefore, tooling.

Production at Meriden for each new model year, as detailed throughout this book, usually began in August when the workforce returned from summer shutdown. That way, a stock of new bikes for the vital North American market would be ready for the USA's short but lucrative selling season. This time, not only were the drawings and tooling late, but, as has been recounted many times since, when bikes finally started rolling down the production line at Meriden, it was found that the 650cc engine would not fit the frame! A hastily redesigned cylinder head cured that, and the bikes finally staggered into production just before Christmas 1970. Even then, yet more problems arose when the new bikes began to hit the road: the seat was sky-high, engines overheated thanks to a smaller oil capacity than before, swarf was found inside the new in-frame oil reservoir, centre stands collapsed and frames cracked ... and so it went on. No doubt about it, the 1971 model year fiasco was a mortal blow to Triumph as well as BSA.

In the meantime, where did all this leave the C range? In some ways, the 500cc twin was the Cinderella of the new line up. It was barely changed, carrying on with the same frame, brakes and forks as before, just with a few detail changes, such as indicators (see below). Alone amongst the entire range, it represented continuity with the past.

In fact, Triumph seemed to be soft-pedalling the 500s, trimming the range back to just three models: a single Daytona (all markets now received the T100R), the Tiger 100C, and a police spec machine. The civilian single-carb T100S was dropped. This apparently simpler range still hid several variations in specification, with UK machines differing from European bikes, and also those bound for the USA.

Simplifying a range is a sure sign of lower sales expectations, and BSA/Triumph planners cannot have failed to notice that the new DOHC 350 would have been very close to the 500 in performance and price, especially the T100S, which would have looked odd to say the least. After all, who would buy an old pushrod twin when an all-new overhead cam alternative was sat next to it in the same showroom? It's likely

Triumph twins always responded well to polishing (though this isn't a '71).

High-barred Daytona was part of a slimmed-down two-bike range.

that the C range was being wound down with maybe just another couple of seasons to go.

However, it turned out that the decision to keep the 500s going would be a lifeline. Because of the 650's production problems, the Meriden workforce came back from summer shutdown with no bikes to build. Fortunately, thanks to its minimal use of new parts, the 1971 model year 500s could be put straight into production. Schedules were hastily rearranged and the factory concentrated on the 500s, with production running in three batches, starting on 12th September 1970 with JE0001, a T100R destined for Baltimore. Meriden's rapid production soon used up the stock of 500 parts, so the factory carried on building 650cc engine/gearbox units. Some departments were idle for weeks (on full pay) waiting for work, so Triumph management must have been eternally grateful to the C range, to at least enable some bikes to be shipped out and bring in some money.

Engine

There were a few engine changes for 1971. The most useful, from a maintenance viewpoint, was the addition of small access plugs to both sides of the rocker boxes. Sealed by O-rings and sealant, these allowed a feeler gauge to be inserted directly between the rocker and the top of the valve, making tappet adjustment a far easier process. One of the co-authors, as

New hexagonal plug made checking the tappets easier.

a young Tiger 90 owner, remembers advice in the official workshop manual, which seemed to accept that it might not be possible to use feeler gauges at all on pre-'71 bikes. The exhaust valve gap was correct, if memory serves, when "there is the faintest perceptible movement of the rocker arm, accompanied by a slight click."

Some parts were now common across the range, which made sense, all now using 9:1 compression pistons, while the stronger conrods fitted to the Daytona from 1969 may also have been fitted to everything. A one-piece oil pressure relief valve was introduced, but was soon replaced with the earlier version.

During the year the exhausts became a push fit into the head, and the exhaust pipe adaptors were deleted, though at least one source refers to this for the 1972 model year. Klingerite cylinder head gaskets were listed, shown as spares, and are likely to have been used on production models. Loctite or Permatex 300 sealant was now used on many parts, including the rocker box caps and new access plugs.

According to official literature, UK and General Export machines (T100R and T100C) were now fitted with a new combined induction system and air filter, as on the new 650s, but road tests and other evidence does not show this, and the 1971 500s appear to have used the same chrome-banded air filters as before. It's likely that this new arrangement for the '71 model year simply wasn't ready in time, so bikes were sent down the line with the old filters. The Parts Supplement for UK and General Export models does show the supposed new induction box.

Trophy 500 (actually a 1970 bike) – the smaller twins kept the factory going when the '71 650s weren't ready.

Year by Year: 1957-1974

Had Triumph finally licked the pushrod sealing problem?

New Lucas switches for '71 were not a great advance.

Officially (again), UK bikes changed to quieter and more restrictive megaphone silencers borrowed from the Bonneville, while the USA models used the older items.

Frame, cycle parts

There was an increasing use of Cleveloc nuts throughout the bikes. Like Nylocs, they had a self-clamping action once tightened, and were far less likely to come undone in service. Unlike Nylocs, they were all-steel and reuseable. These distinctive fasteners are not available as spares and should be saved whenever possible. All fasteners were now UNC or UNF threads, with nuts in a variety of types – Cleveloc, Philidas, Stiffnut and Nyloc. Refer to pages 82 and 83 of the 1971 Parts Book for details and part numbers of all of the fasteners. This is very useful information for restorers.

No frame changes were recorded, though the fork assembly for UK and General Export bikes carried a different part number to that for US machines. The headlight mounting brackets were new, rubber-mounted to the fork shrouds, with the left shroud having a location for the ignition switch and the right a hole and grommet for the throttle cable or cables.

Wheels were still recorded as 19in front, 18in rear, and the QD wheel option was discontinued – a pity, as it made roadside punctures far easier to fix.

Electrics & controls

The most obvious changes was the addition of Lucas indicators, mounted on the headlight and rear light. New Lucas alloy handlebar switches to suit also included the horn, dipswitch, and headlight flasher on the left cluster, and indicators and engine kill switch on the left. Unlabelled, liable to let in water, and stiff to operate, they were not that popular ... The previous tail reflectors were deleted, and round red Lucas RER 14 reflectors now appeared on the grab rail. All bikes now had side reflectors, not just the US ones.

A new handlebar was needed to accommodate the new switchgear, usually rubber-mounted, with only the western USA bikes using a solid mounting (and a different fork crown to suit). Alloy brake and clutch levers were now integral with the new switches, and the Daytona had a twin-rotor twist grip.

The ammeter was dropped, its place on the headlight taken by a light switch and central indicator warning light flanked by shrouded warning lights for ignition/oil pressure and main beam. That was the Daytona – the T100C didn't have the indicator light. The offroad 500 used the Lucas MCH66 headlight unit, whereas the T100R stuck with the SS700P unit. The rear light changed to the Lucas 679 pointed type in an alloy housing.

All bikes were fitted with a front brake stoplight switch, while the 'Clearhooter' horn under the fuel tank and the Zener diode with its distinctive finned heatsink was still found beneath the headlight. The 1971 650s now carried the diode under the right-hand side panel, with the panel itself acting as the heatsink.

In another break with tradition, the traditional grey-faced Smiths instruments

Triumph 350/500 Unit Construction Twins Bible 1957-1974

New black-faced Smiths speedo and rev counter were part of the 1971 changes.

gave way to simpler instruments with black faces. Fully rubber-mounted, they were still made by Smiths, and the part numbers were as follows: Speedometer SSM5007/02A (mph) or SSM5007/03 (km/h); Rev Counter RSM3003/13A.

Tinwork

Mudguards were the usual mix of painted (T100R) or polished stainless steel (T100C), now drilled to accommodate the new rear light. Despite the rationalised range, UK/General Export and USA bikes still had different fuel tanks – 3-gallon and 2.25-gallon, respectively. Four different part numbers are listed, likely to differentiate paint schemes as well as size. The literature also refers to a larger oil tank, though fixings were unchanged.

Colours

Colours for this year were Olympic Flame with Black, together with white lining, though some illustrations of UK bikes showed White, rather than Black, as the companion colour. Once again, variations abound, and care is needed to confirm the original scheme for your machine if evidence of old finishes is available. Original bikes often show the scalloped colour scheme, using Black over Olympic Flame with White lining.

On the tank there is usually a simple script transfer of the model, while the side panel more reliably has the full model name. The oil tank continued to show the minimum oil level and oil grade transfers.

Notes for 1971

The Parts Book was again separated into Home & General Export and USA sections. It contains numerous errors so ensure that you also use the supplementary parts list for the year.

1972

Models covered: T100R, T100P
Production:
   1972 Triumph Tiger 100R
     (Daytona Super Sports)   5423
   1972 Triumph Tiger
     100P (police)   485
Engine/frame model year letter: 'G' eg HG32303

If 1971 had been a year of radical change and chaos, then the '72 model year was one of retrenchment. There were very few changes to the C range, and in fact production increased from the disastrous slump of the previous year. Meriden was still frantically trying to get acceptable 650s on sale, with several changes made to lower the seat. With all this going on, and the promised DOHC 350 now dropped, the 500cc twins would no doubt have been seen as the only dependable model in the range.

Despite that, the range was trimmed again, with the long-running T100C dropped, though it was still referred to in the Parts Books and the owners manual, very confusing! The T100C, or Trophy 500, was about to give way to the new TR5T Trophy (see below) but it still seemed an odd decision to drop the bike, with the trail bike market booming, especially in North America – over 2000 T100Cs had been built in its final year.

Some 1971 changes carried over into '72, notably the indicators, new switchgear,

Left to right: racers Ray Pickerell, Paul Smart and Percy Tait pose for the 1972 brochure. The bike is a Daytona.

102

Year by Year: 1957-1974

Russ Gurney's lovely '72 Daytona in a modern picture worthy of a Triumph brochure.

Three warning lights now: ignition/oil, indicators and high beam.

Spring-mounted rectifier, to protect it from vibration.

push-in exhausts and (for UK bikes) megaphone silencers, while US machines continued to use the traditional style. All bikes had linked exhaust down pipes and the official literature still referred to a new induction air box and filter, though it doesn't appear to have been fitted in practice.

The kickstart was a new part, angled outwards to clear the new silencers. From April 1972 the rear fuel tank mount was modified to reduce stresses placed on the mounting (Bulletin 4/72).

The Daytona came with either UK 3-gallon or US 2.2-gallon fuel tanks – some illustrations show knee grips fitted, others don't.

The colour scheme was shown as Cherry Red over Cold White, Gold lined with the fuel tank scheme as for 1966 bikes, though once again this may not be the actual one used. Mudguards were Cherry Red overall with Cold White stripes lined in Gold.

Notes for 1972

The Parts Book (99-0954) and the supplementary lists show parts for both the T100R and T100C, but the factory records appear to show that no T100C models were built as all references are for T100R or T100P. Parts book corrections for the 1972 Parts Book can be found on Bulletin #72-03P. Factory records do include a three-figure tyre fitting code but this has proved impossible to decipher.

1973

Models covered: T100R, T100P, TR5T
Production:
  1973 Triumph
    Trophy TR5T   2549 Machines
                    (Trophy Trail/Adventurer)
  1973 Triumph
    Tiger 100R   2365 Machines
                    (Daytona Super Sports)
  1973 Triumph Tiger
    100P   180 Machines
                           (Police Models)
Engine/frame model year letter: 'H' eg JH32303

The TR5T

A new C range model was the big news for 1973 – after the debacle of 1971 and with sales of the 500cc twin still holding up reasonably well, BSA/Triumph seemed to realise that far from being a Cinderella of the range, the 500 was crucial. The slow selling Trophy 250 had been dropped, the DOHC 350 would never see production, and Triumph needed to offer a mid-size bike as well as the 650 twins and 750 triples, so the venerable 500 was needed more than ever.

That the new model was for on/off-road was hardly a surprise. As mentioned above, the trail bike market was growing fast, especially in North America, and the 500 twin had a long history of successful off-road competition. This had segued into the fashionable street scrambler sector, with the Trophy 500 able to maintain credibility in both camps. In the USA, an on/off-road Triumph 500 was part of motorcycle folklore, and if the company was to survive it needed to take advantage of the fact.

When it appeared, the TR5T, variously named as the Trophy Trail or Adventurer, was clearly not a lightweight enduro or trail bike – these were overwhelmingly singles, mostly two-strokes, and with capacities of 250cc or less. But neither was it a cosmetic street scrambler – many factories had sought to cash in on the macho image of off-road racing by selling standard roadsters with wide bars, high pipes, and a general air of dirt track indestructibility.

For a start, the TR5T used its own frame, derived from that of the BSA Victor scramblers, with the engine oil carried in the large top tube. The engine had various modifications to enable it to fit, including different rocker boxes, extended cylinder head mounts and altered cylinder head studs. The engine itself was the familiar twin with the same 9:1 compression as the Daytona, but with a single 28mm Amal Concentric and softer cams. To suit its more off-road role, Triumph fitted a close-ratio gear set with a low top of 6.57:1, and a 53-tooth final drive sprocket in place of the standard 46-tooth. The result was relatively low gearing for the road, and at 60mph the engine was spinning at just over 5000rpm.

There was more evidence that Triumph intended the new bike to be competent off-road, rather than a cosmetic scrambler. The new Ceriani style forks had 6in of movement, and swivelled around taper-roller head bearings. A 21in front wheel backed that up, with high-mounted front mudguard and Trials Universal knobbly tyres at both ends. The front

Specific BSA-derived frame, 21in front wheel and bash plate for the dual-purpose Trophy Trail.

Year by Year: 1957-1974

TR5T proved to be a more capable off-roader than the old Trophy.

Conical front drum brake was okay off-road, but weak on tarmac.

brake was bought in from Rickman, a small 6in single-leading-shoe drum which may have worked well on Rickman's small two-strokes but proved seriously inadequate for the heavier, faster, Trophy Trail, especially on the road. The rear brake was the conical-hub drum, familiar from the larger Triumphs. What the TR5T didn't have was the older Trophy's stylish two-into-two high-level exhaust. Instead, the twin down pipes fed into a single matt black silencer tucked underneath the gearbox – lighter perhaps, but more vulnerable off-road.

With wide-ish braced bars and an alloy tank, it was a good looking machine which looked ready for deserts yet had indicators and a comfortable three-quarter length seat. Finally, at 344lb kerb weight, it was 25lb lighter than the old Trophy – not as light as a two-stroke trail bike, but still a useful saving.

Engine

Meanwhile, the faithful T100R saw very few changes. A balance pipe was added to the inlet manifolds to improve low speed running, with clips to keep it in place. The air induction box, which the factory literature showed fitted to UK machines, but which does not seem to have been in practice, was officially dropped, with the familiar chrome-banded pancake filters taking its place.

New noise regulations from 1st January 1973 required bikes manufactured after this date to comply with a new standard. Daytonas built after DH 30706 now featured more restrictive silencers, though those made earlier in the '73 model year carried on with the previous year's

Triumph 350/500 Unit Construction Twins Bible 1957-1974

Daytona was still a good looking machine, but this was its last full year of production.

The Daytona was still a good all-round useable bike.

Squared-off rear light marks out the post-1972 bikes.

exhausts. Factory Bulletin 2/73 details the part number changes but is not illustrated.

Cycle parts

The headlamp supports and shrouds were reinforced at the headlamp mountings, while the fuel tank lost its centre seam along with the covering styling strip – this applied to both 3-gallon and 2.25-gallon tanks. UK and General Export machines showed a single fuel tap with reserve capability, while US machines had separate main and reserve taps. As previously, orange reflectors were fitted under the front of the tank.

Mudguards were now chrome-plated rather than painted, with matching chrome stays, and the rear mudguard was shortened – some General Export bikes continued to use the longer guard.

A new squared-off Lucas rear light (L917) incorporated side reflectors which allowed the indicators to be moved, with new wiring to suit. The Daytona's Lucas alloy switches now had longer levers, and the dip and kill switches swapped sides – this made dipping the lights trickier, but put a stop to inadvertently flipping the kill switch while groping for the indicators. The TR5T by contrast, benefited from a new style of Lucas left-hand cluster, with easier to use dip, indicator and horn button. Handlebar levers were steel and ball-ended.

The rev counter drive gearbox was a new one-piece item, now fitted as standard, driven by a new one-piece drive gearbox and fixed by a Welch washer. A later service bulletin detailed that the Welch washer was discontinued and the drive gearbox changed to incorporate a threaded cap plug.

Colours

There appeared to be a choice of colours for 1973 Daytonas. Ice White over Hi-Fi Vermillion with Black lining, or Gold over Astral Blue with Black lining. In theory, only US models were offered in the Vermillion scheme. The brakes were Matt Black for UK/General Export, polished for the USA. The TR5T majored on chrome and polished alloy, but also had a Black side panels and Hunting Yellow panels on the fuel tank.

Notes for 1973

The parts supplement published on 1st November 1972 indicated that there were new part numbers for both the crankcases and

frame, but it's not clear what, if any, changes had been made.

Production
Three prototype TR5Ts were built 23rd June 1972 at Meriden: GH15001, GH15002 and GH15003. All went to the experimental department, but didn't stay that long – 001 was despatched to Baltimore on 21st August and 003 to Duarte on 11th September, possibly for feedback from the American distributors. The production TR5Ts for 1973 were built in three batches: September '72 (KH16597-KH17096); November '72 (PH19020-PH20753); December '72 (XH20754-XH2068).

Competition
Triumph had an enviable record of success in the International Six Days Trial, taking many victories through the 1960s, though the factory was diverted by success at the Daytona 200 in 1966-68, and financial considerations precluded any works teams in the early 1970s. However, in 1973, with the new TR5T to promote, the company was back, with a team of eight TR5Ts, shared by the British and American teams, and all prepared by the BSA/Triumph USA importer, BSACI.

That year's ISDT was held in the Berkshire Mountains of Massachusetts, which, in Triumph's vital USA market, made this well worth the effort. The bikes were very carefully prepared, every engine blueprinted (and half of them over-bored to 504cc to compete in the 500cc+ class) and all electrical components duplicated. The standard silencer was ditched in favour of a special one mounted just above the swinging arm. To save weight (an important consideration against the lighter two-strokes) the steel side panels and mudguards were replaced with leather screens and plastic guards respectively, helping cut weight to 306lb.

It was well worth all the effort and expense, with riders on TR5Ts taking three gold medals and a silver, the British team taking silver overall, runners-up to the Czechs on their lighter two-stroke CZs. This was Triumph's last factory competition campaign, and it ended well.

1974
Models covered: T100R, T100P, TR5T, T100D
Production
TR5T (Adventurer) 929

> ### What the press said
> **TR5T Trophy Trail – *Cycle World* May 1974**
> Remember how *Cycle World* really liked the Trophy 500 in 1970 but wanted it to lose weight? (see page 98). You might have expected it would love the TR5T, when it tested one of those three years later, but, in the event, the write up was a bit ... well ... lukewarm.
>
> Just like the Trophy, the new bike was praised for its tractability, compact dimensions and low speed smoothness. And it got absolute top marks for stability and handling both on-road and off; the writer gleefully describing riding around the outside of another bike on a left-hand sweeper. The Triumph's secret weapon was superb traction, able to get its power down more reliably than the peaky, buzzy two-strokes.
>
> That was the good news. What *CW* didn't like was the on-road vibration at anything over 50mph. Off-road, the shocks were too stiff and the forks lacked travel, while, at 344lb, the TR5T still wasn't as light as two-stroke trail bikes. The brakes (*CW* was probably being kind) "... weren't the best." The result, *CW* thought was the proverbial curate's egg – good in parts – but not cheap at $1649. Three years earlier, Triumph had asked $500 less for the Trophy.

Tiger T100D (Daytona Mk2) 25
Tiger 100R (Daytona Super Sports) 550
Tiger 100P (Police) 100
Engine/frame model year letter: 'J' eg JK32303

Much has been written about the Meriden factory's proposed closure in 1973, the sit-in which followed, and its eventual re-opening as a workers' co-operative in March 1975. As it was these events which finally spelled the end of the C range, they are worth a brief summary.

As a condition of state funding for the beleaguered motorcycle industry, government officials had insisted that BSA/Triumph merge with Norton to form Norton Villiers Triumph (NVT),

A new dawn for Daytona? Unfortunately, the Series 2 never reached full production.

led by Dennis Poore, Norton's Chairman. From the outside, Norton looked like a dynamic success story compared to BSA/Triumph, but it was in the same position of making the most out of an ageing basic design.

NVT inherited three factories – Wolverhampton (Norton), Small Heath (BSA) and Meriden (Triumph) – and Dennis Poore decided that the new set up was only viable if one of these was closed. He was probably right, as selling one site would cut costs and bring in some cash. Poore chose Meriden for the chop, announcing the decision in a meeting at the factory on 14th September 1973 – it was the most productive of the three factories, with a highly skilled workforce, but also suffered from volatile industrial relations. The plan was that Bonneville production would be moved to Small Heath, and though it's not known whether the C range would have made the same move, NVT's plan only referred to 'superbike' production, so it looks as if the C range would have died when Meriden closed in any case.

The Meriden workforce reacted immediately, imposing a blockade and sit-in the same day as the closure announcement. Production for the 1974 model year had begun in July '73, but it ended on 14th September, though some bikes were assembled from in-stock parts during the sit-in.

Before it agreed to the new NVT regime, BSA/Triumph had made progress since the debacle of 1971, reducing its debt and preparing an ambitious plan for an all-new range of bikes designed by Bert Hopwood.

In the meantime, Hopwood and his long standing colleague Doug Hele updated the existing twins, and their main focus at this time was upping the Bonneville/Tiger from 650 to 750cc – it wasn't something Hopwood was particularly happy about, but the market was moving strongly towards 750s, and American Triumph dealers were adamant that a 750 was what they needed to keep the Bonneville selling. The big twins also had five-speed gearboxes and front disc brakes for '73.

With all this going on, the 500cc twins didn't see much change for the 1974 model year. New silencers had been fitted from January 1973, torpedo shaped with new down pipes with captive head fixing bolts and bracket similar to those of the larger twins, and attached to the pillion footrests using longer bolts. For '74 the oil pressure relief valve was set to operate at higher pressure (now 75-85psi), and was fitted with a coarse mesh filter – part number 70-6595, as fitted to the 750cc triples. Finally, there was a minor change to the wiring inside the headlight to reverse the operation of the indicator switch, and the left-hand side panel was modified to reduce chafing of wiring. The Factory Bulletins of the time detail these minor changes. The colour scheme was Ice White over Argosy Blue, with Gold lining for the T100R, while the TR5T changed to Hi-Fi Vermillion Red panels on the tank. Two batches of TR5T were built: July 1973 (HJ56408-HJ57076) and August 1973 (JJ57067-JJ57336). The final T100Rs (built either late August or early September) were JJ57337 to JJ57887.

A week before Dennis Poore's closure announcement and the sit-in began, a final batch of T100Ps was built, on 6th September – the numbers were JJ57888 to JJ57987. They actually left Meriden the week after the sit-in began, on 21st September. The customer was the Ministry of Defence in Burma.

When the sit-in did begin, 2650 machines were trapped inside the factory, some complete, some half-built, and some of these were Daytonas and TR5Ts. According to correspondence from John Nelson, this included 11 fully built and 24 partly built TR5Ts. The finished bikes were all despatched in July 1974 to UK dealers, while the 24 were all finished off inside the factory, and most were despatched in July 1975, some of them two years after being started!

Front disc brake was the most noticeable change to the T100D.

Year by Year: 1957-1974

TR5T acquired new colour and new name for '74.

T100D – the final C range

Bigger changes had been planned for the Daytona before the sit-in, notably a front disc brake, conical rear hub, and Ceriani style alloy forks, as fitted to the big twins. Work began in August 1973, and the bike given the code T100D, the 'D' standing for 'Disc,' 'Development' or 'Daytona' – opinions vary, though the public title was to be Daytona Series 2.

The pre-production batch was allocated 25 engine/frame numbers, but it's not clear that all of these were actually used. About nine bikes are known to survive, and it has been suggested that some of the pre-production machines were later dismantled for their parts. In fact, use of common parts was part of the thinking behind the Series 2. As well as the forks, front disc and conical rear hub, the silencers were also shared with the T140V.

As well as those parts shared with the big twins, there were changes to the headstock and swinging arm, plus new handlebars, new oil tank, and a choice of 7.5:1 or 9:1 pistons. The T100D also had a modified rocker feed system and used the 750 twin's oil pump, with crankcase modifications to suit, and damping rubbers between the cylinder head fins, plus several other changes (see box).

One of the rare Series 2 Daytonas – nine are known to have survived.

109

Triumph 350/500 Unit Construction Twins Bible 1957-1974

> ### List of new parts for T100D
> Option of 9:1 or 7.5:1 pistons
> B range oil pump with crankcase modifications to accommodate, requiring new rockers, rocker boxes, spindles and feed pipe
> Rocker spindle feed, via the end of the rocker spindle (similar to B range)
> Cylinder head with fin snubber rubbers
> New tappet assemblies
> Six-plate clutch with new clutch driving plates
> T150 forks and instrument binnacle, with new alloy outer members left and right
> Calipers and brake parts as 1973 B range
> Fork springs 97-4595 (yellow/blue red)
> Instruments as 1973 B range
> Handlebars new for T100D, controls mostly 1973 B range
> Wheels, disc, caliper and master cylinder from 1973 B range
> Rear brake conical hub
> New swinging arm
> New oil tank with feed pipes and connectors and filters
> New 2-gallon petrol tank as well as 4-gallon
> Frame with new top head lug, to suit T150 forks
> New silencer and end caps
> New wiring harness

The pre-production bikes were numbered from JJ57989 to JJ58013, and, in the aftermath of Meriden, they were transferred to NVT's spares operation, Andover Norton in Hampshire, where they were completed for sale, most being put together by John Nelson. As for the remaining stocks of old-style T100R Daytonas and TR5Ts, some of these were among the bikes refurbished and sold when the factory blockade was lifted – hence some Daytonas and TR5Ts from this period carry 1975 registrations. Some TR5Ts were also converted to road specification, with lower front mudguard, Dunlop K70 rear tyre, Avon front tyre, and higher gearing.

So that was the end of Triumph's C range, which had started back in 1957 and ended in the messy, complicated situation at Meriden sixteen years later. It's not clear that its demise could be blamed on the sit-in. That was the immediate cause, but the evidence suggests that NVT had no intention of moving production to Small Heath along with that of the Bonneville. At the end, 102,665 350/500cc unit construction twins had left the factory – not bad for what started out as Edward Turner's bathtub.

The final 500cc twin adopted the oil pump as well as other parts from the big twins.

What Might Have Been: the C Range Replacements

Triumph had thought about how to replace the C range, and we've come across three attempts: the Triumph Bandit/BSA Fury 350 (1971); the Triumph Daytona/Thunderbird 600 (1983); and Daytona 500s built from parts (1984). The Bandit/Fury story has been related before, but it's worth retelling, if only for its 'what might have been' status.

In 1968, just as Meriden was phasing out the final Tiger 90 350s, Edward Turner, the man who had designed the original Speed Twin in 1937, as well as the 3TA, presented BSA/Triumph with a brand new 350 twin which he said was ready to put into production. Although long retired, Turner still worked as a freelance designer.

On paper, his latest project looked good. It was an up-to-the-minute DOHC 350 twin, with gear-driven cams, twin carburettors, five-speed gearbox, front disc brake and optional electric start. It weighed, said Turner, slightly less than a Tiger 90, but produced 35bhp. In Triumph's vital North American market, the 350cc market was growing fast, so it looked just the thing.

Stuart McGuigan, who was seconded to the project as a student apprentice, had good memories of the bike: "It was very light and fast. I did ride it briefly – it went well and handled OK. There were flaws, but they were things which could have been sorted. It would have been a good competitor, price and performance wise, much cheaper than the Fury."

Meanwhile, BSA/Triumph chief designer Bert Hopwood and chief engineer Doug Hele had been working on their own C range replacements – 250 and 350cc triples with six-speed gearboxes. As Turner's twin looked further along the development road, the Board gave it the go ahead.

Hopwood wasn't best pleased, knowing that while Edward Turner was a superb stylist and something of a visionary, his engineering could leave something to be desired. Eventually he agreed to assess the new twin, but the report he wrote was damning. The prototype failed to make 35bhp and, according to Hopwood, suffered numerous failures in 5000 miles on the road: crankshafts and main bearings failed, the engine drank oil, and its slim frame flexed. The engine's bottom end, wrote Hopwood,

The BSA Fury 350 (and its Triumph Bandit equivalent) was to have replaced the smaller C range twins.

> ### What the press said
> **BSA Fury 350** *Motorcycle Sport Quarterly*
> "The Fury, at the time of our test, lacked the tractor-like lugging power of its Japanese contemporary when the revs dipped low ... my impression was that a little more mid-range torque was needed was confirmed by the factory men, and I'm fairly sure it'll be there by the time you swing aboard ... Conversely, up near the top end, the Fury is happy as a lark when rolling 80-85mph. Imagine a five-speed 350 with a 90mph fourth gear!"

was "hopelessly skimped," and the forks, "fundamentally unsafe." Stuart McGuigan's memory is that the prototype was ridden "tens of thousands of miles" before the crankshaft failure, but whatever the mileage was, the whole project was taken over as an official BSA/Triumph project.

Doug Hele, one of the industry's great development engineers, went about completely redesigning the bike. There was a new crank, chain drive for the overhead cams and a new, more substantial, frame, while BSA/Triumph's standard forks and conical hub brakes replaced the Turner originals. The result looked production ready when the company launched it as part of the brave new world of its 1971 range. Indeed, it's thought about 60 pre-production bikes were built, and some production tooling had already been ordered. American journalists Bob Braverman of *Cycle Guide* and Bob Greene of *Motorcycle Sport Quarterly* were given an early ride, on both road and track – Greene thought the bike (to be sold as the Triumph Bandit as well as the BSA Fury) lacked the low speed pulling power of a Honda CB350, but that it thrived on revs and performed well.

Alas, that was as far as it got. BSA's financial problems of 1971/72 meant there just wasn't the cash to go ahead with production, and the new 350 was rapidly cancelled. MD Lionel Jofeh ordered that the production tooling be destroyed – that was before he resigned in disgrace, having presided over BSA's commercial collapse, and, despite his record, the ex-MD walked away with a substantial payoff.

If it had gone into production as planned, the Bandit/Fury could well have spelled the end for the existing C range bikes. With a claimed 34bhp at 9000rpm, it would have been very close in performance to the Tiger 100. But it would also have cost more. Although a target price of $900 was talked about, group accountants told the American importer BSA Inc that "a reasonable price" would be $1600, when a Trophy 500 was priced at just $1160 and a Honda 350 just $800 ... So, even if the Fury had made it to full production, would it have sold well at such a premium, or made any profits for BSA? With hindsight, it looks unlikely. Whatever the price, the logical thing at an early stage would have been to make the engine stretchable to 500cc, and thus a genuine replacement for the C range, but there's no evidence that this was built into the design.

Daytona 600

Triumph resurfaced after the 1974/75 sit-in as an independent workers' co-operative, partly financed by a government loan, and supplying Bonneville and Tiger twins to NVT – the Daytona 500 never made it back into production. The Meriden co-op, as some knew it, would keep production going against the odds for another eight years.

By 1983 it was in desperate straits, though, having been hard hit by exchange rate movements which made the British bikes expensive in the USA, still a vital export market. But Triumph had a plan, to sell off Meriden, move to a smaller factory and launch a new water-cooled 900cc twin, which was already in prototype form. In the meantime, it had to maintain interest in the older twins, and, at the Motorcycle Show at Birmingham's NEC in April 1983 unveiled some new variants. The eight-valve TSS and custom TSX, launched the

Just one Daytona 600 was assembled in 1983 – Meriden finally closed before it got any further.

What Might Have Been: the C Range Replacements

previous year, would be joined by two new 600cc twins, both derived from the TR65 Thunderbird, with a lower capacity to cut insurance costs. There was a single-carb Thunderbird with high bars, and a twin-carb Daytona 600, both of which were displayed at the show. Only one Daytona was known to have been assembled.

Sadly, this was to be the last public showing of Triumph. Production had effectively ended in late 1982, and, according to Triumph dealer Bill Crosby, many of the show bikes were actually mock ups, without engine internals. In the uncertain economic conditions of 1983, the rescue deal fell through, and so the new generation Daytona never went into production.

The MCS Daytona

Meriden might have been in its final death throes, but in the 1980s (as now) thousands of Triumph twins were still on the road, owned by a loyal band of riders – and they all needed spares. So, while the old British motorcycle died, the spares specialists kept going, often relatively small businesses filling a gap in the market.

Ted Bloomfield was one such. He had specialised in British bikes right through the 1960s and '70s, and now ran the Motorcycle Shop in Leytonstone, East London. Always on the look out for spare parts, he bought up a vast tranche of 500cc spares from Meriden, and, when the Metropolitan Police moved from Triumph to BMW patrol bikes, he bought its big spares stock too – by 1984 he had an astonishing £2 million worth of spares in stock, including frames, tanks, and crankcases. In fact, enough to assemble complete new bikes – not just Daytonas, but T140 Bonnevilles as well. He decided to put the Daytona back into production.

The plan was to build one new bike a week, and the first new T100R engine was stamped 58001, the second 58002, though, unlike Meriden, there was no two-letter prefix.

MCS of Leytonstone planned to build a run of Daytonas, probably to 1973 spec.

According to the single-sheet brochure, the bikes would have been to 1973 spec, with indicators and front drum brake.

Sadly, the remanufacturing plans never got off the ground, and that really was the end of the C range. Of course, it wasn't the end of the names 'Triumph' or 'Daytona,' thanks to John Bloor, but that's another story.

Visit Veloce on the web – www.velocebooks.com
Details of all books • Special offers • New book news • Gift vouchers

3

Living with a 350/500 Triumph

Choosing, buying, owning, restoring

If you're thinking about buying a 350/500 Triumph as your first classic bike, then you've made a good choice. Quite apart from all the good qualities of the C range, they were a very popular bike when new.

Since then, countless thousands have been crashed, written-off, or left mouldering in the backs of garages as unrestorable boxes of bits. Nevertheless, many have also survived, not least because their desirability as a classic bike means that many sad examples – thought not worth saving a decade or so ago – have since been brought back to life. The upshot is that there is invariably a good selection of bikes being offered for sale, and, if the first one you look at is a disappointment, don't worry, because there are plenty more.

Parts availability is also mostly good (see below) and the C range is more affordable to buy than the bigger Triumph twins; though prices have increased, in line with the increasing interest in classic bikes. We're unlikely to see much more growth, but a C range Triumph will certainly hold its value now.

It's also worth remembering that this really was a range of machines, from the touring 3TA to the rorty Daytona 500, so there's also a good choice of models (again, more details below). If in doubt as to which would suit you best, think about the sort of riding you want to do.

Is it for me?

If you've already owned a classic British bike, then feel free to skip this section – if you haven't, it is worth reading. Like any classic, the smaller Triumph twins need a lot of care and attention compared to a modern machine, and you would have to be quite committed to use one for everyday riding. Of course, young bloods of the 1960s and early '70s did exactly that, but they were keen enough to take on the intensive maintenance which went with it, or were willing to live with the oil leaks and unreliability which resulted from neglect.

A modern bike typically needs servicing every 4000 or 8000 miles, with just the odd oil check and chain adjustment in between, but old bikes aren't like that. The engine oil should be changed every 1000-1500 miles, and there are the tappets, primary chain, carburettor/s and ignition system to look after. Of course, sensible

Bikes are often a mix of original and non-standard parts.

Living with a 350/500 Triumph

Triumph 350/500 twins are relatively small, light and easy to ride.

Single-carb Tigers are the great all-rounders.

upgrades like electronic ignition and better oil filtration reduce the need for maintenance, but, like any old bike, the 350/500 Triumphs do require a different mindset of the owner – keeping an eye out for small problems like a blown bulb or something coming loose is all part of the experience.

A few other caveats apply to the riding experience. Triumph twins do vibrate, but the smaller ones probably less so than legend would have you believe. By contemporary standards, the brakes were quite good, especially the twin-leading-shoe front drum fitted to later bikes, but they will never match a modern disc for power. Similarly, the six-volt electrics have dimmer lights and less certain charging than you might be used to. The 12-volt system (1966-on) is better.

Finally, if you're worried about kickstarting, don't be. These Triumphs are quite easy starters, and don't need a rider with bulging thigh muscles. They certainly like a bit of technique, something you learn from experience, but are less finicky than the big four-stroke singles.

Upsides

Having got the dull but necessary warnings out of the way, we can get onto the upsides of owning a smaller Triumph twin, and the good news is that there are plenty of them. These are not fast bikes, but all of them, apart from the 3TA, have brisk acceleration (especially the Daytona) and will have no trouble keeping up with modern traffic on A and B roads. Motorways are a different matter, as sustaining 70mph or more is asking quite a lot of machinery this old. They are better suited to slower, twistier roads, and apart from the occasional shimmy from earlier frames, they handle very well indeed.

Size has a lot to do with this. By modern standards, these are physically small bikes, about the same size as a modern 250. The seat height is only around 30 inches, they are slim and narrow and weigh only around 160kg, making them featherweights by modern standards. Edward Turner designed the very first 3TA to be easy to ride and handle, and those same attributes carried on right to the end. All have comfortable, 'neutral' riding positions, and, of course, they all look great.

Practicalities

Triumph twins might not be cheap to buy any more, but they are surprisingly cheap to run. Ridden sensibly they will easily average 60-70mpg, slightly less from the Daytona, but keep down to 50mph on one of the 350s and you might see over 80mpg. These bikes have relatively low power outputs, so they're not that hard on consumables either – tyres, brakes, chains and sprockets will all last well, unless a previous owner has skimped by fitting cheap replacements.

The spares backup is excellent, and there are plenty of specialist parts suppliers who can sell you almost every engine part new, and the prices are reasonable – it's labour costs that mount up if a bike is being restored or worked on by a professional.

Very tidy looking engine/gearbox – look at it again after the test ride.

Some parts are getting difficult to find, notably the bathtub or bikini tinwork. There are six different fuel tanks and five different oil tanks, so finding the exact one for your bike could be a challenge. The same goes for genuine mudguards, tool boxes and other sundry items. Pattern part quality can vary, but the long-established suppliers should only be selling sound parts.

Talking of specialists, a huge fund of knowledge has grown up around the 350/500 Triumphs, especially in the UK and USA, where thousands of riders and dealers have had long experience of them. Tap into this by joining the Triumph Owners' Club or the Vintage Motorcycle Club, don't be afraid to ask for advice, either on the forums or face to face, and be a good customer of the specialists who are usually willing to help.

We mentioned earlier that, by modern standards, the 350/500s need a lot of maintenance, and they do, but the good news is that the routine tasks are actually quite straightforward. Changing oils, adjusting tappets and chains (though the primary is a bit messy), the carburettor and (unless you have electronic ignition) the points are all within the capabilities of a home mechanic with a reasonable set of tools. Recommended service intervals are in the workshop manual, but expect to change the engine oil every 1500 miles – preferably 1000 if the original filtration system is still in place – with a similar interval for the tappets.

As for investment potential, as mentioned above, none of the C range Triumphs represent a blue chip investment, but it is nice to know that if you ever decide to sell, you will invariably get all your money back. Single carburettor bikes – 350s or 500s, bathtubs or Tigers – all tend to be valued about the same, with prices depending more on condition than year, model or even strict originality. Non-matching engine and frame numbers will certainly put a dent in any bike's value. Daytonas are worth significantly more than the single-carb bikes, and late model T100Cs are also sought after.

Ready to ride or restore?

This is one of the first things to decide, as old bike purchases range from the familiar autojumble basket case (a collection of well worn and rusty parts that may or may not add up to one complete bike), to a concours machine built to a standard better than new.

Living with a 350/500 Triumph

Fancy restoring it? It'll take time.

Which one suits you best depends on a great many things: budget, available time, inclination and skills. There's an undeniable romance about restoration projects, about bringing a sick bike back into blooming health, and it's tempting to buy something that 'just needs a few small jobs' to bring it up to scratch. But 'small jobs' can turn into big ones once the bike is dismantled, and all restorations take time, which is a precious thing in itself. Will you get as much pleasure from working on the bike as you will from riding it?

Of course, you could always hand the whole thing over to a professional, and there are plenty of specialists who could do an excellent job. But it's a very expensive route, especially if you want a complete restoration done, and the increase in value will very rarely cover the money spent. If you do decide to use a professional restorer, be absolutely clear what you want done. Do you want the bike to be simply roadworthy and useable, 100 per cent original, or better than new?

If you do decide to do the work yourself, then have a think about what skills you have, or

would like to acquire. Can you weld, or paint? Are you confident with electrics, or major engine work? If the bike needs a complete rebuild, you might prefer to handle the chassis yourself, but hand the engine/gearbox over to specialist. Although the engine is relatively simple, it still takes skill to put together properly – that's the difference between an engine that runs well and doesn't leak oil, and one that just runs ... and leaks! Of course, it does help if you have a warm, well-lit garage with a solid workbench and a

This headlight shell is almost past saving.

Many years later, an ex-police 5TA, missing a lot of parts.

Some oil leaks can't be ignored.

117

Triumph 350/500 Unit Construction Twins Bible 1957-1974

3TA and 5TA are the mildest C range bikes.

good selection of tools. The Haynes manual, the original Triumph workshop manual, parts books and instruction manuals will all be invaluable.

If you do any dismantling, take note of the order in which the various spacers, seals and washers go, so that they slip straight back in, in the right order. This applies to wheel bearings as well as the engine/gearbox unit. The frame shouldn't need any repair work apart from blasting and repainting. On a well worn bike, don't forget the stands – the centre stand, in particular, may well be sloppy and need work.

Which model?

As a general rule, the C range was gradually improved over the years, so the later the bike, the better the spec. These bikes do have well known weaknesses, such as the electrics, oil filtration and leaks, but are generally reliable – once the weak points are addressed a 350 or 500 should provide years of trouble-free riding, provided you keep off motorways and keep it well serviced. As previously mentioned, although regular maintenance is vital, it's not over complicated.

So, if you've decided to buy one, which model? To make it easier to decide which one might suit you, the C range is divided here into four categories: tourers (3TA/5TA); single-carb road bikes (Tiger 90/Tiger 100); twin-carb road bikes (Daytona); and competition/off-road bikes (TR5AC, T100C, TR5T, etc).

The tourers

These were the original C range bikes, which kept to Edward Turner's original concept of a clean and easy-to-ride machine with appeal beyond the limited enthusiast market. In a lower state of tune than the other bikes, they are very docile but still able to cruise at up to 60mph – the 18.5bhp 350 could reach about 80mph and the 27bhp 500cc 5TA is significantly faster, though still softly tuned and flexible at low speed. The unique aspect of both, of course, was the voluminous bathtub rear end, which was later slimmed-down into the skimpier bikini and finally lost altogether, although the tourers kept their headlight nacelle right to the end. All of these, plus the big 'Roman helmet' front mudguard were often ditched by impatient teenagers who saw it all as a frumpy, heavy horror which restricted performance. This is why some 3TA/5TAs now turn up without their trademark tinwork – the advantage is they do tend to be cheaper.

Strengths/weaknesses: Flexible, easygoing and economical, with unique styling and presence. The 3TA is quite slow, and the brakes and six-volt electrics on both bikes aren't up to modern standards.

The Tigers

These single-carburettor road bikes – the 349cc Tiger 90 and 490cc Tiger 100 – were in some ways the backbone of the range. In a higher state of tune and (apart from the early T100), without the bathtub, they offered a more sporting alternative to the 3TA/5TA, and the Tiger 100 sold well for several years – today, it's the easiest to find of the whole C range.

The Tiger 90 is one of the rarer models, with 4204 built. Launched in 1963 with the

Living with a 350/500 Triumph

Single-carb Tigers are great all rounders.

skimpier bikini tinwork and no nacelle, its power was increased substantially over the 3TA, to 27bhp at 7500rpm. That was enough for a top speed of 85-90mph, and, although the T90 lacks the torque of the T100, it gives enjoyable performance if you're willing to use the gearbox. The T100 was in a similar state of tune (initially 32bhp, soon rising to 34bhp) but with decent midrange power as well. The early T100A with energy transfer ignition is rare, especially in the UK, but later models such as the T100SS are far easier to find, with over 8000 built.

Both Tigers shared the same updates as the rest of the C range – modified frame in 1965 and '67, the 12-volt electrics in '66, and stronger bottom end from '69.

Strengths/weaknesses: A good compromise between the touring 3TA/5TA and the twin-carb performance. Enjoyable performance, sporting looks, and (from '65) excellent handling. 1969/70 Tiger 100s are the pick of the bunch, the result of ten years' steady development.

The Daytona

The Daytona was the hottest of the C range twins, by far the fastest and most powerful. Inspired by Triumph's victories in the Daytona 200 in 1966 and '67, the bike capitalised on that success by being named after the famous Florida circuit. It wasn't just a marketing ploy either, as the new Daytona owed much to the race bikes.

Full details are on page 71-72, but briefly, the Daytona's frame was based on that of the racers, with a new cylinder head with bigger valves, E3134 camshafts, and the trademark twin Amal carburettors. The result was 39bhp at 7400rpm, enough for a top speed of 104mph and 0-60mph in 7.0 seconds. It was actually faster than Honda's CB450, though not as reliable or oil-tight. There were several worthwhile changes for 1968 (though many early Daytonas will have since been updated as well) including harder wearing nitrided cams, 8in twin-leading-shoe front brake, and Amal Concentric carbs.

Daytonas tend to be valued higher than any of the single-carb bikes, thanks to their glamour, performance, and association with those iconic race wins. If you can find one of the very rare Series 2s, they will be worth even more.

Strengths/weaknesses: Excellent performance, fine handling and (from '68-on) the best front brake. But the engine is more highly stressed and there are two carburettors to keep in tune.

Twin-carb Daytona commands the highest price.

The off-road bikes

'Off-road' is a bit of a misnomer, as the T100C was more of a street scrambler, a road bike which could tackle easy off-road use as well. The other C range bikes in this category, though, were more genuine attempts at dual-purpose on/off-road machines – they were heavier than equivalent single-cylinder trail bikes, but a better compromise on the road. For some they remain the most stylish Triumphs of all time, with a high-pipe glamour and toughness associated with Steve McQueen and American desert racing.

The early TR5A/R and A/C were aimed at the US market only for 1961, and are now very rare, with only just over 1000 built in total. Both were based on the T100A but with the naked styling now associated with 1960s Triumph twins – no bathtub, gaitered forks, and chrome headlight shell. Both had energy transfer ignition, and the A/C was the off-road oriented version, with a bash plate and off-road tyres amongst other changes. Renamed the T100S/C for '62 and the T100C for '66, it gradually became more road oriented, sharing the same updates as the Tigers, and survived right up to 1972.

Its replacement for '73, as Triumph struggled to survive, was the more seriously off-road TR5T (see page 104 for details), with its BSA trail bike frame, 21in front wheel and small alloy tank – it was quite capable on the dirt but the brakes were marginal for road use.

Finally, there are the Cheney Triumphs, using the 500cc twin in Eric Cheney's well respected scrambles frame, made of Reynolds 531 or T45 tubing. One of these with a verifiable competition history would be a real find. Eric Cheney's son Simon still offers spares and builds new frame kits.

Strengths/weaknesses: High-pipe, off-road style, which Triumph made its own. Early rare TR5s will be expensive, T100C is a practical classic, and TR5T is more of a genuine trail bike.

'Off-road' bikes are better described as dual-purpose or street scramblers.

Ammeter will show whether or not the alternator is charging.

Living with a 350/500 Triumph

Points to look for

So you've decided that you really do want a 350 or 500cc Triumph, narrowed the choice to a particular model, and, after hopefully not too much searching, you've found one that sounds like the sort of thing you're looking for. Confronted with the actual bike, what points should you look for? Triumph twins are relatively simple, uncomplicated bikes, but it still pays to give any potential purchase a good examination before parting with cash. A lot of what follows would apply to any secondhand bike, though some of it is specific to the C range.

Experience suggests that there are few really good bikes out there, and you will need perseverance and patience to find a good example of the particular model you're after. However, as mentioned above, these are relatively common classics, so you should find what you want. Any machine you examine should be looked at carefully and sympathetically, but be open and friendly with the seller – a suspicious demeanour might put them on their guard. Finally, watch out for fakes. 3TAs can be dressed up as Tiger 90s, and Tiger 100s fitted with twin carbs to become Daytonas. Some 350s have been converted to 500s. There's nothing wrong with any of this if the seller is honest about it, but a lack of originality should be reflected in the price.

Engine/frame numbers

Engine and frame numbers come up many times in this book, and for a very good reason – they'll tell you whether the bike really is the model it's advertised to be, and whether the engine (or frame) is the original one. That's why many Triumphs are advertised with "matching numbers," because the engine and frame numbers are the same, and, therefore, left the factory together.

The engine number is stamped on the left-hand side, just below the cylinder barrel. The figures should be clear and not 'fuzzy' – if they aren't clear, the number could have been tampered with. From 1969 the engine number was stamped onto a background of 'Triumph' logos, to make tampering more difficult. The model code ('T90,' 'T100,' etc) will be stamped to the left of the number.

Look for the frame number, stamped on the left-hand side of the headstock. This may be more difficult to read, especially if the frame has been repainted or powder coated, but it should still be visible. All the same comments apply. It's worth noting that if the frame and engine numbers don't match, the bike may still be honest and useable, but, being non-original, this should be reflected in the price. Finally, check that these numbers match those on the registration document.

Engine/frame number should tell you a lot.

Frame number should match engine number.

Are the mudguards straight, rust-free, and do they match the tank?

Tinwork

If you're looking at a 3TA, 5TA, or early T100A, check the bathtub, headlight nacelle, and the front mudguard for rust and dents. New front mudguards in most styles are available, and old-stock nacelles do come up, but, at the time of writing, bathtubs and bikinis were not available new.

Mudguards should be straight, free of rust around the rims, and securely bolted to the bike. Apart from the high-level front guard of the TR5T, all are substantial items, with two or three stays. The oil tank should be checked for leaks through the seams, as repair entails removal and flushing out before it can be put right. The fuel tank needs to be checked for leaks around the tap and along the seams, as well as for dents and rust. Watch out for patches of filler. Pinhole leaks can often be cured by Petseal, but anything more serious needs a proper repair. If the tank is beyond saving, new ones are available, though make sure to get the right one for your bike.

Electrics/wiring

Triumph electrics don't have the best reputation, but the 12-volt Zener diode system from 1966 is pretty good, and all bikes can be significantly improved with aftermarket items. Even if it's had later sensible modifications, the electrical system still needs checking. A good general indication of the owner's attitude is the condition of the wiring: is it tidy and neat, or flopping around? The many bullet connectors need to be clean and tight, and many odd electrical problems are simply down to bad connections or a poor earth. Up to 1970, most bikes came with an ammeter, which, at least, gives some indication that all is well in the charging circuit. Finally, check that everything works: lights, horn, indicators (fitted post '71, but sometimes removed by owners), and stop light (water can

Alternator (primary chaincase removed).

Living with a 350/500 Triumph

enter the rear brake switch). Hinge up the seat and check the battery (or in the case of early 12-volt bikes, twin 6-volt batteries): acid splashes indicate overcharging. Do check that the battery is securely kept in place by its rubber strap. If it isn't, the battery can leap upwards over bumps, and short out against the metal seat base.

Running gear

Check the wheel bearings by holding each wheel off the ground (bike on centre stand) and trying to rock it from side to side

Swing the handlebars from lock to lock. They should move freely, with not a hint of roughness or stiff patches. To check for play, put the steering on full lock, grip the front wheel and, with the front brake on hard, attempt to rock the bike gently back and forth. Swinging-arm bearings sometimes get neglected (ie not greased), so check for wear by grasping the rear end of the arm on one side and trying to rock it from side-to-side. There should be no perceptible movement. Grasp the bottom of the forks and try to rock them back and forth – play here indicates worn bushes. There should be no leaks around the forks or rear shocks.

Engine/gearbox

You can tell a lot about the likely condition of a Triumph twin without hearing it run. Look for chewed up screw or Allen bolt heads and/or rounded off bolts; these, plus damage to the casings surrounding them, are all signs of careless ownership.

Oil leaks are not inevitable. As long as the engine is in good condition and has been properly put together, it should be reasonably

How to check for play in the front forks (will also show up a loose steering head).

Checking steering head bearings.

Check swinging-arm for play.

123

Is the exhaust system sound with good chrome?

oiltight. Look for leaks at the barrel/crankcase joint, around the pushrod tubes, and the underside of the crankcase. If there's a serious leak that should be obvious after the test ride.

Now it's time to start it, and, as stated elsewhere, if in good condition it should fire up within two or three kicks. Reluctant starting is mostly likely to be (if electronic ignition hasn't been fitted) simply maladjusted contact breaker points and ignition timing, but it could also be a worn-out top end.

Once started, the engine should idle evenly on both cylinders. If it sounds and feels lumpy and uneven, then contact breaker or carburettor adjustments are the most likely cause, but a knowledgeable owner should already have these spot-on.

Some tappet noise from the top end is normal (unless it's an obvious harsh tapping), but knocking or rumbling from the bottom end is not (this will mean a complete engine rebuild for sure). Also listen to the primary drive – any clonks or rumbles here? Don't buy a bike that's making these noises unless it's cheap. While the engine is idling, hinge up the seat, remove the oil tank cap and take a peek inside – you should see a spurt of oil being returned to the tank, which increases with revs. If there's nothing, switch off immediately, as this means the oil pump isn't scavenging, and damage

Living with a 350/500 Triumph

Subtle oil leak, probably from the head/barrel joint.

could ensue. This is usually down to the ball-valve in the pump not seating properly, and is relatively simple to put right, but the bike can't be run until it is.

Look back at the silencers and blip the throttle. Blue smoke means the engine is burning oil and is a sign of general wear in the top end, which isn't unusual – all parts to put that right are available.

Bikes without air filters should be avoided, as you don't know what the motor has ingested.

Blue smoke (this is a Bonneville, but smoke is smoke) indicates top end wear.

125

Test ride

The test ride should not last less than 15 minutes, and you should be doing the riding – not the seller riding with you on the pillion. It's understandable that some sellers are reluctant to let a complete stranger loose on their pride and joy, but it does go with the territory of selling a bike, and so long as you leave an article of faith (usually the vehicle you arrived in) then all should be happy. Take your driving licence in case the seller wants to see it.

A Triumph twin in good condition should give good acceleration in the mid-range. The low powered Twenty-One/3TA will seem slow, but all bikes should pull cleanly. Despite all the talk of vibration, these engines are reasonably smooth and free-revving up to 4-5000rpm.

The clutch is heavier than on some modern bikes, but take up should be smooth and positive. Nor should it drag or slip, despite the tales of all Triumph clutches dragging. To check this, select first gear from a standstill. A small crunch is normal, but a full-blooded graunch, followed by a jerk forward, means the clutch is dragging. However, the cure is usually down to careful adjustment rather than the wholesale replacement of parts.

Triumph gearboxes work well, with a clean, positive shift. Watch for stiffness, notchiness and whining. They're also reliable, and, given regular oil changes, should not give trouble, but false neutrals or slipping out of gear, are sure signs of trouble.

These are relatively light bikes with stiff suspension, very agile and easy to flick through corners. Any vagueness and weaving is usually down to worn forks, rear shocks or tyres – it's not inherent. They should never feel soft and wallowy – if they do, the suspension condition is your first thing to recheck. If the bike pulls to one side in a straight line, the wheels may be out of line.

Don't expect modern braking power from the cable-operated drum brakes, which were adequate when new, but need taking into account when riding in fast, heavy traffic. The twin-leading-shoe front drum fitted from 1969 is the best of the lot, while the TR5T's smaller conical hub brakes are weak for modern roads. Whatever the brake, the lever should not feel spongy, shouldn't 'pulse' (the sign of an out-of-round drum), or reach close to the bars on a hard stop.

When you get back from the test ride, examine the engine and gearbox again for leaks.

Cables are cheap to replace, but stiff or damaged controls are expensive.

Modifications and Improvements

Even the keenest owners, riders and supporters of the C range Triumphs would admit that they are not perfect, and a number of modifications can improve reliability and performance without losing the general character of the bike. Modifications are listed in the order shown as some are probably more useful than others, but the success or failure of any them is not guaranteed! All modifications are, of course, a personal preference, and should be done only after some thought as to what you intend to achieve. For example, do you really want to boost performance at the expense of low speed running and easy starting? Many owners of older bikes now put ease of use and reliability above higher performance, but not everyone does. Triumph twins were and are famously tuneable: one race-prepared Tiger 90 could reach 8500rpm and top 120mph!

If you are making changes, care should be taken not to dispose of or damage parts so that the machine can be returned to standard in the future. John Healy and Don Hutchinson, the USA Triumph experts, assisted with additional information in this section.

Engine improvements

Generally, the engine is reliable without modification, as long as the state of key components, such as the main bearings and crankshaft sludge trap, are sound. Weak points, such as the timing side oil feed on pre-1969 machines, can be improved, in this case by the 'Devimead' type conversion offered by several companies, notably SRM Classic Bikes.

Dynamic balancing will smooth the crankshaft vibration inherent to parallel twins. Until 1968, 350cc engines featured steel con-rods, while 500cc machines all have RR.56 Hiduminium alloy rods.

Improving performance

Converting 3TA and T90 engines to 500cc to improve performance may initially seem relatively easy, but actually involves replacing the pistons, con-rods, barrels, heads, carb and, sometimes, the exhausts. If the 3TA seems slow, consider fitting the camshafts, higher compression pistons and cylinder head from a T90 instead. One of Triumph's service bulletins (no: 240) actually gives comprehensive details of all the parts needed to do this.

Fitting lower or higher compression pistons from other machines in the range is possible – just bear in mind that there are many variations of cylinder head, valves, camshafts and gearing, and only the correct combinations will improve overall performance. Almost all the camshafts feature three keys to allow some variation in valve timing.

Barrels in original sizes are becoming rare, together with standard pistons. An option is to have the barrels sleeved to standard and then bored to suit the pistons available – unfortunately, this will often double the cost, but it does give the barrels a new lease of life.

Ignition

All early models will benefit from replacing the distributor with one of the compact ignition units from Electrexworld, which replaces the Lucas alternator with an efficient and compact energy transfer unit which can supply basic lighting, and simplifies the ignition and lighting circuitry. Especially suited for competition or occasional use machines – although it does replace the distributor, the distributor body can be retained for an original look. www.electrexworld.co.uk

Distributor-era bikes can also be converted to the later system of twin points in the timing cover, if all the suitable parts can be obtained. Triumph's Technical Bulletin 13 details this, along with other factory approved modifications.

Electronic ignition

This is surely one of the most common modifications for any Triumph twin, and for several good reasons. Replacing the standard points with electronic ignition gives more precise ignition timing, so better running and easier starting. Once set up, it will never need adjusting, and the change is discreet, with no external signs that it has been done. Several alternatives are now available for all models.

Boyer Bransden's system fits all post-1962 points ignition models, though the bike should be 12 volts to get the best from the system, and fitting will be easier if you undertake the two jobs at the same time. The control box fits neatly under the fuel tank between the frame tubes, secured with a large cable tie or tape. The connections to the coils can then be kept short, while the location keeps the box and connections dry and allows some cooling air to reach the unit. Setting up the ignition can be time-consuming, but, once done, it's set for life.

The crimp-on bullet connectors supplied with the Boyer ignition kit can be distorted by heat, so these should be changed to spade, British bullet, or Japanese connectors, soldered in place and carefully insulated. With care it's possible to re-solder the wiring directly to the PCB connector. Smear silicone on the cover plate flange and fill the wiring entry point to weatherproof everything.

Another point to beware of is that the Boyer unit will fail if the battery becomes disconnected or the Zener diode fails, allowing the voltage to rise to exceed the maximum, so regularly check that these connections are clean and tight. If the engine stops after a short period of erratic running, the main fuse and ignition box connections are the first things to check. Misfiring at high revs is usually the result of a flat battery. Fitting the power box as described above is the best solution. If you want to carry a spare ignition unit, there's space within the headlight shell to keep it safe and dry.

Lead free

All petrol (certainly in the UK and USA) has been unleaded for many years now, and although the C range was designed for what used to be known in Britain as four- or five-star leaded fuel, this isn't the disaster it might seem. Many bikes will already have been converted to harder valve seats which can cope with unleaded fuel, and current thinking is that valve seat recession should only be a problem when bikes are ridden hard. Riding more gently, and keeping an eye on tappet clearances, is worth doing, then simply replacing valve seats with harder types when the time comes. The octane value of Super Unleaded is little different from that of the old four star petrol, though the adoption of lower compression pistons would enable worry-free use of standard Premium Unleaded.

Filtration

The standard filtration system relies on wire gauzes in both the sump and oil tank, together with the action of the centrifugal sludge trap in the crankshaft. A modern cartridge-type filter will greatly improve filtration as well as increase oil capacity and oil cooling. Anglo Nihon and Paul Goff, amongst others, offer a filter kit, and, with a suitably shaped bracket, the replaceable filter can be fitted neatly under the gearbox, attached to the frame by the footrest bolt. Replacement spin-on filters of less depth make this mod very discreet. Magnetic drain plugs do not appear to be available for the C range, but the alternative is to pop a magnet into the oil tank on a length of copper wire so that it can be removed and examined periodically.

One easy and worthwhile modification to the lubrication system is a Morgo oil pump, which claims 20 per cent greater oil flow than the original pump. It is a direct replacement for the Triumph unit, and bolts straight on after removing the timing cover for access.

Modifications and Improvements

The oil feed to the rockers can be improved by enlarging the centre hole of the rocker shaft so that the flow is not restricted to the ends (beware that the shaft is hardened and difficult to drill). Also be aware that over tightening the oil pipe domed nuts can crush the upper copper washer against the bolt, restricting the flow. You can ease the inside of the washer with a triangular file. Access to the bolts becomes restricted once the head steadies are located, and Locktite is advised to keep everything in place.

Tappets/rocker boxes

Mushroom-headed tappets with light alloy Allen key adjusters are sometimes available, and these ease tappet adjustment, though you will need to remove the rocker box to fit them. They are also thought to increase valve and valve guide life, reducing the tendency of the tappets to hammer the valve tip. The light alloy nuts can strip easily, but can be replaced without removing the rocker boxes.

The tappet covers are easily lost, coming loose thanks to vibration and disappearing into the nearest hedge, which you don't notice until stopping for fuel 50 miles down the road. Ensure that the retaining clip (fitted from 1963) is actually in contact with the cap and indenting the serrations.

Post-1968 rockers can be replaced with the earlier items, where oil is directed to the tappets through drillings rather than relying on splash lubrication. Later (1970-on) rocker spindles have an oil scroll, and are suitable for use with the later rockers. If you intend to use the 1968 parts it is recommended to file (deepen) the oil path indentation on the end, and to use an additional thin washer between the rocker and the Thackery spring washer so that oil is directed towards the tappets/valves where it is needed.

Metal-backed rocker box gaskets are available which do not compress like the standard paper versions. Using gasket cement in place of a gasket is not recommended as this may lead to the tappet adjustment being reduced or eliminated, in addition to the angle of tappets to the valves changing beyond the design limit. Ensure the hole for the pushrods in each gasket is large enough to prevent the rods rubbing – if necessary elongate the holes slightly with a suitable wad punch.

Pushrods

For performance engines it is recommended to fit larger diameter pushrods, which can be still alloy, but steel capped at both ends. This sounds contrary to the usual principle of lightening valve train parts to allow higher revving, but the standard rod has a tendency to flex at high revs, preventing the valves from opening fully on lift. Standard pushrods can be lightened by carefully machining the lower end of the cup. The factory Daytona race bikes, of course, had their own solution: hollow pushrods and lightened cam followers.

Carburettors

All the carburettor parts are available for both Monobloc and Concentric types, as well as complete new units, and plunger choke versions are available by request. But rather than replace the whole thing, renew the jets and internals of the original carb. Look up the manual to find the size and jet requirements you need. If you do replace with a new carb, don't throw the original away as these are very difficult to find – clean it and pack it away in an air-tight container. Worn units can be re-sleeved and reconditioned to maintain authenticity.

Clutch

The clutch fitted to the C range is under-stressed and reliable if unworn. Several changes were made over the years, though, so clutch hubs and main shafts may not be compatible. The clutch does benefit from careful assembly and a more rigid billet spring pressure plate with needle-roller lift is available from SRM. Clutch problems are usually the result of wear within the shock absorber and the engagement slots on the clutch hub and basket. Additional problems stem from wear in the release mechanism. Once wear has occurred very little can be done, and replacement is the only solution.

Belt-drive conversions, replacing the primary chain, have long been available for the bigger twins, and pre-unit 500, but at the time of writing don't appear to be on offer for the C range.

Transmission

Most machines were supplied with standard ratio gearboxes, though some competition models featured different ratios depending on their market.

If a bike's gearing seems too low (ie it feels 'buzzy' at speed), the overall ratio can be raised by fitting a larger gearbox sprocket (one or two more teeth). Two teeth will raise the overall gearing by 12 per cent, which is quite a step for the 350s, though, if you are content with more sluggish performance, this does give more relaxed cruising. Gaining access to the gearbox sprocket does involve removing the alternator, primary drive, and the complete clutch, not to mention special tools for some stages of the operation. The six small screws retaining the access plate behind the clutch are often punched and need drilling.

Post-1966 bikes have a removable rear sprocket, which allows finer adjustment of the gearing – a smaller rear sprocket will raise the gearing, a larger one will reduce it, and, combined with a different gearbox sprocket, this gives plenty of choice. As mentioned above, alternative ratios were supplied for the gearbox internals, in standard, close or wide ratios, which do not affect the overall gear ratio. Early 3 and 5TAs feature plain bushes on the gearbox lay shaft – if these need replacing, consider using needle-roller bearings, as fitted to the Tiger 90 and 100.

Improving electrics

Pre-1966 bikes will greatly benefit from changing to a 12-volt system, which can be achieved in several ways. Fit the 1966 or later wiring scheme, including the Zener diode in a suitable location – a heat sink hidden behind the left hand panel neatly re-creates the 1966 location. The later finned Zener heat sink is also effective, but either can be replaced with a modern encapsulated regulator/rectifier. You can retain the original rectifier for show, using dummy wiring to complete the deception.

An alternative is the excellent Boyer Bransden Power Box (or similar). It is a self-regulating rectifier which includes an internal current and voltage storing rectifier, and is a simpler way to convert to 12 volts. This small box, usually fitting on the back of the battery carrier, will power conventional or electronic ignition, and claims to supply the lights as well, with or without a battery, though some think it is only really suitable for daylight use. The Power Box certainly simplifies the electrics, eliminating the ammeter, fuse, ignition switch, rectifier and Zener diode, though you will need to arrange an ignition kill switch.

When converting to 12 volts, the coils, battery, all bulbs and the horn will have to be replaced as well – feeding 12 volts to the Lucas 6V 8H horn will destroy it. With care and time a non-working horn can be dismantled, serviced and revived – www.taffthehorns.com is a helpful specialist. If fitting a modern horn, mount it out of sight under the fuel tank, and keep the original with dummy wiring for the sake of appearance.

Wiring

When rewiring, modern 2mm cable is recommended, as is running dedicated earth wires to the headlight, tail light, engine and coils. Carefully crimped, soldered and finished with a little heat shrink tubing, the standard British bullet connector is reliable, especially if filled with Vaseline or silicone grease before pressing together, and the correct tool is essential. Try to keep to the wiring colours used in the appropriate diagram for the year, as this will help you to trace problems you or the next owner may encounter. There is a wiring convention for British machines, and you will soon learn the primary colours.

All connections will eventually become loose, either due to corrosion, heat or metal fatigue. To minimise these failures plan the wiring carefully to reduce the number of connections to an absolute minimum, and arrange the wiring to avoid hot spots and excessive flexing. Think of replacing the bullet connectors after ten years, and re-wiring after 20 years. Pay attention to giving wires additional support or insulation where movement and abrasion occurs – for example, the wiring to the coils can short out on the sharp edges of the petrol tank over time.

Alternator

The six-volt Lucas RM19 three-wire alternator is not able to provide sufficient charge when running with the dip beam on continually, which is required in some countries. A rewired RM19 will work with a 12-volt system, though for long daylight runs alternate between running with the lights on and off, in order to let the Zener diode and battery rest. Monitor the ammeter to judge current flow.

Lighting

Improving the lighting is possible by fitting the halogen conversion from Paul Goff, and the

Modifications and Improvements

LED tail light bulbs – the main advantage of the latter is that they will never blow! Uprated pilot bulbs (21 watts) are also available, and a good option if touring where daytime lights are mandatory. The 21-watt bulb is also small and easy to carry as a spare. The Neolite headlamp unit supplied by Hitchcocks Motorcycles (www.hitchcocksmotorcycles.com) is also well thought of, with an excellent beam pattern and intense light provided by the modern Philips bulb.

Cycle parts
Suspension

Dual or variable rate fork springs are available (LP Williams) or could be made for you by a spring specialist, such as Faulkner Springs www.dfaulknersprings.com. The grade of oil used in the standard pre-'68 forks has little effect, with no shuttle damping, though Triumph did recommend experimenting with grades. Whichever oil you use, do not exceed the recommended quantity. The oil has a dual role of lubrication and as a hydraulic stop. It is possible to fit the shuttle damping to post-'64 machines, fitted as standard later on. The works manual details this modification.

If working on the forks, it is not necessary to have the special fork assembly tool. A suitably sized jubilee clip can be used to grip the stanchion while compressing the spring before fitting the complete unit to the steering yokes. The jubilee clip can then be removed, allowing the spring to extend to its normal position. A suitable C-spanner is needed to remove and tighten the chromed oil seal/spring holder, but, if this isn't available, a workable clamp can be made using a block of wood and a suitably sized hole saw.

Fork judder will be caused by worn sintered bronze bushes (though loose steering head bearings feel similar on braking). The bushes are straightforward to replace once the forks are dismantled.

The rear shocks were factory fitted with 100lb or 145lb springs, which are suitable for carrying pillion passengers, but changing to 90lb springs (as detailed in one of the factory's Performance Bulletins) will improve the handling for solo riding/racing.

Frame

As detailed in the main section of this book, the C range frame saw several changes over the years in a process of gradual development, and some changes can be retrofitted. All early bikes benefit from the 1965-on frame brace and tank, if these can be sourced, or from welding in a brace, as used by the factory for 1966. All bikes built before the 1967 model year have a tendency to shimmy when cornering, especially when not on the power, thanks to a lack of support for the swinging-arm. Some owners have even modified the 1967 swinging-arm arrangement by having additional plates welded to the frame with later parts. This is a serious conversion which will be difficult to do well and difficult to undo later. Please don't do this if the bike is in good condition – buy a post-1968 bike instead where it's all been sorted for you by the factory.

Tyres

Unfortunately, there is little tyre choice in the 18in size (3.25 and 3.50), and Dunlop K82s are well thought of. Replace any tyre you suspect to be over ten years old or is obviously cracked – your life is at stake! While the tyre is off always assess the inside of the rim for corrosion, and check the spoke locations before fitting a new tyre and new tape. Discard any tube which has been repaired, as a blow out is not what you want, at any speed.

Wheel bearings

Sealed bearings are usually available to replace the open wheel bearings, and a good bearing supplier will be able to advise if you can provide a sample. It is a good idea to have suitable drifts made to drive in the new bearings squarely and without damage. Popping the bearings in the freezer overnight and heating the hub with a hot air gun will make fitting easier. Bearing Locktite is also a good idea if you suspect there has been a problem.

Brakes

Early C range bikes can be fitted with the fully-floating brake shoes, part numbers W1406 and W1407. Look carefully at the floating shoe slipper as this often becomes indented and ineffective. A common modification is to fit the twin-leading-shoe front brake from the later bikes, which will greatly improve performance but at the loss of originality. It should be possible to modify the standard plate to twin-leading design internally as there's room within the hub. This could be done on a spare plate and its components without altering the original.

The standard single-leading-shoe brake is quite adequate for normal classic use if serviced and set up properly. Have the drum skimmed, the linings replaced with modern compound, and then machined to fit. Ask to have the linings biased to improve the servo action, and ensure that they are chamfered on the leading and trailing edges. Check the springs are in good condition and that the internal surface of the drum is not contaminated with grease or oil.

After assembly, loosen the fixed anchor point and the spindle nut, apply the brake hard and, while maintaining pressure, tighten the spindle nut and then the anchor. This procedure will position the shoes at the optimum position. The hole in the brake plate for the fulcrum can be carefully elongated with a file to increase the amount of adjustment available. If you do this, you will be in illustrious company – Johnny Giles did the same to improve brake performance on his ISDT bike.

Ensure that the operating arm is at right angles to the cable when the brake is applied, and that the handlebar lever is not flexing on the bar. All of this will help to maximise the performance of the standard unit, but even when it is tip-top, stopping from speeds over 60mph can get exciting!

5

How Meriden Worked

John Nelson was Triumph's Service Manager, and had a detailed knowledge of how the Meriden factory worked.

Interview with Justin Harvey-James, August 2011

"I am always amazed by the vast range of questions that are asked regarding the production of motorcycles from the original factory in Meriden. Most can only be answered from the 'incomplete' records made at the time, and the memories of the dwindling few that worked there, and still exist (and retain their memories)!

"My first statement is that there was no one at the factory who was detailed to study and record each individual machine and function so that he could recall precisely 60 years later. What records that were kept were for business and legal purposes.

"Secondly, Triumph was not just a motorcycle assembly shop from bought in finished components as were many other makes. When I joined in 1950 they made their own pistons, frames, gears, shafts, clutches, wheel hubs. They polished and plated their wheel rims, handlebars, silencers in modern paint, polishing and plating shops. The machine shops manufactured almost every part for engines and gearboxes, and all was subject to very strict inspection and quality procedures.

"So how did it all work? In the 1950s and '60s, Edward Turner was in charge. Each year he approved design changes and new models down to every nut and bolt. Most proposed changes were submitted by Sales for acceptance following market trends and distributor and dealer requests. Once agreed, the new season's models were specified by the Design Department, and a specification issued for each model by part number, detailing quantity, material, etc, indicating 'new' where appropriate.

"When these were issued, Sales issued a programme of forthcoming sales requirements which went to the Purchase and Production departments. Purchase had to schedule deliveries of raw materials to cover manufacturing requirements in time for Production to commence at the proposed date. Tallies were issued to each section in the factory detailing quantities for each individual component in scheduled batches for delivery in time for inspection, and transfer to the central 'finished' stores. The finished stores was in a central position in the assembly area, midway between the engine and gearbox assembly tracks, and the motorcycle final assembly line.

"By this time, the Sales departments (Home and Export) had collected the forward orders for the forthcoming season, and converted these into coloured cardboard tallies (white for Home and General Export, and pink for Overseas markets), detailing individual model, destination, distributor or dealer, additions to specification, packing and despatch, etc. All these tallies were collected in single model and destination batches and passed down to Production and Planning to be attached to the bare assembled frames, forks and wheels and handlebars, as the machine was placed on the final assembly track.

"Engineering Excellence," according to this brochure for Meriden.

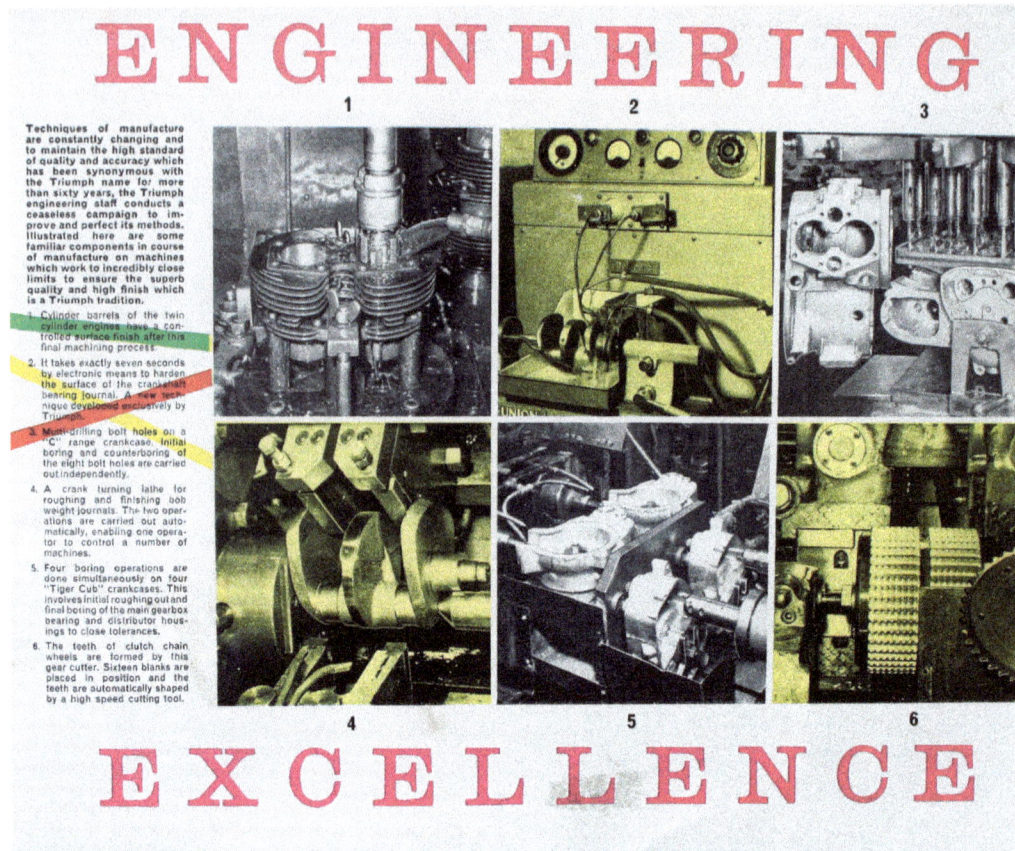

"Meanwhile, the engine assembly track, on the other side of the finished stores, was commencing build of the new season's specification engines. Nothing had a frame or engine number at this point. As the engine 'grew,' and after the pistons and barrels had been fitted, the designated operator sequentially stamped each individual letter and number on the crankcase, whilst standing by the engine at waist height (not easy!) and then recorded it in the build book.

"Passed on to the next operators, the engine was then completed, collected in a batch at the end of the track, and then shipped in batches round to the final assembly track, and fitted into the next frame going down the line. The engines were picked from the engine bench supply in random order and it was not until the last operation on the finished motorcycle, just before it was passed down to the testers, that the frame number (taken from the engine number) was stamped by hand, using individual stamps on the head lug (later an adhesive label). This number entered on the tally, and then into the build register. On rare occasions, due to frame hold-ups, large stocks of engines gathered awaiting build, and no attempt was made to ensure they were segregated and then fitted in chronological order. An engine was a bike, which was an invoice, and an income.

"When passed test (or rectification, and then re-test), the machines were delivered to the Despatch Department, stripped as required for shipment, packed, crated – or delivered by truck – as specified. A despatch record of every machine was also logged by the Despatch Department, the completed tallies were then returned to Sales, the final records completed ... and the invoices despatched. During every stage of the above procedures, there were a large complement of progress chasers, based in the Production Department, whose sole job was to ensure the material from the 'rough stores' was presented to the various machining sections in time for each batch manufacture, heat treatment, plating/polishing in accordance with the schedule, and available in time in the central stores for each day's supply to the tracks in accordance with the day's model build programme. And as you will appreciate, the constant supply of finished material for the Spares Department.

How Meriden Worked

"Everyone knew the programme, and what they were building, normally starting with 650cc 6Ts, TR6, T110, and T120, in those days, and eventually the 750cc TR7 and T140s. In the early days, 350/500s and police and military bikes were usually at the end of the sequence. Then it was all round again and no going back to earlier models.

"New models were usually introduced immediately following the annual works holiday, when a skeleton staff had been retained to install the new jigs and fixtures to be used for subsequent production, and a number of dummy runs made to solidify any new installation procedures required for the return and start-up when the operators returned – so all was ready to go! This was the time when the routine changed to supply the US with early consignments of the new models, so they could be shipped and distributed and displayed across the USA in time for the spring selling season. Imagine what happened when the new frame from Umberslade was introduced three months late, and then the engine couldn't be installed. The entire selling season was lost, and the decline set in.

"The records that I have show factory deliveries to Tri-Cor and JoMo between the years 1958 and 1965.

C range crankcases were bored and counter-bored for eight holes simultaneously.

Year	Production	Tri-Cor	Income (£)	JoMo	Income (£)
1958	23,633	2797	458,333	1756	260,920
1959	26,532	3267	491,816	2458	345,309
1960	28,859	3799	600,672	2787	438,949
1961	27,914	1478	232,917	1009	152,999
1962	16,083	2460	410,214	2047	333,361
1963	14,718	4295	738,914	3378	584,303
1964	16,348	4802	909,013	4773	859,673
1965	16,658	8807	1,888,692	6531	1,324,803

Tri-Cor and JoMo sales figures includes all models, including Cubs, 350/500, Tina/T10 and 650s. 'Income' figures are factory invoice value. 'Production' is the total Meriden output figures for the periods shown.

"Another important feature about the US market, when investigating US models, is that both distributors – Johnson Motors in the West and Tri-Cor in the East – were there to sell the machines. They offered dealer update parts to shift the products, altered machines within their own warehouses, sold them as models the factory had never heard of. The competition between the two main distributors was who could clear last year's stock the soonest, so don't ask me about anything that turns up there after 50 years or more. Whatever it is, it left the production line to spec!"

John Nelson

Production process

As John indicates, production at Meriden was in batches of similar machines. Most were for export, and some produced to special order for police, government and military duties, and reading the despatch books is an education in manufacturing for export.

Once machines had passed final testing they were taken to the packing department, partially dismantled, or, in some cases fully dismantled, and then carefully packed in purpose-designed crates.

The crates used by Triumph were supplied by GB Developments of Kenilworth – the handlebars, footrests and front wheel would be removed before the machine was then secured into the crate. Home market bikes would generally not be packed but transported complete by lorry, while those destined for Ireland were fully dismantled (referred in the industry to as CKD, Completely Knocked Down) as this exempted them from the import duties on complete vehicles. As for the US market, shipping time was 14 days to Tri-Cor and 21 days to Johnson Motors.

Although great attention is paid to Triumph sales in the US, they were actually sold all over the world, and huge numbers of machines, especially 3TAs and 5TAs, were sent to very disparate markets, often sold as escort or military machines to royalty, democratic governments and even the Khmer Rouge. Today, these bikes survive in Vietnam, Burma, Bhutan, Nepal, Puerto Rico, Peru, Pakistan, Tenerife, New Zealand, Guam, Canada, Singapore and many other countries – some have been brought back to the UK. Have a look at the Pakistan website www.pakwheels.com – it's a modern buying/selling site, but classic machines do appear. At the time of writing, a 1961 pre-unit T120 Bonneville was advertised (albeit for $12,000).

Notwithstanding John Nelson's comments about US bikes and how many were modified before sale, home market machines do at least seem to be standardised, and were ordered by dealers in advance as potential sales. The Triumph brochure would have been printed to coincide with production for the coming year in order to stimulate public interest. Some home market machines were made to special order, for factory publicity, the police or MoD duties, and these had differing finish and fittings over standard.

For example, the factory records include a single order sheet for a batch of 3TAs. This shows these machines made in small sub-batches before a change was made to fulfil a particular requirement, ie colour or electrical arrangement. So, although the written record shows some 135 3TAs made in this batch, only this sheet details the differences applied to each sub-batch. But it also makes identifying the exact specification of any machine a potential nightmare because no other order sheets from this period appear to have survived. So we don't know what colours and specifications the Tiger 90s supplied to the Ministry of Supply in Ghana were, or what was the specification of Burmese Police bikes, and was the 3TA sent to the King of Nepal special in any way? One of the royal Nepalese bikes has survived, and, at the time of writing, is undergoing restoration in Finland.

Required daily production by 1965 was 60 machines but this figure increased gradually to 1968 when it peaked at 140 a day (one every few minutes)!

Justin Harvey-James

Final machining of the bores.

APPENDIX I

Specifications

1957 Twenty One
Bore x stroke	58.25 x 65.5mm
Capacity	349cc
Compression ratio	7.5:1
Carburettor	Amal Monobloc 375/25
Power	18.5bhp @ 6500rpm
Primary drive	
Type	Duplex chain
Engine sprocket	26T
Clutch sprocket	58T
Gear ratios:	
1st	13.00:1
2nd	9.32:1
3rd	6.30:1
4th	5.31:1
Final drive	
Type	Chain ⅝ x ⅜
Gearbox sprocket	18T
Rear sprocket	43T
Engine speed in top gear:	760rpm @ 10mph
Electrics	6-volt alternator
Tyres	F: 3.25-17 R: 3.25-17
Brakes	F: 7in drum R: 7in drum
Frame type	Tubular steel, single downtube
Steering head angle	n/a
Fuel capacity	3.5 gallons
Oil capacity	5 pints
Dimensions:	
Wheelbase	51.75in
Ground clearance	5in
Length	80in
Width (at handlebars)	26in
Seat height	28.5in
Weight	340lb

1959 5TA
Bore x stroke	69 x 65.5mm
Capacity	490cc
Compression ratio	7.0:1
Carburettor	Amal Monobloc 375/3
Power	27bhp @ 6500rpm
Primary drive	
Type	Duplex chain
Engine sprocket	26T
Clutch sprocket	58T
Gear ratios:	
1st	11.56:1
2nd	8.35:1
3rd	5.62:1
4th	4.80:1
Final drive	
Type	Chain ⅝ x ⅜
Gearbox sprocket	20T
Rear sprocket	43T
Engine speed in top gear:	670rpm @ 10mph
Electrics	6-volt alternator, 7in headlight
Tyres	F: 3.25-17 R: 3.50-17
Brakes	F: 7in drum R: 7in drum
Frame type	Tubular steel, single downtube
Steering head angle	n/a
Fuel capacity	3.5 gallons
Oil capacity	5 pints
Dimensions:	
Wheelbase	51.75in
Ground clearance	5in
Length	80in
Width	26in
Seat height	28.5in
Weight	350lb

1960 Tiger T100A
Bore x stroke	69 x 65.5mm
Capacity	490cc
Compression ratio	9.0:1

Carburettor	Amal Monobloc 375/35
Power	32bhp @ 7000rpm
Primary drive	
Type	Duplex chain
Engine sprocket	26T
Clutch sprocket	58T
Gear ratios:	
1st	11.66:1
2nd	8.44:1
3rd	5.69:1
4th	4.89:1
Final drive	
Type	Chain 5/8 x 3/8
Gearbox sprocket	20T
Rear sprocket	43T
Engine speed in top gear:	670rpm @ 10mph
Electrics	6-volt alternator, energy transfer ignition
Tyres	F: 3.35-17 R: 3.50-17
Brakes	F: 7in drum R: 7in drum
Frame type	Tubular steel, single downtube
Steering head angle	n/a
Fuel capacity	3.5 gallons
Oil capacity	5 pints
Dimensions:	
Wheelbase	51.75in
Ground clearance	5in
Width	26in
Seat height	29.25in
Length	80in
Weight	363lb

1961 TR5 A/C

Bore x stroke	69 x 65.5mm
Capacity	490cc
Compression ratio	9.0:1
Carburettor	Amal Monobloc 375/35
Camshaft	'Q' Racing
Power	38bhp @ 7000rpm
Exhaust system	2 into 1 downswept
Primary drive	
Type	Duplex chain
Final drive	
Type	Chain 5/8 x 3/8
Electrics	6-volt AC Direct, energy transfer ignition
Headlamps	Detachable sports
Instrumentation	Speedometer, tachometer
Tyres:	
Type	Dunlop Trials F & R
Sizes	F: 3.25-19 R: 4.00-18
Brakes	F: 7in drum R: 7in drum
Frame type	Tubular steel, single downtube
Fuel capacity	3 gallons
Oil capacity	6 pints
Dimensions:	
Wheelbase	53.5in
Ground clearance	6in
Seat height	30.25in

1963 Tiger T100SS

Bore x stroke	69 x 65.5mm
Capacity	490cc
Compression ratio	9.0:1
Carburettor	Amal Monobloc 376/273
Power	34bhp @ 7000rpm
Primary drive	
Type	Duplex chain
Engine sprocket	26T
Clutch sprocket	58T
Gear ratios:	
1st	13.86:11
2nd	9.26:1
3rd	6.75:1
4th	5.70:1
Final drive	
Type	Chain 5/8 x 3/8
Gearbox sprocket	18T
Rear sprocket	46T
Engine speed in top gear:	763rpm @ 10mph
Electrics	
Tyres	F: 3.25-18 R: 3.50-18
Brakes	F: 7in drum R: 7in drum
Frame type	Tubular steel, single downtube
Steering head angle	n/a
Fuel capacity	3 gallons
Oil capacity	5 pints
Dimensions:	
Wheelbase	53.5in
Ground clearance	7.5in
Length	84.25in
Width	26.5in
Seat height	30in
Weight	336lb

1966 Tiger 90

Bore x stroke	58.25 x 65.5mm
Capacity	349cc
Compression ratio	9.0:1
Carburettor	Amal Monobloc 376/300
Power	27bhp @ 7500rpm
Primary drive	
Type	Duplex chain

Appendix I – Specifications

Engine sprocket	26T
Clutch sprocket	58T
Gear ratios:	
1st	14.96:1
2nd	9.71:1
3rd	7.36:1
4th	6.04:1
Final drive	
Type	Chain ⅝ x ⅜
Gearbox sprocket	17T
Rear sprocket	46T
Engine speed in top gear:	808rpm @ 10mph
Electrics	
Tyres	F: 3.25-18 R: 3.50-18
Brakes	F: 7in drum R: 7in drum
Frame type	Tubular steel, single downtube
Steering head angle	n/a
Fuel capacity	3 gallons
Oil capacity	6 pints
Dimensions:	
Wheelbase	53.5in
Ground clearance	6in
Length	83.25in
Width	26.5in
Seat height	30in
Weight	337lb

1968 Tiger 100

Bore x stroke	69 x 65.5mm
Capacity	490cc
Compression ratio	9.0:1
Carburettor	Amal Concentric 626
Power	34bhp @ 7000rpm
Primary drive	
Type	Duplex chain
Engine sprocket	n/a
Clutch sprocket	n/a
Gear ratios:	
1st	14.09:1
2nd	9.18:1
3rd	6.95:1
4th	5.70:1
Final drive	
Type	Chain
Gearbox sprocket	18T
Rear sprocket	n/a
Engine speed in top gear:	763rpm @ 10mph
Electrics	12 volts, alternator
Tyres	F: 3.25-18 R: 3.50-18
Brakes	F: 7in tls drum R: 7in drum
Frame type	Tubular steel, single downtube
Steering head angle	n/a
Fuel capacity	3 gallons
Oil capacity	6 pints
Dimensions:	
Wheelbase	53.5in
Ground clearance	7.5in
Length	83.25in
Width	26.5in
Weight	337lb

1970 T100C

Bore x stroke	69 x 65.5mm
Capacity	490cc
Compression ratio	9.0:1
Carburettor	Amal Concentric 626
Power	38bhp @ 7000rpm
Primary drive	
Type	Duplex chain
Gear ratios:	
1st	14.10:1
2nd	9.20:1
3rd	6.90:1
4th	5.70:1
Final drive	
Type	Chain ⅝ x ⅜
Mph/1000rpm	13.65mph @ 1000rpm
Electrics	12 volts, alternator
Tyres	F: 3.25-19 R: 4.00-18
Brakes	F: 7in drum R: 7in drum
Frame type	Tubular steel, single downtube
Fuel capacity	2.25 gallons (US)
Oil capacity	6 pints (US)
Dimensions:	
Wheelbase	54.5in
Ground clearance	7.5in
Width (handlebars)	32in
Seat height	32in
Weight (kerb)	369lb

1972 Daytona T100R

Bore x stroke	69 x 65.5mm
Capacity	490cc
Compression ratio	9.0:1
Carburettors	2 x Amal 626
Power	39bhp @ 8000rpm
Primary drive	
Type	Duplex chain
Engine sprocket	26T
Clutch sprocket	58T
Gear ratios:	
1st	14.10:1
2nd	9.16:1

3rd	6.97:1		
4th	5.70:1		

Final drive
  Type   Chain
  Gearbox sprocket   18T
  Rear sprocket   46T
Engine speed in top gear: 760rpm @ 10mph
Electrics
Tyres   F: 3.25-19 R: 4.00-18
Brakes   F: 8in tls drum R: 7in drum
Frame type   Tubular steel, single downtube
Steering head angle   n/a
Fuel capacity
  UK: 3 gallons
  US: 2 gallons
Oil capacity   5.8 pints
Dimensions:
  Wheelbase   55in
  Ground clearance   7.4in
  Length   84in
  Width   29in
  Seat height   30in
  Weight   356lb

1974 Adventurer TR5T

Bore x stroke   69 x 65.5mm
Capacity   490cc
Compression ratio   7.5:1
Carburettor   Amal Concentric 626
Power   n/a
Primary drive
  Type   Duplex chain
  Engine sprocket   26T
  Clutch sprocket   58T
Gear ratios:
  1st   14.39:1
  2nd   9.38:1
  3rd   7.11:1
  4th   5.82:1
Final drive
  Type   Chain ⅝ x ⅜
  Gearbox sprocket   18T
  Rear sprocket   47T
Engine speed in top gear: 775rpm @ 10mph
Electrics   12 volts, alternator
Tyres   F: 3.00/21 R: 4.00/18, Trials Universals
Brakes   F: 6in drum R: 7in drum
Frame type   Tubular steel, single downtube

Steering head angle   n/a
Fuel capacity   2 gallons
Oil capacity   5 pints
Dimensions:
  Wheelbase   54in
  Ground clearance   7.5in
  Length   85in
  Width   n/a
  Seat height   32in
  Weight   322lb

1983 MCS Daytona (not produced)

Bore x stroke   69 x 65.5mm
Capacity   490cc
Compression ratio   9:1
Carburettor   2 x Amal Concentric
Power   n/a
Primary drive
  Type   Duplex chain
  Engine sprocket   26T
  Clutch sprocket   58T
Gear ratios:
  1st   14.1:1
  2nd   9.16:1
  3rd   6.97:1
  4th   5.7:1
Final drive
  Type   Chain ⅝ x ⅜
  Gearbox sprocket   18T
  Rear sprocket   46T
Engine speed in top gear:
Electrics   12 volts, alternator
Tyres   F: 3.25 x 19 R: 4.00 x 18
Brakes   F: in drum R: in drum
Frame type   Tubular steel, single downtube
Steering head angle   n/a
Fuel capacity   2.5 gallons
Oil capacity   6 pints
Dimensions:
  Wheelbase   53.5in
  Ground clearance   7in
  Length   83in
  Width   27in
  Seat height   30in
  Weight   356lb

Source: 1983 sales leaflet

APPENDIX II

Contacts, Clubs and Sources

This is not an exhaustive list, and there are plenty more Triumph spares suppliers and restoration specialists – we've concentrated on UK and US businesses. Some of them sell spares only, but they should be able to recommend other businesses for restorations and repairs. All those listed here were active at the time of writing.

Clubs

Triumph Owners' club (Germany)
www.tmoc.de
Triumph Owners Motorcycle Club (Denmark)
www.triumphmc.dk
Triumph Owners Motorcycle Club (Norway)
www.tomcc-n.com
Triumph Owners Motorcycle Club (Australia)
www.tomcc.com.au
Triumph Owners Motorcycle Club (Sweden)
tomccsweden.org
Triumph Owners Motorcycle Club (New Zealand)
www.tomcc.co.nz
Triumph Owners' club (UK)
www.tomcc.org
Triumph International Owners' club (USA)
www.tioc.org

Parts

Ace Classics
www.aceclassics.com
General spares
Boyer Bransden
www.boyerbransden.com
Cheney Racing
www.cheneyracing.co.uk
New frames, parts and complete bikes
Classic British Spares (USA)
www.classicbritishspares.com
Dealer Decals (UK)
www.dealerdecals.co.uk
Original dealer decals
Don Hutchinson
www.hutchinsoncycle.com
General spares
Electrexworld
www.electrexworld.co.uk
Klempf's British Parts
www.klempfsbritishparts.com
Paint supplier (UK)
www.msmotorcyclesuk.com
Paint supplier (USA)
www.hutchinsoncycle.com
Tri-Cor England (UK)
www.tri-corengland.com
General spares
Tri-Supply (UK)
www.trisupply.co.uk
General spares

Literature

Brochures – classicbike.biz to view Triumph brochures and other material
Parts Books – www.classicbritishspares.com and use Parts Book library tab to view Triumph Parts Books
Vintage Motorcycle Club Library (VMCC) – www.vmcc.net for brochures, Parts Books, workshop manuals, bulletins, magazines, books and road tests.

The VMCC Library holds the world's largest collection of publicly available motorcycle literature, covering all makes and models of Veteran, Vintage, Classic and contemporary motorcycles and scooters over 25 years old. Includes the original Factory Records for Ariel, BSA, Levis, Norton and Scott, as well as Triumph. The full-time staff can assist with dating, registration and research inquiries. Email at library@vmcc.net or phone +0044 1283 540557.

American magazines. *Cycle and Cycle World* have digitised their back catalogues of magazines and for a small annual subscription these can be viewed. www.covertocover.cycleworld.com and www.cyclenews.com
Dutch military 3TAs – www.triumph3ta.nl – excellent website all about these bikes, in English or Dutch.

Haynes Workshop Manual for Triumph 350/500 twins – www.haynes.co.uk

Modern Records Library at Warwick University (UK) – Meriden factory records, including sales, costs, salaries, all the minutia of company finances!

Auctioneers
Bonhams: www.bonhams.com
Cheffins: www.cheffins.co.uk
H&H: www.classic-auctions.co.uk

APPENDIX III

Production and Sales Figures

Note: Production figures differ from sales for each year because of the time gap between the two. Production schedules had to be arranged weeks in advance of sales to enable parts delivery to be arranged for production. JoMo and Tri-Cor refer to bikes sold by Johnson Motors and Triumph Corporation respectively. Police H refers to bikes sold to UK police forces, Police X to export police machines.

Year-by-Year Production Totals

(For model by model production figures, see main text)

Year	Total
1957	760
1958	4724
1959	6028
1960	7098
1961	6628
1962	4474
1963	2738
1964	3509
1965	4537
1966	7556
1967	8297
1968	8138
1969	7861
1970	9514
1971	4804
1972	5908
1973	5094
1974	1604

Home/Export Sales Figures (1957-68)

1957	**T21**
Home	244
Export	294
Total	538

1958	**T21**
Home	2374
JoMo	275
Tri-Cor	351
Export	1263
Total	4263

Triumph 350/500 Unit Construction Twins Bible 1957-1974

1959	3TA	5T	5TA
Home	2220	45	1867
JoMo	10	92	
Tri-Cor	1	226	
Export	853	66	562
Total	3084	111	2747

1960	3TA	5TA	T100A
Home	1697	1592	1209
JoMo	24	33	122
Tri-Cor	30	77	114
Export	988	544	327
Total	2739	2246	1772

1961	3TA	5TA	T100A
Home	1575	1171	1013
JoMo	14	14	12
Tri-Cor	6	32	26
Export	1401	371	72
Total	2996	1588	1123

1962	3TA	5TA	T100A	T100SS
Home	1737	342	53	716
JoMo	0	0	0	422
Tri-Cor	0	20	0	486
Export	509	163	7	185
Total	2246	525	60	1809

1963	3TA	5TA	T90	T100SS	T100SC	T100SR
Home	433	152	693	215	2	0
JoMo	0	0	28	42	208	71
Tri-Cor	0	0	0	240	185	34
Export	337	184	34	155	0	0
Total	770	336	755	652	395	105

1964	3TA	5TA	T90	T100SS
Home	481	222	632	403
JoMo	0	0	0	615
Tri-Cor	0	0	0	572
Export	614	42	243	153
Total	1095	465	674	1743

1965	3TA	5TA	T90	T100SS	T100SC
Home	279	189	774	324	0
JoMo	0	0	0	1127	0
Tri-Cor	0	0	0	863	1
Export	463	233	27	280	0
Total	715	422	801	2594	1

Appendix III – Production and Sales Figures

1966	3TA	5TA	T90	T100SS	T100SC	T100SR	T35W
Home	447	247	777	832	0	0	0
JoMo	0	0	0	0	1326	737	0
Tri-Cor	0	0	0	0	822	1277	0
Export	265	246	46	700	0	0	1
Total	712	492	823	1532	2148	2014	1

1967	3TA	5TA	T90	T100SS	T100R	T100C	T100T	T100SC	T100SR	T35W	T50W
Home	42	52	186	135	19	30	277	0	0	0	0
JoMo	0	0	0	0	0	0	0	976	904	0	0
Tri-Cor	0	0	0	0	0	0	0	1402	1987	0	0
Export	108	51	228	77	479	0	78	345	0	1099	1
Total	150	103	414	212	498	30	355	2723	2891	1099	1

1968	3TA	5TA	T90	T100S	T100R	T100C	T100T	T100
Home	2	0	347	312	1	18	363	0
JoMo	0	0	0	0	1106	904	0	0
Tri-Cor	0	0	0	0	1336	2201	0	0
Export	0	0	160	507	443	263	195	0
Police H	2	0	26	7	0	0	0	0
Police X	1	7	195	0	75	11	0	0
Total	5	7	685	826	2994	3402	558	139

APPENDIX IV

The Triumph Factory Records

Justin Harvey-James' guide to how the factory records can help a restoration

Most of the surviving Triumph factory records are held by the Vintage Motorcycle Club (VMCC) at its library in Burton-on-Trent. A microfilm copy is also held by the Triumph Owners' Club, and other materials are retained by Warwick University, Birmingham Central Library, Solihull Library, and a number of individuals and organisations both in the UK and in America.

Factory production records are divided into model ranges, then Engine Records, Build Records and Despatch Books, all contained in some 200 volumes covering the entire production period of Triumph at Meriden from 1942 until approximately 1983. The original books are quite difficult to decipher, but most Triumph enquiries at the VMCC take only a few minutes to complete.

Most of the records are hand written in either pencil or fountain pen and take time and experience to decipher.

Engine Record books (from 1950) show the engine assembly date and the changes to specification applied to all subsequent engines at a particular engine number. The books go into some detail as to the various gearbox ratios and ignitions used, and are essential to identify models such as the T120C, T120TT and police machines.

Assembly Books show the model of each machine made, its date of assembly, the order number it relates to, and some of the options fitted. Although bikes were recorded in sequential order, they would not necessarily have been assembled in sequence, and the date of assembly of adjacent numbered machines can be separated by several days!

Despatch Books show the order number, invoice and destination of each machine, with sometimes additional notes but never any specification details. USA bikes show the destination as Tri-Cor or Johnsons Motors; those for the UK show the dealer.

Dating your Triumph

The VMCC is able to provide a comprehensive research, dating and registration service for most makes of motorcycle from 1900 onwards, offered to both members and non-members, including certified copies of the factory records.

Many UK owners assume that the registration number dates the bike, but this is not necessarily so!

Many bikes were not registered until they

Don't forget, engines carry more than just the overall number.

Appendix IV – The Triumph Factory Records

Engine/frame numbers are a key identifier.

were sold, which could take two years or even more.

Most bikes left the factory soon after assembly, though a few were stored, in which case the despatch date could be several months after the build date. Press and display machines were either not recorded in the despatch book or sent to selected dealers up to two years later ...

A few machines, such as the pre-production Tiger 90 and 100A, were converted from other models, and other machines were supplied for conversion to race machines and special duties. So, you may unwittingly (and happily) have a particularly historic machine.

C Range engine/frame number series

Year	Range
1957	H1 to H760
1958	H761 to H5480
1959	H5481 to H11511
1960	H11512 to H18611
1961	H18612 to H25251
1962	H25252 to H29732
1963	H29733 to H32464
1964	H32465 to H35986
1965	H35987 to H40527
1966	H40528 to H48728
1967	H48729 to H57082
1968	H57083 to H65572
1969	H65573 to H67331

During 1969 model year the engine numbering system changed to a mixture of letters and numbers indicating month and year of manufacture. There were factory errors at times, and the chart below is only a guide to the letter codes.

A	January	C	1969
B	February	D	1970
C	March	E	1971
D	April	G	1972
E	May	H	1973
G	June	J	1974
H	July	K	1975
J	August	N	1976
K	September	P	1977
N	October	X	1978
P	November	A	1979
X	December	B	1980

The numbering was still sequential, but was shared between the various models and sizes of twins so that the different ranges were now combined under a common system. As before, production for each model year began after the summer shut-down.

The engine/frame numbers above, denoting the start and end of annual production, are based on the numbers quoted in many sources, which, in turn, are derived from the factory records and parts books – information supplied by the late John Nelson confirmed these numbers. But the end of one model year production and the beginning of the next was not set in stone, and machines made close to the change-over period need to be checked carefully. The engine/frame number should be used with care, and purely as a guide to year specification.

One other point about engine numbers. When completed and given their numbers, engine/gearbox units were stacked on pallets, ready for transfer to the main assembly line for building into frames. However, the pallets weren't always used in sequence, so it's possible that some engines waited for some time before being transferred, while later engines (with later numbers) 'jumped the queue.' It could be that an earlier spec engine found itself in a later spec frame.

Engine/frame numbers explained

These numbers should still be your main point of reference for dating the machine. No complete standard machines intentionally left the factory with different engine and frame numbers. The engine number was stamped in two operations: the model code ('T90' etc) was usually (though not always) made by a single stamping, and the figures should be neatly aligned and even. The 'H' numbers were individually stamped, and, therefore, variable to a degree. Look closely at the font and style of the lettering, as it is very distinctive and changes over time! Even if some of the numbers are obscured or lost, it's possible to work out from the batch production record what model of machine you have.

To be safe, before committing to purchase a bike, contact the VMCC or Triumph Owners' Club with details of the engine/frame number. There are some particularly good fakes out there, especially for the more collectable models.

Look, too, for the casting date marks. These small circular marks (the size of a small button) usually show a two-figure year code (eg '63') which is surrounded by a series of raised lines to indicate the month. You will find casting date marks on the crankcase halves, visible just behind the clutch and the exhaust timing pinion. Crankcases are also marked as a pair with numbers on the lower engine mounting – if these are not matched then it is likely that one half has been changed during the life of the machine. The crankcase casting pattern was made up of a number of interlocking parts, allowing one part of the crankcase to be changed without affecting the remainder.

Interim changes

As mentioned above, the engine and frame numbers can only be a guide to year specification. As the bikes were made in batches, separated by other models, there are often subtle variations in specification from one batch of the same model to another, where later specification parts were used as they became available. Changes were also made during the year, for example as part of a warranty claim (eg 1963 fuel tanks), or by the dealer to shift old stock, or at the request of the owner before acceptance. There is anecdotal evidence that alternative parts were fitted if the correct items weren't available on the assembly line, but, according to John Nelson, this did not happen, as sufficient parts were prepared to complete each batch of machines.

The Parts Books are another guide to details of the range, updated usually for each new model year. The pages of the Parts Book start in the drawing office as annotated drawings on A3 paper, with small parts drawn actual size, the finished drawing was then photographed

Casting marks are further dating aids – this dates from 1970.

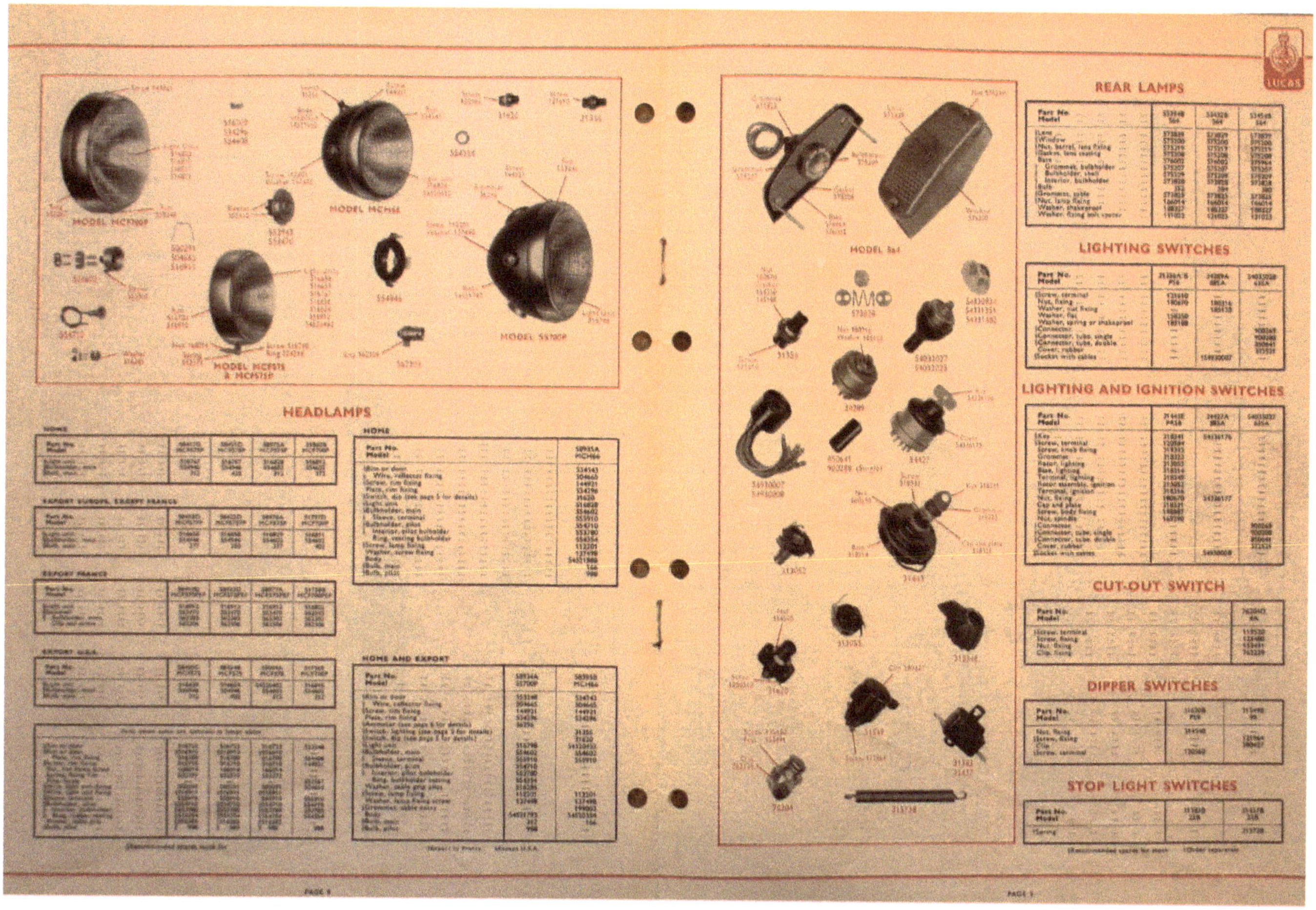

Appendix IV – The Triumph Factory Records

A Lucas brochure – a useful source which electrical components were fitted, and their part numbers

and reduced in size to create the final Parts Book page. Rather than redraw everything from scratch every year, the old drawings would be brought out and modified to show any new parts. This wasn't an infallible system and mistakes were made, with some new parts missed out, so care needs to be taken when using the Parts Book during your restoration. The Parts Books also won't necessarily cover machines built with different specifications for small batches. It is more useful to note any change in part number as this will mean a new or modified part was used, even if the image in the Parts Book is unchanged.

American dealers would be provided periodically with a Bulletin detailing those parts applicable to or omitted from US bikes, and these supplementary sheets are essential reading for restorers. Many of these bulletins are held by the VMCC Library.

The DVLA

This section applies only to UK owners – every country has its own registration authority, and

Registration number indicates when a bike was first registered, but discovering its build date needs research.

Triumph 350/500 Unit Construction Twins Bible 1957-1974

in Britain it's the Driver Vehicle and Licencing Authority (DVLA), the butt of many jokes and frequent frustration, some of it justified, some not.

The DVLA website www.direct.gov.uk can also be helpful to identify if a registration is current, and this can be correlated with the registrations for the county/area to verify a machine's identity. Local records sometimes still exist which can also lead to interesting facts. Copies of the old logbook (if they exist) will also show the original colour scheme, and any changes made during the life of the machine affecting taxation class.

Occasionally machines lose their original registration number (years spent dismantled, the parts in boxes and the number plate lost is the usual cause), but it is possible to recover this as long as the registration is available and you have sufficient documentary evidence to present a case that this is the same bike which originally had that number. Sometimes registrations can also be traced from the factory records. At the time of writing, Richard Wheadon was Registrar of the Triumph Owners' Club and an expert in this field, and can conduct research on your behalf. Contact him tomccregistrar@clara.co.uk. He will need a photograph or rubbing of your engine and frame numbers. Richard can also help in the dating and verification of any postwar Triumph.

Original receipts are good evidence of age and other information – this 1965 Tiger 90 was being traded in for a Hillman Imp!

APPENDIX V

Magazine Road Tests/Features

Contemporary road tests (not more recent 'classic' features) of C range Triumphs – this list is by no means exhaustive! *Moto Revue* articles are in French, *Das Motorrad* in German.

Model	Magazine	Date/issue
Twenty-One introduction	*Motorcycling*	28 Feb 1957
Twenty-One introduction	*The Motorcycle*	28 Feb 1957
Twenty-One road test	*The Motorcycle*	7 March 1957
Twenty One	*Cycle* (USA)	Dec 1957
10,000 miles on a Twenty-One	*Motorcyclist Illustrated*	Jun 1958
21,000 miles on a Twenty-One	*Motorcyclist Illustrated*	Jan 1959
Twenty-One road test	*Motorcycling*	30 Apr 1959
5TA road test	*Cycle* (USA)	May 1959
5TA road test	*The Motorcycle*	14 May 1959
5TA in Thruxton 500 race	*Motorcyclist Illustrated*	Sept 1959
T100A road test	*Motorcycling*	22 Oct 1959
T100A road test	*Moto Revue* (French)	No 1509
T100A road test	*Motorcycling*	10 Mar 1960
3TA road test	*Motorcycle Mechanics*	Jun 1960
3TA & 5TA service tips	*Motorcycling*	28 Jul 1960
Tri-Greeves description	*Motorcycling*	26 Jan 1961
5TA road test	*Motorcycle Mechanics*	Apr 1961
Tiger 100SS ISDT test	*The Motorcycle*	21 Sept 1961
TR5AC	*Cycle* (USA)	Oct 1961
Tiger 100	*Moto Revue*	No 1531
Tiger 100SS road test	*Motorcycling*	26 Oct 1961
C range overhaul	*Motorcycling*	21 Mar 1962
5TA road test (w/fairing)	*Motorcycling*	16 May 1962
Tiger 100SS impressions	*Motorcycle News*	27 Jun 1962
3TA road test	*The Motorcycle*	26 Jul 1962
T100 SR	*Cycle World*	Aug 1962
T100C	*Moto Revue*	No 1627

Model	Magazine	Date/issue
Tiger 90	*Motorcycle Sport*	Dec 1962
Tiger 90 road test	*Motorcycling*	7 Nov 1962
Tiger 90 road test	*The Motorcycle*	23 May 1963
5TA road test	*Motorcycling*	15 Jan 1964
Tiger Cub/90/100 road test	*Motorcycle Mechanics*	Jun 1965
T100 SC	*Cycle* (USA)	Sept 1965
3TA Dutch military	*Motorcyclist Illustrated*	Apr 1966
Daytona race winner	*Motorcycle Sport*	May 1966
Daytona race report	*Cycle World*	Jun 1966
T100A supercharged sprinter	*Motorcycling*	19 Mar 1966
Tiger 100 road test	*Motorcycle News*	1 Jun 1966
Tiger 100 road test	*The Motorcycle*	18 Aug 1966
Tiger 90 road test	*The Motorcycle*	22 Sept 1966
Tiger 90 riders' report	*The Motorcycle*	13 Oct 1966
Daytona T100R	*Cycle* (USA)	Feb 1967
Daytona T100R road test	*Cycle World*	Feb 1967
Tiger 100 road test	*Motorcycle Sport*	Mar 1967
Daytona racer test	*Cycle World*	Jun 1967
Daytona race report	*Motorcyclist Illustrated*	May 1967
Daytona impressions	*Motorcycle Sport*	Nov 1967
Daytona road test	*The Motorcycle*	3 Nov 1966
Daytona road test	*Motorcycling*	5 Nov 1966
Daytona race report	*Motorcycling*	1 Apr 1967
Daytona road test	*Motorcycle News*	24 May 1967
T100C road test	*The Motorcycle*	13 Jul 1967
	Triumph World Wide No 1 (Company magazine)	Oct 1967
Amal Concentric carb description	*The Motorcycle*	25 Oct 1967
Tiger 100 riders' report	*The Motorcycle*	15 Nov 1967
	Triumph World Wide No 2 (Company magazine)	Feb 1968
Daytona T100R road test	*Cycle Guide*	Feb 1968
Tiger 100 road test	*The Motorcycle*	29 May 1968
	Triumph World Wide No 3 (Company magazine)	Jun 1968
T100C road test	*Cycle*	Aug 1968
Tiger 100 road test	*Motorcyclist Illustrated*	Aug 1968
Daytona T100T road test	*The Motorcycle*	9 Oct 1968
	Triumph World Wide No 4 (Company magazine)	Nov 1968
Tiger 100 road test	*Les Motards*	No 12

Appendix V – Magazine Road Tests/Features

Model	Magazine	Date/issue
Daytona road test	*Motocyclisme*	No 2
T100C road test	*Modern Cycle*	Feb 1969
Tiger 100 road test	*Motorcycle Mechanics*	May 1969
Daytona racer test	*Motorcycle Mechanics*	Aug 1969
Daytona road test	*Motorcycle Sport*	Apr 1969
Tiger 100 road test	*Motorcycle Sport*	Aug 1969
Tiger 100S road test	*Motorcycle Sport*	Mar 1970
	Triumph World Wide No 8 (Company magazine)	May 1970
	Triumph World Wide No 9 (Company magazine)	Sept 1970
Daytona road test	*The Motorcycle*	4 Nov 1970
Bandit/Fury description	*The Motorcycle*	11 Nov 1970
Bandit/Fury description	*Cycle World*	Feb 1971
Bandit/Fury technical description	*The Motorcycle*	3 Feb 1971
Daytona road test	*Motorcycle Mechanics*	Aug 1971
Daytona road test	*Motorcycle Mechanics*	Mar 1973
TR5T road test	*Motorcyclist Illustrated*	Apr 1973
TR5T	*Dirt Rider*	May 1973
Daytona road test	*Motorcycle Mechanics*	May 1973
TR5T road test	*Bike*	May/Jun 1973
TR5T ISDT bike	*Cycle*	Jun 1973
TR5T road test	*Modern Cycle*	Jun 1973
Daytona T100R vs Yamaha TX500 test	*Cycle*	Jul 1973
TR5T road test	*Cycle World*	May 1974

APPENDIX VI

Bibliography

A selection of reference books on Triumph in general as well as the C range in particular. Many are out of print now, but should be available used online.

Ayton, Cyril (ed), *Triumph Twins from 1937*, Bay View Books, 1990

Bacon, Roy, *Triumph T90 & T100 Unit Twins*, The Promotional Reprint Company, 1996

Brooke, Lindsay & David Gaylin, *Triumph Motorcycles in America*, Motorbooks 2018 (also original 1993 version)

Cycle World on Triumph 1967-1972, Brooklands Books, 1988

Cycle World on Triumph 1972-1987, Brooklands Books, 1987

Hancox, Hughie, *Tales of Triumph Motorcycles and the Meriden Factory*, Veloce Publishing, 2013

Henshaw, Peter, *Triumph 350 & 500 Unit Twins*, Veloce Publishing, 2014

Hopwood, Bert, *Whatever Happened to the British Motorcycle Industry?*, Haynes, 1998

Koerner, Steve, *The Strange Death of the British Motorcycle Industry*, Crucible Books, 2012

Morley, Don, *Classic British Scramblers*, Osprey, 1986

Morley, Don, *Classic British Trials Bikes*, Osprey, 1984

Nelson, John, *Triumph Tiger 100/Daytona*, Haynes Publishing, 1988

Meriden: Historical Summary 1972-1974, Norton Villiers Triumph Limited, 1974

Pearson, Gregory, *The Complete Grand National Championship Volume 1 1954-1969*, DTG Publications, 2009

Rosamund, John, *Save the Triumph Bonneville*, Veloce Publishing, 2009

Shilton, Neale, *A Million Miles Ago*, GT Foulis & Co, 1982

Simon, Ted, *Jupiter's Travels,* Penguin, 1980 (iconic travel book – around the world on one of the last Tiger 100Ps)

Sintich, Claudio, *Road Racing History of the Triumph 500 Unit Twin*, Panther Publishing, 2010

Vale, Matthew, *Triumph Twenty-One to Daytona*, Crowood Press, 2008

Wilson, Steve, *British Motorcycles Since 1950 Vols 5 & 6*, Haynes Publishing, 1992

Woolridge, Harry, *Triumph Speed Twin*, GT Foulis & Co, 1989

Visit Veloce on the web – www.velocebooks.com
Details of all books • Special offers • New book news • Gift vouchers

Also from Veloce Publishing

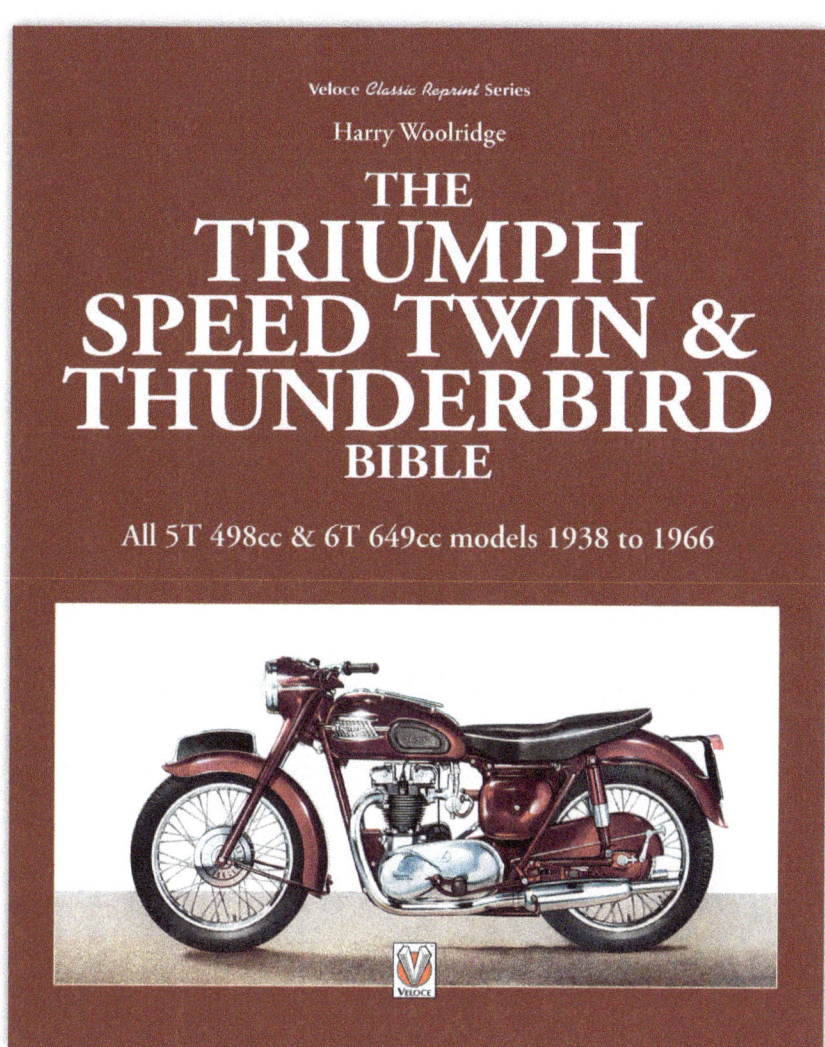

Triumph Speed Twin & Thunderbird Bible
Harry Woolridge

New in paperback!
The Triumph Speed Twin & Thunderbird Bible reveals the definitive history of two of Triumph's most popular motorcycles in the 40s and 50s. From development history to sporting achievements, this book is packed with detailed information – everything an owner or would-be owner of one these classic twins needs!

ISBN: 978-1-845849-82-5
Paperback • 25x20.7cm • 144 pages
• 150 colour and b&w pictures

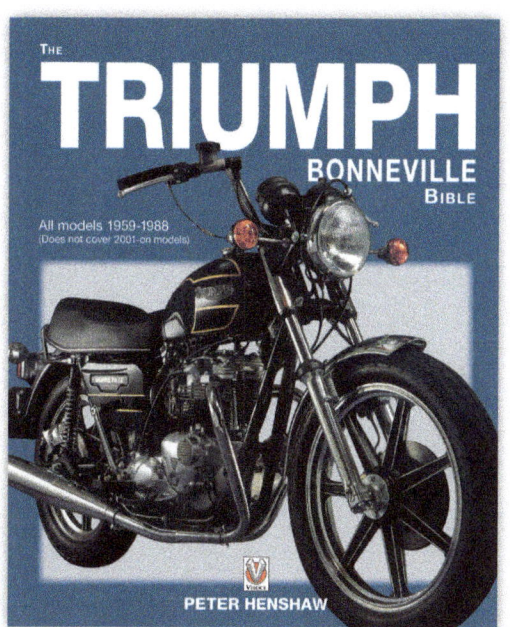

The Triumph Bonneville Bible
Peter Henshaw

The story of the Triumph Bonneville – its conception, design and production, how it compared to the competition (British and Japanese), and how it was seen at the time. With insights into the company that built it, from the boom times of the 1960s, through struggles in the 70s, and eventual closure in the '80s, plus guidance on buying a Bonneville secondhand, this is the fascinating history of a British icon.

ISBN: 978-1-845843-98-4
Hardback • 25x20.7cm • 160 pages
• 262 pictures

For more information and price details, visit our website at
www.veloce.co.uk • email: info@veloce.co.uk • Tel: +44(0)1305 260068

Also from Veloce Publishing

Tales of Triumph Motorcycles & the Meriden Factory
Hughie Hancox

A Veloce Classic Reprint.
A delightful and often humorous account of life with the Triumph motorcycle company in its heyday. Hughie Hancox started work with the Triumph Engineering Company (manufacturer of Triumph motorcycles) in 1954 and, apart from a short break for national service, stayed with the company until its closed in 1974. In his time with Triumph, Hughie worked in the Experimental, Service, Product Road Test, Toolroom, Final Production Assembly and Service Repair Shop departments before joining the staff in the Service Office. He also served as a Technical Writer/Advisor/Customer Relations "Trouble Shooter." Even his National Service was spent with the "White Helmets" motorcycle display team! Here, Hughie tells the story of his life in the famous Meriden factory and of his many adventures with Triumph motorcycles and Triumph people and, by doing so, records the fascinating inside story of one of Britain's greatest motorcycle marques.

ISBN: 978-1-787115-49-1
Paperback • 25x20.7cm • 144 pages
• 90 pictures

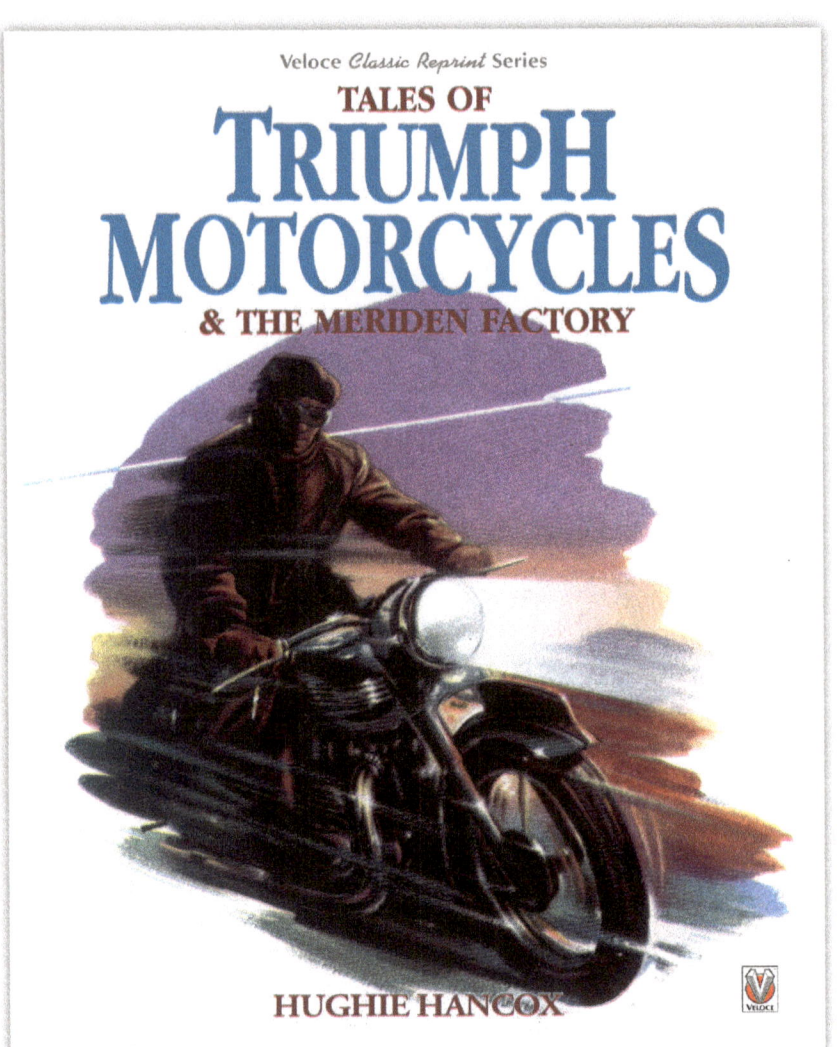

Triumph Production Testers' Tales – from the Meridan Factory
Hughie Hancox

Long time Meriden worker and Triumph restorer, Hughie Hancox, describes everyday life in the Triumph Production Testing team from 1960 to 1962. A story packed with amusing anecdotes, and guidance on fixing problems still found today on the 1960s models. An intimate and entertaining account of Britain's most famous motorcycle factory.

ISBN: 978-1-845844-41-7
Paperback • 25x20.7cm • 160 pages
• 183 colour and b&w pictures

For more information and price details, visit our website at
www.veloce.co.uk • email: info@veloce.co.uk • Tel: +44(0)1305 260068

Also from Veloce Publishing

The Norton Commando Bible
Peter Henshaw

The story of the Norton Commando – its conception, design and production, and how it compared to the competition (British and Japanese). With insights into the company that built it, and guidance on buying a Commando secondhand, this is the fascinating history of a true British icon and an essential guide for restorers.

ISBN: 978-1-78711-006-9
Hardback • 25x20.7cm • 144 pages
• 163 colour and b&w pictures

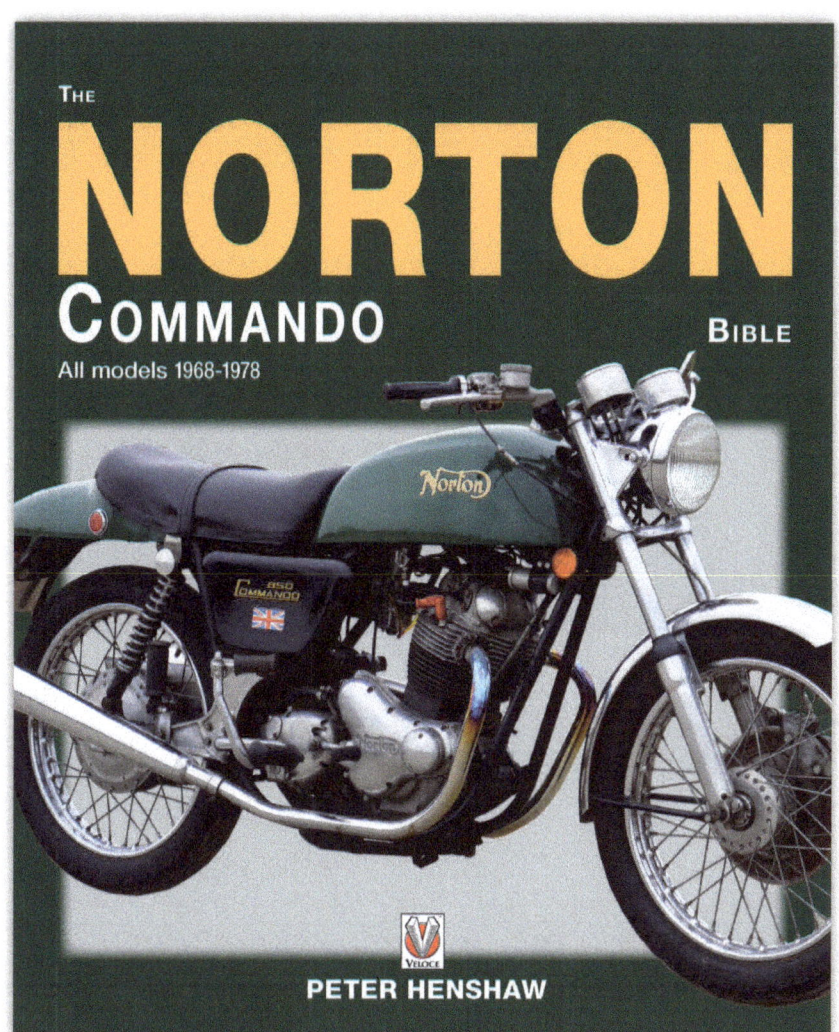

The BSA Bantam Bible
Peter Henshaw

Now in paperback!
The BSA Bantam Bible covers the year-by-year evolution of the BSA Bantam, a simple commuter bike that thousands learnt to ride on. It became the standard GPO 'telegram bike' in the 1950s and was a huge success, with 100,000 built in the first four years of production.

ISBN: 978-1-787111-36-3
Paperback • 25x20.7cm • 160 pages
• 167 colour and b&w pictures

For more information and price details, visit our website at
www.veloce.co.uk • email: info@veloce.co.uk • Tel: +44(0)1305 260068

Also from Veloce Publishing

Essential Buyer's Guides
Peter Henshaw

Having one of these books in your pocket is just like having a real marque expert by your side. Benefit from the author's years of bike ownership, learn how to spot a bad bike quickly, and how to assess a promising bike like a professional. Get the right bike at the right price!

ISBN: 978-1-84584-136-2
Paperback • 19.5x13.9cm • 64 pages
• 104 colour and b&w pictures

ISBN: 978-1-84584-165-2
Paperback • 19.5x13.9cm • 64 pages
• 105 colour pictures

ISBN: 978-1-845847-55-5
Paperback • 19.5x13.9cm • 64 pages
• 102 colour pictures

ISBN: 978-1-84584-134-8
Paperback • 19.5x13.9cm • 64 pages
• 127 colour pictures

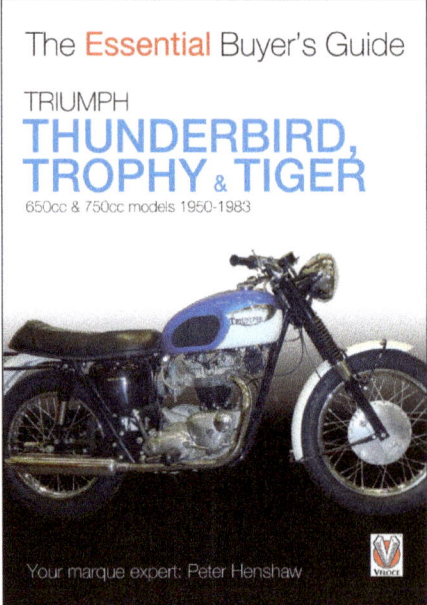

ISBN: 978-1-845846-09-1
Paperback • 19.5x13.9cm • 64 pages
• 104 colour pictures

For more information and price details, visit our website at www.veloce.co.uk • email: info@veloce.co.uk • Tel: +44(0)1305 260068

Index

Amal:
  Concentric 82
  Monobloc 9
American differences 47, 54
Andover Norton 43, 108
Army 3 Day Trial 62

'Bathtub' 12-13, 14-16, 52
'Bikini' 34, 42, 52-53, 64
Blakeway, Gordon 33, 34, 40, 48
BSA 19, 45, 60, 69, 76, 81, 88, 90, 98, 99, 104
BSA Fury 99, 111, 112
Burnett, Don 41
Buying secondhand:
  Electrics/wiring 122
  Engine/frame numbers 121
  Engine/gearbox 123-125
  Running gear 123
  Test ride 126
  Tinwork 122

C range, year by year:
  1957 7-17
  1958 17-20
  1959 20-23
  1960 23-27
  1961 27-34
  1962 34-41
  1963 41-50
  1964 50-56
  1965 56-62
  1966 62-70
  1967 70-81
  1968 81-88
  1969 88-94
  1970 94-98
  1971 98-102
  1972 102-104
  1973 104-107
  1974 107-110

Choosing a 350/500:
  3TA/5TA 118
  Daytona 119
  Off-road models 120
  T90/T100 118, 119

Dating 146-149
Daytona 200 race:
  1962 41
  1966 69, 70
  1967 80, 81
  1968 88
Daytona Beach 27
Dutch army bikes 76-78
DVLA 149

'Easylift' stand 11, 18, 37
Ekins, Bud 69
Electrics
  6-volt 10
  12-volt 63, 64, 122
Engine breather 95
Engine design 7-9
Engine/frame numbers 121, 147-149

Frame brace 56
Fuel tank mounting 45, 56, 57, 74

Gearbox design 9
Giles, Johnny 33, 34, 41, 48-50, 55, 69, 81
Greene, Bill 41, 56

Harley-Davidson 60, 69, 88
Hele, Doug 59, 69, 72, 73, 80, 83, 108
Hopwood, Bert 108

Interim changes 148
ISDT:
  1962 40, 41
  1963 49, 50
  1964 55

1965 61, 62
1966 68, 69
1967 81
1973 107

Living with a 350/500 114-126

Maintenance 114-116
McGuigan, Stuart 111, 112
Meriden factory:
  Production process 133-135
  Records 146
  Sit in 107, 108
Modifications/improvements:
  Brakes 131
  Carburettors 129
  Clutch 129
  Electrics 130-131
  Electronic ignition 128
  Frame 131
  Ignition 128
  Lead-free fuel 128
  Oil filters 128-129
  Performance 127-128
  Pushrods 129
  Rocker boxes 129
  Suspension 131
  Tappets 129
  Transmission 129-130

Nelson, John 50, 66, 68, 83, 110, 133-135
Norton 69, 98
Norton Villiers Triumph (NVT) 107, 108

Oil pressure switch 89-91

Peplow, Roy 27, 33, 34, 41, 49, 55, 60, 68, 81
Personal Export Scheme 88
Production debacle (1971) 99, 100

Prototypes:
  350 DOHC twin 111, 112
  '67 x 70' 500 59
  T21 16

Queens Award for Export 76, 85, 95

Racing 22, 33, 34, 49, 56
Registration numbers 50
Restoration 116-118
Rolling road testing 87

Small Heath 69, 108, 109
Spares 115, 141-142

Tait, Percy 74, 80, 83, 102
TDC slot 57
Triumph models:
  3TA 20, 21
  5TA 20, 21, 23
  Bandit 99, 111, 112
  Bonneville 50, 71, 81, 88, 94, 95, 101, 108
  Daytona 71, 72
  Daytona 600 112, 113
  MCS Daytona 113
  T21 7-19
  T90 42, 43, 87
  T100A 22, 23-25, 27, 30
  T100C Trophy 98
  T100D 109, 110
  T100SC/SR/SS 34-37
  TR5 AC 27-29
  TR5 AR 28, 29
  TR5T 104, 105, 107
Turner, Edward 13, 15, 16, 25, 52, 62, 66, 110

UNF threads 83, 89-90
Unit construction 7, 8

van de Linden, Kees 77, 78